APR '98

Teacher Change
and the
Staff Development Process

A Case in Reading Instruction

Teacher Change
and the
Staff Development Process

A Case in Reading Instruction

EDITED BY
Virginia Richardson

TEACHERS
COLLEGE
PRESS

Teachers College, Columbia University
New York and London

Published by Teachers College Press, 1234 Amsterdam Avenue, New York, NY 10027

Library of Congress Cataloging-in-Publication Data

Teacher change and the staff development process : a case in reading
   instruction / edited by Virginia Richardson.
         p.   cm.
   Includes bibliographical references and index.
   ISBN 0-8077-3361-X (cloth : acid-free paper).—ISBN
0-8077-3360-1 (paper : acid-free paper)
     1. Reading teachers—In-service training—United States.
   I. Richardson-Koehler, Virginia, 1940–
   LB1731.T36   1994
   371.1'46—dc20   94-12291

ISBN 0-8077-3360-1 (paper)
ISBN 0-8077-3361-X (cloth)

Printed on acid-free paper
Manufactured in the United States of America

01   00   99   98   97   96   95   94   8   7   6   5   4   3   2   1

Contents

Preface

"In order to tell this story in all its complexity, you will have to write a book." These words were spoken by Tom Russell of Queens University, Canada, as he was responding to a set of papers from the Reading Instruction Study (RIS) at the annual meeting of the American Educational Research Association. This book is a result of Tom's suggestion, and all of those involved in the project thank Tom for his encouragement and helpful suggestions over the years.

RIS, funded by the Office of Educational Research and Improvement (OERI), U.S. Department of Education, began in 1986 and ended in 1992. It was a complex project, involving many, many individuals. In addition to the authors represented in this book, the project involved teachers in six schools and their principals. It is to these professionals that I dedicate this book. They have taught me much of what I now know about teacher change, staff development, and reading instruction. Their dedication to and caring for their students give me hope for the future of our children, for our educational system, and for the democratic ideals that we pursue.

Alasdair MacIntyre stated, in *After Virtue* (1984): "We are never more (and sometimes less) than the co-authors of our own narratives" (p. 213). While each of the chapters in this book is identified by individual or joint author, this story is co-authored by a large number of teachers, faculty members, graduate and undergraduate students, and friends and colleagues in the United States and Canada. Some of these names may be found in the Appendix to Chapter 1; however, space would not permit us to name them all. My thanks to all of you who were involved in composing this story.

My thanks, also, to those in the funding agency, OERI, Department of Education, who facilitated the funding of the project: Elizabeth Ashburn, Clara Copeland, and many others within the bureaucracy who ensure that the money comes through, and work is disseminated. Those were hard times in the federal social agencies, and I appreciate the dedication with which these people approached their work. I would like to think that we have produced, with a modest amount of money, some understanding of teaching and teacher change that will be useful to others considering such changes.

And last, to the loyal and caring members of my immediate family, Gary, Derek, Kurt, and Paul, and my parents, Bruce and Helen Richardson, I thank you for your love and support.

REFERENCE

MacIntyre, A. (1984). *After virtue* (2nd ed.). Notre Dame, IN: University of Notre Dame.

Teacher Change
and the
Staff Development Process

A Case in Reading Instruction

1

Launching a New Form of Staff Development

PATRICIA L. ANDERS AND **VIRGINIA RICHARDSON**

We imagine you have picked up this book because of an interest in any one of the topics inferred by the title. Perhaps you are a curriculum specialist or a principal responsible for a district's or a school's staff development program. Or maybe you are interested in how to facilitate or bring about teacher change. Research may be an area of interest; perhaps you are curious about the methodology used to conduct inquiry in teacher development. You may also be interested in reading comprehension and want to be a better teacher or teacher educator in all matters pertaining to the teaching of reading comprehension. We hope this book will respond to these and other interests as well.

This book represents a collaborative effort to study the teaching of reading comprehension using research-based practices. It is the result of a research project designed in response to an Office of Educational Research and Improvement (OERI) request for proposals (RFP). The study addressed five questions: What are research-based reading comprehension practices? To what degree are teachers using these practices? What are the barriers to the use of research-based practices? Does a school-based staff development program affect teachers' practices? Does a teacher's participation in the staff-development program affect student reading performance?

The purpose of this first chapter is to explain how we came together to respond to the request for proposals, what we wondered about as we formulated our response to the request, how we created the questions we wanted to investigate, the tensions we felt as we developed our program of research, the staff development program we designed, and the ways that this program of research has affected our thinking and professional lives. We think these topics are appropriate and important to explain because the "how" of what we did is different from that of most projects. We imagine that those wanting to do a similar project would find themselves working through a process similar to ours. Hence, we ask your indulgence as we tell our story, which serves to frame the next eight chapters. The last chapter will pick up where this chapter leaves off, and reflects what we think we have learned and what we and others perceive as possibilities for the future.

THE REQUEST FOR PROPOSALS

A request for proposals arrived at the University of Arizona during the summer of 1986, and it included four topics related to the teaching of reading. The fourth topic, of particular interest, read as follows:

> 4. Implementation of Current Research Knowlege of Reading and Literacy.
> OERI encourages examinations of the degree to which teachers use current research knowledge of reading and literacy and of the factors that prevent their doing so. OERI also encourages investigations into the ways in which the use of current research knowledge affects reading achievement, particularly of students in the elementary grades who are from middle socio-economic backgrounds. Findings would suggest more effective teaching strategies and more effective methods of training teachers. (Office of Educational Research and Improvement [OERI], 1986, p. 5)

Having been a reading specialist responsible for staff development to help content area teachers incorporate reading strategies into their instruction of content, I (Anders) was naturally drawn to this topic. My experience in that position led me to believe that telling teachers about exciting and innovative new practices did not necessarily lead to implementation of those practices. I felt there was a clear need to better understand the nature of teachers' beliefs, teachers' practice, and teacher change.

At the same time, I was working on another project with Candace Bos, a professor of special education. I talked with her about the request for proposals and she suggested that a collaborator representing teacher education would be needed to adequately conceptualize the project. Hence, we looked for a colleague with whom we could collaborate to help better understand the conditions under which teachers might adopt and adapt research-based practices.

Virginia Richardson was that person. She had recently joined the faculty of Teaching and Teacher Education at the University of Arizona and was reputed to be interested in "reflective practice." I didn't really know very much about the literature of reflective practice, but it seemed to have something to do with how teachers think about what they do and why they choose to use one practice, but not another. The concept seemed to have potential for helping us to understand barriers to the use of research-based reading comprehension practices. Instinctively, I also thought that a collaboration between a researcher representing a reading perspective and a researcher representing teacher education would be appropriate.

After I talked with Virginia, a collaborative project between teacher education and reading was conceived. As the proposal began to take shape, we became aware of the need for an even more interdisciplinary effort, and made the decision to involve faculty from all departments in the college, including educational philosopher Gary Fenstermacher, then dean of the college. The appendix at the end of this chapter displays the organization of our project as it finally evolved, including the individuals who participated and their current affiliations.

Most of us were trained in hypothesis-driven research; however, as we read the request for proposals and mulled over what our project might be, it became increasingly clear that we did not have hypotheses to test. We needed a different sort of project.

The remainder of this chapter describes the issues and tensions with which we dealt as we grappled with who we are as teachers and researchers; what we thought we knew and did not know about both teaching and research; and how best to inform the profession about teachers' ways of thinking and doing.

THE RESEARCH BASE

The perspective we brought to this project was informed by two broad areas of inquiry. We were impressed with the substantial body of research on the teaching and learning of reading that had been conducted, completed, and disseminated. Clearly, the RFP required that recent research on reading be an important part of this study. In addition, our experience and knowledge of the teacher education literature provided a knowledge base from which to begin. Our interpretation of this literature in 1986 is summarized below.

Instructional Reading Research

Two events conjoined in the late sixties and early seventies to change the world of reading research. The first event was the publication of Ken Goodman's (1967) article "Reading: A Psycholinguistic Guessing Game" and the second event was the bringing together of cognitive psychologists to create the Center for the Study of Reading at the University of Illinois. With these two events, a shift took place from an emphasis on decoding remediation to comprehension processes and practices.

Goodman (1967) posited that reading was more than accurate decoding, which was a major tenet of previous theories; rather, he suggested that a reader used a linguistic cuing system. He described the cuing system as consisting of grapho-phonic, syntactic, and semantic cues. Moreover, he theorized that certain cognitive functions (selecting, predicting, confirming, and integrating) were integral to the reading process. As his theory was refined, he included the influence of social context on a reader's comprehension (1984). Goodman and his colleagues describe the reading process as transactive—a socio-psycholinguistic process whereby readers construct meaning rather than "get" meaning from the written word.

Cognitive psychologists were also developing theories to explain the mental activity of reading. Dominant among those most often cited was the work of the schema theorists. Schema theory suggests that knowledge is structured in large, complex, abstract units of organized information called schemata (Rumelhart, 1981). Learners understand text by determining how the ideas they read relate to their existing schemata or knowledge. This description of the reading process, which grows out of information-processing research, implies that comprehension is a constructive process by which readers interpret text according to their own understandings, or sometimes misunderstandings (Spiro, 1980).

Changes were taking place in the methods of conducting reading research. The inquiry of both basic and applied researchers was moving from the laboratory and an emphasis on individual students to asking whether the processes of instruction made a difference in the quality and quantity of meaning that students constructed (Pearson & Johnson, 1978). The new constructivist theories were tested in classrooms rather than in the laboratory.

Reading researchers' initial steps into classrooms were taken to investigate the efficacy of a particular theory-based practice. For example, a tenet of schema theory is that learning occurs when background knowledge is activated and linked with new information. One instructional research question, then, was "how can a teacher best activate students' background knowledge?" To answer a question like this, practices such as brainstorming were investigated for usefulness and influence on the quality of students' comprehension. The intention of this instructional research was to provide some level of confidence that if the practices were implemented, student achievement in reading would improve.

Becoming a Nation of Readers (Anderson, Hiebert, Scott, & Wilkinson, 1985) summarizes many of those practices. Included among the many recommended practices were the following examples of reading research—supported findings that suggest the information and knowledge base available to teachers:

1. The quality and quantity of readers' prior knowledge can be predicted, and instructional lessons can be designed to accommodate that prior knowledge (e.g., Anderson & Smith, 1987; Langer, 1982).
2. Strategies can be designed to activate prior knowledge, organize prior and forthcoming knowledge, and set purposes for reading comprehension and learning of concepts in content area classrooms (Anders, Bos, & Filip, 1984; Pearson & Gallagher, 1983).
3. Comprehension instruction does work—students do learn to comprehend whether the instruction is by direct instruction (Rosenshine & Stevens, 1984), explicit instruction (Pearson & Gallagher, 1983), reciprocal teaching (Palincsar, 1984), or whole language (Goodman, 1984; Goodman, Watson, & Burke, 1987).
4. The structure, coherence, unity, and appropriateness of text influence the quality of reader comprehension (Anderson & Armbruster, 1984; Beck, 1984; Meyer, 1985).

These findings suggested that if we could teach teachers to use these and similar practices, their students' reading comprehension would improve. It is not surprising that this is the sense we made of this body of literature. The process/product orientation (see Chapter 8) of the last 20 years contributed to this linear, causal type of thinking. Our optimism was tempered, however, by reports decrying the reading achievement of students and the status of reading comprehension instruction.

For example, despite an emphasis on reading comprehension research and the plethora of research-based practices for teachers to use, test scores in reading, particularly in the upper elementary grades, were not rising as expected (National Assessment of Educational Progress, 1984). Further, naturalistic studies indicated that many teachers were teaching very little reading comprehension (e.g., Bozsik, 1981; Coyne, 1981; Durkin, 1978; Neilson, Rennie, & Connell, 1982). This issue seemed to be the crux of what we were to investigate. Why weren't students improving in their reading achievement? Was it because teachers didn't use research-based practices? If so, why didn't they use these practices? We were troubled by the apparent gulf between research and theory, and teaching practices. How could we get to the bottom of this issue?

Teacher Education Research

The second general area of inquiry we drew on to inform our perspective was the research on teaching, learning, and schooling that would help us understand why teachers use the practices they do. Our reading of that literature suggested the following five considerations: the ethos of the school, the nature of the practices the teachers are supposed to adopt, teachers' belief systems, school-level practices, and staff development.

School Ethos. Lortie (1975) described the ethos of the school as consisting of three aspects: conservatism, presentism, and individualism. This, he felt, is due in large part to the anxiety surrounding the uncertainty about classroom outcomes, and the lack of an agreed-on professional knowledge. The conservatism norm implies that teachers may not accept organizational objectives because they rely on personal values and past experience rather than on imposed goals, objectives, and methods. The presentism norm is indicated by teachers not planning for long continuous periods, nor feeling assured about their future performance.

The individualism norm suggests little reliance on others for sources of knowledge, skills, or experience except during the first two years of teaching (Fuchs, 1969). Trial and error and the individual personalities of teachers are the bases for developing good practice. Since students, circumstances, and personalities of teachers differ, there is a tolerance for widely different practice as well as strong egalitarian norms. Differences in practice are therefore viewed as "matters of philosophy" (Metz, 1978).

These norms can be described as part of the culture of the teaching profession (Feiman-Nemser & Floden, 1986). Within this culture, the individual teacher's beliefs differ on such issues as the effectiveness and appropriateness of different classroom practices, the purposes of instruction, and the ways in which students learn. This culture could strongly affect the curriculum and practices chosen by teachers.

Practices Recommended in the Literature. Another consideration is related to the characteristics of the research-based reading comprehension literature. Certain of these characteristics may limit teachers' inclination to adopt the recommended practices. For example, methods textbooks, teachers manuals for basal reading programs, professional books, and the educational journals may not regularly explicate the relationship among theory, research, and practice (Beck, 1984; Tierney, 1984). Teachers may not realize that such a triad exists to inform instructional decisions. Further, many staff development programs may be fragmented and exclude the research and theoretical connections.

The research itself may negate teachers' experience and therefore be rejected, or the research may be overgeneralized to contexts far beyond those in which it was conducted. Such overgeneralization, in many cases, renders the research unusable or inappropriate for context-specific use. An example of this problem is the concept of "wait time." Research on this concept has been conducted in elementary and secondary classrooms and in various content areas (Tobin, 1987). The first study, however, was conducted in high school science classes (Rowe, 1974), and indicated that when teachers gave students more time to answer questions during recitation, the responses from pupils were qualitatively better. On the basis of this research, wait time has been accepted as a universal prescription for effective teaching, rather than as a practice that may or may not be applicable in a particular context. For younger students in different types of classes, increased wait time may bore students and thereby cause serious classroom management problems. Such a negative result would be predicted by Kounin's (Kounin & Doyle, 1975) research and theory suggesting that instruction must move along at a relatively brisk pace to keep students on task. The classroom management imperatives help to explain why many teachers who are trained in wait time quickly revert to their previous pace.

Belief Systems. A third consideration that informed our perspective, and one that is related to the teacher education literature, is the importance of teachers' belief systems. In 1985 the literature was not yet extensive, but the existing studies led us to conclude that ignoring teachers' beliefs in implementing change could lead to disappointing results. Teachers' implicit theories vary from teacher to teacher (Munby, 1984) and may be at odds with those of curriculum developers and administrators. For example, Olson (1981) found that eight teachers who were implementing a new science curriculum "domesticated" it to match their own implicit theories of effective instruction.

Work on how teachers and professionals think in action helped us to understand that teachers' implicit theories might affect behavior, and that those beliefs and theories can be modified to accept new and different research-based practices. Schön's (1983) discussion of reflective practice, for example, suggested that practitioners' knowledge-in-action is intuitive, tacit, and based on the experiences of trial and error. Reflection in action, or the ability to think about the knowledge-in-action process while it is taking place, helps practitioners deal with situations of "uncertainty, instability, uniqueness, and value conflict" (p. 50).

School-level Practices. We also considered the research related to school-level features that were linked to teachers and their thinking. Research on effective schools provides information on the characteristics of schools that are particularly effective in increasing student learning (Bossert, 1985; Corcoran, 1985; Purkey & Smith, 1983). One such characteristic is the degree of collegiality among teachers (Little & Bird, 1983).

Schools with high collegiality provide opportunities for teachers to discuss their practices with each other, offer each other support and critical feedback, and conduct experiments to test their practices.

Rosenholtz (1986) and colleagues investigated the school factors that affected teachers' commitment. She concluded that teachers' perceptions of their work are strongly affected by the organizational context in which they work. For example, teachers who were identified as leaders in collaborative schools were those who "moved others toward fulfilling their instructional purposes." In noncollaborative schools, teacher leaders were defined as those who earned their reputation "by engaging in noninstructional activities, either by union-related leadership, or by their empathetic responses to colleagues' classroom or personal problems" (p. 243). The degree of collaboration in a school was also found to be important in whether schools adopted innovations. Huberman and Miles (1984) found that change occurred in schools with norms that supported collaboration, cohesive relationships, and a reasonable tolerance for diversity.

To our way of thinking, then, it seemed that practices existed to help children learn to comprehend, but that several potential "barriers" existed regarding teachers' adoption of those practices. The barriers suggested to us from the literature were several. For example, perhaps teachers had little or no opportunity to talk to each other and, hence, the cultural norm of individualism was continually reinforced. What would happen if that norm were challenged and teachers were provided an opportunity to talk? Or, perhaps, teachers don't *use* research in the ways that researchers mean when they ask "do you use research"? Teachers may well use practices that are based on research, but judge their worth by a notion of "what works" rather than the quality and quantity of empirical evidence supporting the practice. We also wondered about the nature of teachers' beliefs about reading comprehension and the teaching of reading comprehension. Tabachnick and Zeichner (1984) had suggested that teachers acquire fundamental perspectives and understandings in their preservice programs and hold onto them during their years of teaching. There was a sense in the literature that teachers were "recalcitrant" and difficult to change. Was that one of the factors contributing to OERI's conclusion that teachers were not using research-based practices?

Staff Development. The literature on staff development also informed our thinking. We were familiar with traditional modes of staff development, those that are designed to import specific information to teachers for the purpose of changing their behavior. The negative history surrounding those types of staff development (Guskey, 1986), however, was discouraging. It seemed that a different tack was needed. Our vision was to create a process that was neither top-down nor bottom-up, but allowed for the introduction of specific knowledge and ways of thinking that were "new" to at least some of the participants.

Further, we were convinced that the staff development needed to account for teachers' beliefs (Hollingsworth, 1990; Munby, 1984; Russell & Johnson, 1988) and also needed to provide opportunities for articulating linkages between beliefs and practices. One intriguing line of inquiry was the work of Fenstermacher (1986) in the area of "practical argument." The notion of the practical argument suggested a context in which we could discover teachers' reasoning for their practices. We theorized that if part of their justification was empirical (i.e., testable assumptions about instructional practices), we would have a beginning point for the discussion of research-based practices.

This literature, our experiences, and the process of our team working in collaboration resulted in the development and accomplishment of our project. This method is consistent with the qualitative tradition. Validity may be enhanced by bringing different views together to both create the project and interpret the findings.

THE PROJECT DESIGN

To review, the purpose of our project was to investigate five questions:

1. What are the practices recommended in the research for the teaching of reading comprehension?
2. To what degree are teachers using these research-based practices to teach reading comprehension?
3. What are the barriers to the use of research-based practices?
4. Does a school-based staff-development model affect teachers' use of research-based instruction of reading comprehension?
5. Does a teacher's participation in the staff development program affect student reading achievement?

These questions suggest a sense of uncertainty and a tension between qualitative and quantitative research traditions. Arriving at these questions and the subsequent design of the study was not accomplished without trepidation, concern, and caution. Tensions among us centered around the following issues: What was our responsibility to the teachers and students we would ask to participate? Would our research method conform to accepted standards and rules regarding the conduct of research? What was meant by the term *practice*? What would a "practical-argument" staff development process look like? And, finally, could we actually observe changes in student achievement in such a short time? These issues and related tensions pushed and pulled at us as we wrote our proposal and as we conducted our study.

We only briefly describe the research processes and methodology here, since these are presented in the chapters that follow. Table 1.1 is a matrix of the years of our study and the questions that framed the study. Within each cell of the matrix is the activity that was conducted to provide information related to each question. The column headings list the focal area of the questions and the corresponding chapters in this book, in which the research related to each question is addressed in more detail.

The Participants

We planned to work with intermediate-level (grades 4, 5, and 6) teachers in five schools. We were looking for middle-class schools with relatively heterogeneous student populations where both the principal and the teachers were willing to spend time and energy examining reading comprehension instruction. We approached the research offices of two school districts near our university and provided them with the required information to gain access to their schools. After receiving approval from both offices, we talked with one of our consultants, Robert Wortman, a school principal with a long history in the area who is attuned to local principals, faculties, and schools. We wanted to approach schools that would be willing to listen to our proposal. We also wanted to work in schools that were not already overburdened with many other projects. We chose to ask seven principals to allow us to talk to the teachers in their schools. All seven principals agreed. We visited the teachers in those schools and explained our proposal and what we would be asking them to do. Much to our surprise, six schools wanted to participate. We resolved the problem of having more schools wanting to participate than we had planned for by deciding that we could handle an additional school because the schools were located near each other and were relatively small. The sixth school was then designated a "pilot" school. The teachers in this school gave us feedback on our plans and we piloted certain aspects of our staff development with them.

More about these teachers and the activities they engaged in is presented in subsequent parts of this chapter and throughout the book. Suffice it to say that 39 grade 4, 5, and 6 teachers were involved in the project. They ranged in experience from a first-year teacher to one with over 30 years' experience.

Table 1.1 The Data by Question: RIS Study

			QUESTION		
Semester	1. Recommended Practices (Chap. 4)	2. Teacher Use of Practices (Chap. 3)	3. Barriers to Practices (Chaps. 5 & 7)	4. Effect of Staff Development on Teachers (Chaps. 2, 6, & 8)	5. Effect of Practices on Reading (Chap. 9)
FALL 1987	Literature Review	Baseline observations: all teachers	Survey: School Context Interview: Principals		Student Achievement: ITBS
SPRING 1988	Literature Review		Interview: Teachers	Staff Development: Pilot School	Student Achievement: ITBS
FALL 1988		Baseline Observation: New teachers videotape		Staff Development: 3 schools. Practical arguments	Student Achievement: Illinois
SPRING 1989		Observation and Survey: Survey all schools		Interviews: Teachers	Student Achievement: ITBS & Illinois
FALL 1989				Staff Development: Control Schools	Student Achievement: Illinois
SPRING 1990		Observation: Control			Student Achievement: ITBS & Illinois

Addressing the Questions

The purpose of this section is to discuss each of the five proposal questions in terms of our plans to answer it and our resolution of the issues within each question.

Question 1. To answer the first question—"What are the practices recommended in the research for the teaching of reading comprehension?"— we conducted a literature search. Three problems confronted us as we conducted this review. The first problem was basic: What is a practice? The use of this term was problematic because it lacked an operational definition. What distinguishes a practice from a method, an activity, or a teaching strategy? Some members of our team thought it could be defined very broadly. For example, a practice might be "using the basal," "reading in the content areas," or "questioning for comprehension." Others suggested that a practice was a very specific activity such as using particular types of worksheets, doing oral reading, or having students make predictions on the basis of story titles or pictures.

For the project, we resolved these questions by using two resources: our own experience, and the use of the term in the literature. If an author labeled an activity a practice, we also identified it as a practice. Most of the time, however, practices were called something else—such as skill, strategy, or method—and were identified as practices by members of our research team. The operational definition of a practice that emerged included three elements. First, it is observable. It is an activity a teacher undertakes to provide an opportunity for reading comprehension to take place. Second, it is describable. One who understands the practice can explain to another how to accomplish it. Third, it is linked to a theoretical notion of the reading process—that is, it is not just another good idea. Rather, it is a practice that engages readers in an activity that is assumed to be critical and necessary for enacting the reading comprehension process.

Our second concern regarding the literature review had to do with the confidence ratings assigned to each practice. How confident were we of our readers' evaluations? To mitigate this concern, we evaluated each practice a minimum of two times and when there was a disagreement between evaluators, two evaluators met to negotiate a resolution between the differing evaluations. Hence, we implemented a "holistic scoring" of sorts to predict the usability of a given practice in a classroom and to evaluate the quality and quantity of research supporting that practice.

The third concern related to what is *not* in the published literature. For example, some studies may have found no significant differences between the control and experimental groups when testing a practice and would therefore not be published. Hence, as researchers making recommendations to teachers we had access to only part of the story. This is a limitation of research and publication processes; however, it is a reality that must be acknowledged.

Question 2. The next question—"To what degree are teachers using these research-based practices to teach reading comprehension?"—was asked because of our ambivalence about the assumption that teachers do not use research-based practices. Most of the teachers in our project were using current basals. The authors of basals are, for the most part, participants in the research community, and many are leaders in conducting instructional reading research. Also, the Tucson area has a very active reading association (the Tucson Area Reading Council of the International Reading Association) and a large and active grass-roots organization, Teachers Applying Whole Language (TAWL). Members of our research team regularly made presentations at these meetings and we could attest to the presentation of research-based practices at those meetings. These experiences caused us to question the assumption that teachers did not use research-based practices. Hence, we observed teachers, and the methods we used are described in Chapter 4.

One decision to be made when designing the observational study was *when* to observe the teachers. Our qualitative methodological approach suggested that it should be when the teacher said he or she was teaching reading comprehension. Hence, we only observed when invited, and when the teacher could plan for our observation. This provided us with confirmation of what the teacher defined as teaching reading comprehension. As reported in Chapter 8, the teachers' definition of teaching reading comprehension changed during the course of our study and that was confirmed by the lessons they chose for us to observe.

Another decision revolved around the type of observational record to be used. In general, classroom observational studies can be viewed on a continuum: On the one end are studies in which researchers identify all the variables of interest, usually in the form of a checklist, and observers note and/or rate the frequency of occurrence, presence/absence, or duration of those variables during classroom observations. On the other end of the continuum are those studies in which researchers describe and analyze classroom events by transcribing what transpires during an instructional segment and then examining patterns that recur across these observational data. We were again driven by the more qualitative approach—the latter end of the continuum—for several reasons. Since the identification of reading comprehension practices was proceeding simultaneously, firm definitions of practices were not available to guide the development of instruments needed for the former type of classroom observation. Also, it was desirable to identify the context of instruction in which research-based reading comprehension practices were used to arrive at a sense of how the practices related to the larger instructional focus of the lesson. Two types of contexts were potentially important: the sequence of the practice within a teaching activity, and the structure of the teaching situation (large group, small group, or individual). Further, this type of approach to observation allowed for the inclusion within the data of unanticipated classroom events and, therefore, unexpected practices. (For a description of the results of the research, see Chapter 3.)

Question 3. "What are the barriers to the use of research-based practices?" was addressed by investigating teacher beliefs and knowledge about reading and the teaching of reading and also by considering school-level factors that may inhibit or enhance teacher change.

The interview we conducted is detailed in Chapter 5. A couple of interview-related activities are not described in that chapter and may be of interest to readers. One is that both principal investigators practiced conducting the interview before visiting the teachers. It was important that the interviewer not impose her own language on the conversation; in effect, the informant leads the interviewer to behave linguistically or verbally in ways the informant considers appropriate. Practice was needed to conduct the interviews in ways that would be consistent.

Since much of the study was conducted using a qualitative methodology, we were aware that the beliefs of the researchers could affect the process. To understand and reduce this bias, it was important for us to be aware of our beliefs. Hence, each of us was interviewed by a third party. This provided us with the experience of being in the role of an informant and also provided us with a sense of our own beliefs about the reading process and the teaching of reading. We learned that each of us perceived the reading comprehension process and the teaching of reading differently. Virginia tended to believe that what the author meant in writing a text is important, and that the reader should make an attempt to understand that meaning. Patty was inclined to believe that meaning is constructed by a transaction between the reader and the author and that a justified meaning might be constructed that had not occurred to the author.

The two principal investigators also differed on other aspects of the interview. For example, Virginia believed that teaching math is different from teaching reading, but Patty thought "teaching is teaching." We found these differences interesting in light of the collaborative nature of our project. A requisite condition of collaboration is negotiation, and the fact that we differed on our beliefs about the teaching of reading (and a variety of other topics) suggests that the capacity to acknowledge and deal with others' differences is critical to a collaborative venture. Further, we demonstrated and exemplified this negotiation process during the staff development process.

Barriers to teachers' use of research-based practices may have also existed in the schools themselves. For that reason, we needed a sense of the schools in which we were working. To learn about the schools, we employed three procedures. First, with the help of Sharon Conley, we used a teacher questionnaire. Bacharach, Bauer, and Conley (1986) had previously used the Organizational Climate Survey in 83 school districts in New York State. Second, we collected qualitative data on each of the schools. Third, an interview with each of the principals was conducted to get a sense of his or her beliefs concerning the reading curriculum and teacher practices and change.

Chapter 7 describes the findings from this phase of our study. The analysis of these data provided an interesting description of the schools we were to work in, especially in terms of the two "experimental" schools. One of the schools, Jones, was described as being very collegial and open to new information. The second experimental school contrasted sharply with the first. We worried about these differences because the effective schools literature had led us to believe that these differences could make a substantial difference in the process and results of our staff-development program. While there were differences in the processes of the programs in the two schools, as described in Chapter 7, the results were similar (see Chapter 8).

Question 4. In hindsight, answering the fourth question, "Can a school-based staff-development model affect teachers' use of research-based instruction of reading comprehension?" turned out to be far bigger and more important than anything we could have imagined. It changed our lives as researchers and teachers in ways that we never could have predicted and that is why we chose to write a book about staff development.

Remember that we wanted to frame our staff development process in terms of Fenstermacher's practical argument (1986); however, we did not know what that would mean. As conceptualized by Fenstermacher (1986) and Green (1976), practical arguments are philosophical statements. Morine-Dershimer (1987) had used the construct to analyze interview data already collected. As a result, we needed to create our own methodology.

Chapter 6 describes the methodology we employed: however, several issues needed to be resolved to get to that point. For example, could the

practical arguments be conducted in a group, or did they have to be conducted individually? We turned to our pilot school to try out the practical
argument. Interested teachers met with us for an afternoon. Two teachers
had volunteered to be videotaped while teaching reading comprehension.
They also consented to having their respective videotapes shown to their
colleagues and to the researchers. We then discussed the tape with each
teacher, using the practical-argument ways of thinking as a guidepost for
the discussion.

The teachers really enjoyed the discussion. They commented on what
an unusual event it was to consider their instruction in such a reflective
and professional way and enjoyed seeing each other teach and also enjoyed
listening to each teacher's critical analysis of what she was doing on the
videotape. This experience bolstered our confidence that the practical-
argument framework, the collaborative viewing of the tape, and the discussion that took place while watching the tape were of value.

This initial experience also suggested that perhaps the practical argument could take place in a group setting. We tried it once at Jones School,
but the results were not very satisfying. Despite the reputed collegiality of
the school, discussing practices in the way that we had with our pilot school
faculty seemed uncomfortable for the teachers at Jones and they did not
seem to be enthusiastic participant observers. Hence, we regrouped, and
quickly decided that the practical-argument sessions needed to be conducted with only the teacher and the researchers present.

The practical-argument individual sessions were one part of our staff
development program; the other part was group sessions held with the
faculty of each school. The group sessions were videotaped and became
an important part of our data. In-depth description of those sessions can
be found in Chapter 6. Several issues emerged as we conducted these sessions. For example, as researchers, we were troubled by the difficulty of
participating in the sessions as colleagues of the teachers and also playing
the role of researchers. We found the dual identity (teacher and researcher)
sometimes conflicting. In retrospect, our conflicting feelings might be
explained by the ambivalence with which we approached staff development. On the one hand, our goal was to share the research-based practices
we had found. On the other, we shied away from being authoritative; rather,
we wanted to be constructivist and collaborative. We believed it was important for teachers to want to know about the practices and for the practices
to be relevant to their day-to-day teaching.

Another potential explanation for our discomfort might have been the
nature of some of the discussions. At times, we would leave the sessions
concerned that the discussion was more like group therapy than staff development. It is easy to understand why this was the case. The norms of

our schools, and we believe most schools, mitigate against teachers' openly and critically sharing and analyzing their practices. Learning to do that sort of thinking and articulating is a trying experience. Indeed, when we consider our own colleagues in the College of Education and their reluctance to talk about why they teach classes in the ways they do and to substantively critique their instruction, we are not surprised that teachers with far less verbal experience in talking about teaching would suffer similar feelings of discomfort.

This led to another question—how directive should we be? Actually, this problem worked itself out as the program progressed. When we were directive, teachers responded in a way that was qualitatively different from when we were conversational and collegial. The former resulted in teachers' behaving as students at a lecture, while the latter resulted in all of us engaging in problem solving and critical thought (Richardson, 1992).

We described our project as collaborative. It was perceived as collaborative on several levels. Clearly it was a collaboration between two people representing two rather different fields of inquiry—reading and teacher education. As principal investigators we also called on the collaborative efforts of colleagues representing the entire educational research enterprise. The project was identified as collaborative because we worked with our graduate students in a way that was not typical in our college. We considered the graduate assistants colleagues and they participated fully in the conduct of the study, as evidenced by their contributions to this book.

Our work with the teachers was also collaborative in several ways. We invited teachers to participate and were as clear as we could be about the purpose of the study. To some, and in retrospect, this may not be truly collaborative because perhaps teachers and researchers should create the research questions and methodology together. Nonetheless, given our understanding of collaboration at the time, the constraints of funded research, and the uncertainty with which we approached the process, we came as close to being collaborative as we felt we could.

What is evident to us and what we want others to know is that we were, throughout this project, conducting inquiry into our own ways of thinking and doing. We were sometimes in conflict with ourselves and with each other as we attempted to sort out what was going on during a change process. As we conducted this project, analyzed the overwhelming amount of data, and reflected on what we learned, we realized that the questions we were asking and the questions that were inferred by the request for proposals were coming from the wrong direction. They suggested a one-way, top-down process: an extension of the process/product approach to knowledge generalization and change in practice (i.e., What are the research-based practices? When they are found, give them to the teachers). Instead, we designed a project that was constructed as we learned. It was qualitative. It was teacher research, or staff-developer research, in that we were conducting inquiry on our own practices. It was a life-altering experience.

Question 5. The final research question was one we were very nervous about: "Does a teacher's participation in the staff development program affect student reading achievement?" We were nervous because we knew OERI would be very interested in this question. After all, how could they justify funding us and other reading research if it didn't make a difference for children? But being able to find such differences required that we alter our approach from one that was primarily a qualitatively designed study to one that was more quantitative.

We approached the question initially by attempting to answer it from three levels of data. P. David Pearson, a consultant to the project, helped us to see that we could and should collect and analyze data at a global level. That was easy because the Iowa Test of Basic Skills was administered each spring and the schools would make the results available to us. Second, Pearson suggested that we use a more local measure and offered to help us use the Illinois Test. Finally, he suggested we should have a third, nonstandard measure. Whenever teachers tried a practice, they should design some measure of the success of that practice.

Chapter 9 explains the findings of the two standardized measures. The third measure, however, was never conducted or collected. As explained by Anders and Richardson (1992), the teachers in this study were very attuned to the importance of "objective" measures. They were not convinced during the time that we worked with them that their own evaluations of practices or student learning could be adequately "objective."

CONCLUSION

We write this introductory chapter to invite you to read the remaining chapters in this book and to consider both the history and the future of staff development. Indeed, if schools are to respond to the demands of the next wave of educational reform, staff development is a critical consideration.

Our own voyage into the realm of teacher change, staff development, schools, and studying ourselves as researchers, teachers, and collaborators has been a process that has taken us on a new professional tack. We believe we have learned some things that will challenge your own thinking and your own ways of working. We look forward to your reactions and to the voyage ahead.

APPENDIX: Staff Organization: RIS Study

Principal Investigators
Patricia Anders, University of
    Arizona
Virginia Richardson, University of
    Arizona

Project Coordinators
Carol Lloyd (Years 1&2),
    University of Nebraska at Omaha
Deborah Tidwell (Year 3),
    University of Northern Iowa

Graduate Students
Carol Christine, Center for Edu-
    cational Development, Phoenix
Ann Batchelder, University of
    Texas, El Paso
Pamela Brown Clarrige, Tucson
    Unified School District
Marjorie Gallego, Michigan State
    University
Mary Lynn Hamilton, University of
    Kansas
Peggy Placier, University of
    Missouri
Marynell Schlagel, Principal,
    Tucson Unified School District
And Others

*University of Arizona Faculty
    Associates*
Candace Bos
John Bradley
Gary Fenstermacher, Dean, College
    of Education
Judy Mitchell
Lois Coleman (Visiting Faculty)

Consultants
Sharon Conley, University of
    Arizona
Yetta Goodman, University of
    Arizona
Gerry Duffy, Wentworth College
John Guthrie, University of
    Maryland
Judith Langer, State University of
    New York, Albany
David Pearson, Dean, University of
    Illinois
Laura Roehler, Michigan State
    University
Michael Townsend, Aukland
    University, New Zealand
Robert Wortman, Principal, Tucson
    Unified School District

REFERENCES

Anders, P., Bos, C., & Filip, D. (1984). The effect of semantic feature analysis on the reading comprehension of learning disabled students. In J. A. Niles (Ed.), *Changing perspectives on research in reading, language processing and instruction* (33rd Yearbook of the National Reading Conference, pp. 162–166). Rochester, NY: National Reading Conference.

Anders, P., & Richardson, V. (1992). Teacher as game-show host, bookkeeper, or judge? Challenges, contradictions, and consequences of accountability. *Teachers College Record, 94*(2), 382–396.

Anderson, C. W., & Smith, E. L. (1987). Teaching science. In V. Richardson-Koehler (Ed.), *Educators' handbook: A research perspective* (pp. 84–111). New York: Falmer.

Anderson, R. C., Hiebert, E. H., Scott, J. A., & Wilkinson, I. A. G. (1985). *Becoming a nation of readers: The report of the Commission on Reading*. Washington, DC: National Institute of Education.

Anderson, T. H., & Armbruster, B. B. (1984). Studying. In P. D. Pearson (Ed.), *Handbook of reading research* (p. 657). New York: Longman.

Bacharach, S., Bauer, S., & Conley, S. (1986). Organizational analysis of stress: The case of elementary and secondary schools. *Work and Occupations, 13*(1), 7–32.

Beck, I. L. (1984). Developing comprehension: The impact of the directed reading lesson. In R. C. Anderson, J. Osborn, & R. J. Tierney (Eds.), *Learning to read in American schools: Basal readers and content texts* (pp. 3–20). Hillsdale, NJ: Erlbaum.

Bossert, S. (1985). Effective elementary schools. In R. Kyle (Ed.), *Searching for excellence* (pp. 39–54). Washington, DC: National Institute of Education.

Bozsik, B. E. (1981). *A study of teacher questioning and student response interaction during pre story and post story portions of reading comprehension lessons*. Unpublished doctoral dissertation, University of Pittsburgh.

Corcoran, T. (1985). Effective secondary schools. In R. Kyle (Ed.), *Reaching for excellence* (pp. 71–98). Washington, DC: National Institute of Education.

Coyne, M. (1981). *An investigation of reading comprehension instruction and content instruction in fourth grade social studies*. Unpublished doctoral dissertation, University of Pennsylvania.

Durkin, D. (1978). What classroom observations reveal about reading comprehension instruction. *Reading Research Quarterly, 14*(4), 483–533.

Feiman-Nemser, S., & Floden, R. E. (1986). The cultures of teaching. In M. C. Wittrock (Ed.), *Handbook of research on teaching* (3rd ed., pp. 505–526). New York: Macmillan.

Fenstermacher, G. D. (1986). A philosophy of research on teaching: Three aspects. In M. C. Whitrock (Ed.), *Handbook of research on teaching* (3rd ed., pp. 392–407). New York: Macmillan.

Fuchs, E. (1969). *Teachers' talk. Views from inside city schools*. New York: Doubleday.

Goodman, K. S. (1967). Reading: A psycholinguistic guessing game. *Journal of the Reading Specialist, 6*(4), 126–135.

Goodman, K. (1984). *What's whole about whole language?* Toronto, Canada: Scholastic.

Goodman, Y., Watson, D., & Burke, C. (1987). *Reading miscue inventory.* New York: Richard Owen Press.

Green, T. (1976). Teacher competence as practical rationality. *Educational Theory, 26,* 249–258.

Guskey, T. R. (1986). Staff development and the process of teacher change. *Educational Researcher, 15,* 5–12.

Hollingsworth, S. (1990). Prior beliefs and cognitive change in learning to teach. *American Educational Research Journal, 26,* 160–190.

Huberman, A. M., & Miles, M. B. (1984). *Innovation up close.* New York: Plenum Press.

Kounin, J. S., & Doyle, W. (1975). Degree of continuity of a lesson's signal system and the task of involvement of children. *Journal of Educational Psychology, 67,* 159–164.

Langer, J. A. (1982). Facilitating text processing: The elaboration of prior knowledge. In J. A. Langer & M. Smith-Burke (Eds.), *Reader meets author—bridging the gap: A psycholinguistic and sociolinguistic perspective* (pp. 27–44). Newark, DE: International Reading Association.

Little, J. W., & Bird, T. (1983). *Finding and founding peer coaching: An interim report of the application of research on faculty relations to the implementation of two schools improvement experiments.* Boulder, CO: Center for Action Research. (ERIC Document Reproduction Service No. ED 221-141)

Lortie, D. (1975). *Schoolteacher.* Chicago: University of Chicago Press.

Metz, M. (1978). *Classrooms and corridors: The crisis of authority in desegregated secondary schools.* Berkeley: University of California Press.

Meyer, B. J. F. (1985). Prose analysis: Purposes, procedures and problems. In B. K. Britton & J. B. Black (Eds.), *Understanding expository text* (pp. 11–64). San Francisco: Jossey Bass.

Morine-Dershimer, G. (1987). Practical examples of the practical argument: A case in point. *Educational Theory, 37*(4), 395–408.

Munby, H. (1984). A qualitative study of teachers' beliefs and principles. *Journal of Research in Science Teaching, 21,* 27–38.

National Assessment of Educational Progress. (1984). *The reading report card: Progress toward excellence in our schools. Trends in reading over four national assessments. 1971-1984.* Washington, DC: U.S. Department of Education. (ERIC Document Reproduction Service No. ED 264-550)

Neilson, A., Rennie, B., & Connell, A. (1982). Allocation of instructional time to reading comprehension and study skills in intermediate grade social studies classrooms. In J. A. Niles & L. A. Harris (Eds.), *New inquiries in reading research and instruction* (31st Yearbook of the National Reading Conference, pp. 81–88). Rochester, NY: National Reading Conference.

Office of Educational Research and Improvement. (1986). *Application for grants under the educational research grant program: Research grants on reading and literacy* (CFDA Number 84.117). Washington, DC: Author.

Olson, J. K. (1981). Teacher influence in the classroom. *Instructional Science, 10,* 259–275.

Palincsar, A. M. (1984). The quest for meaning from expository text: A teacher-guided journey. In G. Duffy, L. Roehler, & J. Mason (Eds.), *Comprehension instruction: Perspectives and suggestions* (pp. 51–264). New York: Longman.

Pearson, D., & Gallagher, M. (1983). Instruction of reading comprehension. *Contemporary Educational Psychology, 8,* 317–344.

Pearson, P. D., & Johnson, D. D. (1978). *Teaching reading comprehension* (pp. 1–5). New York: Holt, Rinehart, & Winston.

Purkey, S., & Smith, M. (1983). Effective schools: A review. *Elementary School Journal, 83*(4), 427–437.

Richardson, V. (1992). The agenda-setting dilemma in a constructivist staff development program. *Teaching and Teacher Education, 8*(3), 287–300.

Rosenholtz, S. (1986). Educational reform strategies: Will they increase teacher commitment? *American Journal of Education, 95*(4), 543–562.

Rosenshine, B., & Stevens, R. (1984). Classroom instruction in reading. In P. D. Pearson (Ed.), *Handbook of reading research* (pp. 745–798). New York: Longman.

Rowe, M. B. (1974). Wait-time and rewards as instructional variables, their influence on language, logic, and fate control: 1. wait-time. *Journal of Research in Science Teaching, 2,* 81–94.

Rumelhart, D. E. (1981). Schemata: The building blocks of cognition. In J. T. Guthrie (Ed.), *Comprehension and teaching: Research reviews* (pp. 3–26). Newark, DE: International Reading Association.

Russell , T., & Johnson, P. (1988). *Teachers learning from experiences of teaching: Analyses based on metaphor and reflection.* Paper presented at the annual meeting of the American Education Research Association, New Orleans.

Schön, D. (1983). *The reflective practitioner.* New York: Basic Books.

Spiro, R. J. (1980). Constructive processes in prose comprehension and recall. In R. J. Spiro, B. C. Bruce, & W. F. Brewer (Eds.), *Theoretical issues in reading comprehension* (pp. 245–278). Hillsdale, NJ: Erlbaum.

Tabachnick, B., & Zeichner, K. (1984). The impact of the student teaching experience on the development of teacher perspectives. *Journal of Teacher Education, 21,* 165–167.

Tierney, R. J. (1984). A synthesis of research on the use of instructional text: Some implications for the educational publishing industry in reading. In R. Anderson, J. Osborn, & R. J. Tierney (Eds.), *Learning to read in American schools* (pp. 63–78). New York: Random House.

Tobin, K. (1987). The role of wait time in higher cognitive level learning. *Review of Educational Research, 57*(1), 69–96.

2

The Place of Practical Argument in the Education of Teachers

GARY D FENSTERMACHER

The purpose of this chapter is to set forth the notion of practical argument as it applies to the activity of teaching. Of particular interest is how practical argument can be used to assist teachers in becoming more reflective about their practice. In addition, this chapter examines the value of practical argument for linking practice to sound educational theory, incorporating new knowledge and understanding into one's teaching, and becoming more aware of how teachers' beliefs affect the character of their instruction. The chapter concludes with a consideration of practical argument as a form of staff development, a form quite different from what is ordinarily thought of as staff development.

This chapter is divided into six sections. The first, third, and fifth sections examine the notion of practical argument. Each of these three sections is more detailed than the previous one, leading to an increasingly sophisticated description of practical argument. The intervening sections explore the educational applications of practical argument. The second section points out how practical argument may assist teachers in becoming more reflective about their instructional practices. In the fourth section it is argued that the concept of reflective teaching, standing by itself, is not sufficient for advancing a robust conception of what it means to educate students. This section then provides an examination of two essential adjuncts to reflective teaching, a morally grounded theory of education and a consideration of new knowledge and understanding in teaching and in content areas. Finally, the sixth section links the concept of practical argument with staff development in teaching. The chapter ends with some views on how the success or failure of staff development depends on the beliefs teachers have about their work, and how practical arguments contribute to teachers' understanding of their beliefs.

This chapter provides a significant share of the philosophical underpinning for the Reading Instruction Study (RIS) described in this book. RIS is a complex study, grounded in several general theories about teaching and learning, as well as in specific theories about reading, research methodology, and the philosophy of teaching. It is this last component that is the subject of this chapter. The philosophy of teaching central to RIS is that the teacher must be viewed as an intentional agent in the classroom, autonomously deciding how theory, research, and context are blended into a basis for instructional actions that advance the knowledge, abilities, and general welfare of the student. The concept of practical argument incorporates these philosophical elements in ways that permit both the analysis of teaching and its improvement. With the overarching framework for this chapter in mind—that the first, third, and fifth sections "unpack" the concept of practical argument, while the intervening sections indicate the uses of this concept for teaching—I begin by taking a first look at practical reasoning.

1. AN OVERVIEW OF PRACTICAL REASONING

Practical reasoning, in its most simple characterization, is the thinking we do about our actions. When we are engaged in practical reasoning, we are connecting the objectives of our action (what we are trying to accomplish) with the ways and means of obtaining these objectives. Sometimes this reasoning is quite conscious, as when we deliberate prior to taking some action that we know has considerable consequence. Sometimes the thought processes are not very deliberate, as when we act out of habit or routine. On other occasions, we reason after acting, pondering why we did what we did or whether we should have done it. Reasoning *post hoc* like this is often a prelude to some future action, whereby we decide to act differently or just the same the next time the occasion arises.

Practical reasoning is always undertaken with respect to some action, or some plan or intention to act. It is different from formal, logical reasoning, which is always propositional in character. Note the difference between the two types of reasoning illustrated below.

Formal:
  Bob is a student in the ninth grade
  All ninth grade students are in this room
  Therefore, Bob is in this room
Practical:
  Eating fruit is good for one's health
  US Department of Agriculture research indicates that we should eat
    several servings of fruit each day
  I have eaten no fruit at all today

>A friend is now offering to share her fruit with me
>{ACTION: I take the fruit and eat it}

The last line, or conclusion, of the formal reasoning example is a statement or proposition describing something about the world. In contrast, the last line of the practical reasoning example is in French braces, to alert you that it is not really a line at all, but an action being taken. Were it possible to do so, it would have been better to have pictures of me accepting the fruit and eating it, in order to avoid the confusion that may arise from having the last line expressed in writing. Practical reasoning always concludes in an action or an intention to act in a certain way.

Because it pertains to action and the reasons connected to an action, practical reasoning is a powerful way to scrutinize teaching practices. However, there is far more involved here than merely thinking back over one's actions. The practical reasoning of interest in this chapter, and to the Reading Instruction Study as a whole, is a particular kind of highly developed reasoning, designed to yield specific results with classroom teachers. It is grounded in Aristotle's ethical theory, as developed in the *Nicomachean Ethics* (named after Aristotle's son, Nicomachus, who is said to have taken the notes that formed this treatise). To those familiar with the *Nicomachean Ethics*, it is most often remembered as the work in which Aristotle asked what is the greatest happiness of humankind, and answered that it is a life of contemplation. Within the larger moral argument that led to this view of human happiness, Aristotle also develops a view of how we reason about action, known as practical reasoning.

For Aristotle, practical reasoning requires the specification of some desire or object of value, something we believe is good for us. This specification forms the initial or major premise of what has come to be called the practical syllogism (e.g., eating fruit is good for one's health). Subsequent premises may specify a number of different things, though the last line before the action is always one that indicates that the situation immediately before me is an instance of all the factors that appear in the previous premises (e.g., a friend is offering to share her fruit with me). When all the premises are set forth and linked to an action that followed from them, the result is known as a practical argument.

The term *practical argument* was coined not by Aristotle, but by a modern-day philosopher. In his presidential address to the Philosophy of Education Society, Thomas F. Green (1976) asked what competencies are needed by a teacher to instruct successfully. He contended that these competencies can be determined

by identifying what is required to change the truth value of the premises of
the practical argument in the mind of the child, or to complete or modify
those premises or to introduce an altogether new premise into the practical
argument in the mind of the child. (p. 252)

It is a simple step to shift from the notion of the practical argument in the
mind of the child to the practical argument in the mind of a teacher, which
is how the concept of practical argument was introduced into contemporary analyses of teaching.

To sum up, a practical argument is practical reasoning set out in a more
structured or systematic form. The premises are grouped together, they are
reasonably well developed, and they relate to the action in a recognizable
way. Following Aristotle, a practical argument contains an initial premise
that sets forth a desired goal, some intermediary premises, and, just prior
to the action, a specification of the situation in which the action takes place.
Section 5 of this chapter expands on the notion of intermediary premises,
describing the format of practical arguments. Before becoming involved
in a more extensive elaboration on practical arguments, it will be helpful
to have a better understanding of what they are meant to do in the context of teaching.

2. THE IMPORTANCE OF PRACTICAL ARGUMENT IN TEACHING

Put in the most simple terms, practical arguments are useful in teaching
because they call on the teacher to set forth the premises that provide an
account of the teacher's actions. As already noted, to specify these premises,
the teacher must state what he[1] was trying to accomplish (the end thought
worthy of attainment), what reasons he had for linking his actions to this
end, and what he thought was the context or situation that led to his acting the way he did. This specification of premises calls for considerable
reflection on the part of the teacher.

Reflection is a vital practice in teaching because of the way most teachers learn to practice their profession. Some learn from parents who were
teachers, others from courses in teacher education, still others from observing and receiving advice from more experienced teachers. Moreover,
as Lortie (1975) noted nearly two decades ago, the practices of many teachers can be accounted for by the way they were taught as students. These
sources of teaching practice pose some troublesome problems (see Buchmann & Schwille, 1983; Feiman-Nemser & Buchmann, 1986). To the extent
that we learn from those who taught us and those who served as our
advisers and mentors, as well as from the experience of teaching itself, our

understanding of teaching and learning is derived from the very culture in which it takes place. Thus the beliefs we have about teaching, learning, schools, and students, as well as all the other critical ingredients of education, are formed and shaped by the settings in which we work. Why is this problematic?

Those who have worked in schools know that schools and school policies are a result of many phenomena. There are political, economic, and social pressures on schooling that often oppose that institution's capacity to serve the more nòble purposes of education (anyone familiar with the bureaucracies of large school systems has a good idea of what is meant here). Given these oppositional forces, the experiences that shape a teacher's sense of what it is to be a teacher, and what is required to teach in a particular setting at any given point in time, can be highly miseducative for that teacher. In other words, when a teacher's conception of what and how to teach, and to what ends, is heavily shaped by his experiences in school—a most normal occurrence—that teacher stands a fair chance of failing to educate the learners in his or her charge.

By "failing to educate," I mean that the teacher is neither pursuing nor attaining educative ends, ends that are grounded in the acquisition of enlightenment, the realization of high ideals of human culture, the ability to exercise the responsibilities of informed citizenship, and the capacity to conduct oneself according to common standards of decency, respect, and regard. More is said about this moral basis for education in a later section. For the moment, it may be useful to look at an example of how the systemic character (or regularities, as Sarason, 1990, would say) can thwart the good intentions teachers have for student learning.

Walter Doyle (1977, n.d.; Doyle & Carter, 1987) studies what he refers to as the academic task structures of classrooms. In the course of his work, he noted how students come to view classrooms as places where performances by them are exchanged for grades given by teachers. The intrinsic, educational meaning of the work performed is often lost in the face of the salience of the exchange between performance and grades. Understanding this feature of teacher-student work helps to explain why students are often so interested in the most minute mechanics of assignments. They want to know what readings are expected, by what date, whether a paper is due, and if so how many pages and whether references are required, and what of all of this will appear on the examination, in what form (true/false, short-answer, multiple-choice, or essay).

Many teachers become frustrated, sometimes even angry, when students express so much interest in what seems to teachers to be the minutiae of schoolwork. What teachers often do not realize is that they (usually unwittingly) encourage this attentiveness to minor details by students.

Given the way teachers work in classrooms, within the larger context of the school and its rules and norms, it is not only reasonable that students would behave in this way; they also often perceive it as in their best interest to do so. They understand that the grade is the object of the exercise, and that grades are awarded on the basis of performances of certain kinds. By asking so many questions, they try to reduce the ambiguity and complexity of the tasks set by the teacher, thereby gaining as much clarity as possible about what kind of performance is most likely to yield the desired grade.

If we depend heavily on the teachers we had when we were students as models for how to teach, or on experienced colleagues who serve as mentors and advisers, and on our own experiences as teachers, for learning how to teach, we may quite easily acquire teaching practices that are inimical to what we truly hope to accomplish as educators of children. One of the most powerful ways to prevent our images of teaching and our teaching practices from being captured by the systems where we work is to stand away from our experience and reflect on it. Practical argument contributes to our capacity for reflection, and to the value of reflection for advancing our teaching, by providing perspective on the experiences of teaching, by offering a means to reconsider this experience, and by encouraging the reconstruction of our experience. This statement represents a broad claim for practical argument. To justify it, a deeper understanding of practical argument is required. It is to this understanding that we now turn.

3. HOW PRACTICAL ARGUMENTS ARE DEVELOPED

To understand how practical arguments contribute to the teacher's capacity for reflection, one must understand how they are developed in the setting of the school. In the description that follows, I believe that a good deal of fidelity to Aristotle's ideas remains; however, this work should not be seen as an explication of Aristotle's concept of practical reasoning.[2] It is, rather, an inventive adaptation of Aristotle, intended to achieve his aspirations for an ethics of human conduct while applying quite directly to the teaching practices common to many of today's schools. With this caution in mind, let us proceed to how practical arguments are developed.

It almost always requires at least two people to develop a practical argument (for an interesting exception, see Morgan, 1993). One is the teacher. The other is called simply "the Other" (with the "O" capitalized to distinguish the noun from the adjective). In this chapter, they are often abbreviated T and O. There may be more than one teacher, as well as two or more Others, as is the case for the Reading Instruction Study. The process of constructing a practical argument begins with O observing T's teaching, and then asking T why he did something that O observed him doing.[3] This phase of developing the practical argument is called "elicitation." The Other is seeking to elicit the practical argument in the mind of the teacher.

It is important to understand that T may not be, indeed probably is not, aware of a set of reasons for acting as he did. Practical argument elicitations are typically *post hoc*; they occur sometime after the teacher has engaged in some instructional behavior. The point of the elicitation phase of practical argument development is to have T go back over the teaching incident to see how he explains or justifies it. In so doing, much is often revealed to T about his own reasons for doing what he did, and how these reasons support or fail to support the action that T took.

In the elicitation phase, O avoids, as much as possible, any judgment or appraisal of T's reasons. O's role in this first phase is to invite T to discuss the grounds for his practice, and to encourage him to set out his reasoning in a form that approximates an argument. That is, O gently presses T to state what valued end he was seeking in acting as he did, what he saw as the situation that called for the action he performed, and what links the desired end and the specific situation to the action. These statements are called "premises," and they constitute the first attempt to formulate a practical argument.

A helpful way for T and O to begin the dialogue leading to the development of a practical argument is by viewing together a videotape of T teaching. At some point in the tape, O will ask T why he did something they both saw on the tape. As T responds, O begins the task of constructing the practical argument. Videotape was used extensively in the Reading Instruction Study, and is an essential part of my own efforts to learn more about practical arguments. I carry a video camera into the classrooms of teachers with whom I work, taping about two hours of teaching at a time. At some later time, usually a few days after the taping occurred, the teacher and I sit together after school to view the tape. During playback, I will ask about a particular action, or the teacher will begin to discuss an action. If the subject of this discussion proves worthy of deeper consideration, it becomes the springboard for eliciting a practical argument.

It will be evident to anyone who has taught that a trusting personal relationship must obtain between T and O. If such a relationship is not in force, T may focus on what he believes is most likely to convince O that T did the right thing, or that he believes O wants to hear. Indeed as is clear in the RIS data, T may do this in the early phases of elicitation, despite a reasonable level of comfort with O. In such cases, O presses issues of clarity and consistency with T, at all times with the intention of revealing to both T and to O the *teacher's* rationale for doing what he did.

At some point in the process the character of O's role will shift from one who is trying to draw out of T his reasons for the specified action to that of engaging T in a critical (in the best and most helpful sense of this term) discussion of the premises earlier set forth by T. That is, O takes on a less descriptive and more evaluative role. This second phase is called "reconstruction," because O and T are, together, engaged in the reconstruction of T's original practical argument. Kroath's (1990) notion of the "critical friend" is especially helpful here. The critical friend is one who works with a teacher "to confirm, to support and to provide authority on the one hand, and to challenge, to destabilize and to withdraw authority on the other hand" (p. 5). These dual functions characterize the role of the Other in the reconstruction phase.

The Other is not always the one to initiate this second phase. The teacher may begin to raise questions or pass judgments on his practice before O takes a more evaluative stance to T's action. When this occurs, O either follows T into the reconstruction, or encourages T to remain with elicitation until there is a shared sense that a reasonably complete and coherent account of T's action has been put forth. Because T is often the one to initiate the second phase, and typically contributes to it as or more extensively than O, the reconstruction phase is referred to as "mutual reconstruction," to make clear that the activity calls for a joint effort, and the product is a result of contributions from both participants.

These phases are clearly illustrated in the Reading Instruction Study. As indicated in Chapter 10, some of the teachers in the elicitation phase began by giving "external" reasons why they acted as they did. That is, they developed their rationales along lines of what they perceived was required or expected of them by external authorities. The teachers may have voiced reasons of this kind at the outset because they believed these would be the explanations most readily understood and accepted by the two Others (who were the primary researchers on the RIS project). It may also be the case that the teachers believed that these externally oriented reasons accounted, to some extent, for why they acted as they did.

The RIS researchers who were acting as the Others encouraged the fuller development of these initially proffered reasons, then began to raise questions about them or followed the teachers as they raised their own questions. If the question-raising is sustained, it marks a clear shift from elicitation to reconstruction. In the case of RIS, reconstruction centered on eliciting and appraising teachers' "internal" reasons for their reading practices. Internal reasons pertain to conduct stipulated by the teachers' own sense of what they should do to advance reading proficiency, rather than to reasons the teachers gave for why and how those in authority—building principals, curriculum coordinators, and school board members—wanted the teachers to teach.

This shift from external to internal reasons for action is a powerful illustration of how practical arguments serve to enhance reflection and increase the teacher's sense of ownership and control over his own practice. However, these results are not achieved merely by eliciting and reconstructing premises that emerge in the course of dialogue between T and O. There is an analytical framework to practical arguments that calls for particular kinds of inquiries on O's part. These inquiries are designed to develop discussion between T and O that accomplishes several important tasks. The first is to ground the initiating or first premise in a morally defensible theory of education. The second is to introduce into the practical argument, if they are not already there in some form, subsidiary premises that bring current knowledge to bear on the instructional practices of the teacher. It will be worth our time to explore these adjuncts to reflective teaching in some detail.

4. CRITICAL ADJUNCTS TO REFLECTIVE TEACHING

There are a number of ways to facilitate reflection about one's teaching, as the work of Clift, Houston, and Pugach (1990); Liston and Zeichner (1991); Russell and Munby, 1992; and Schön (1983, 1991) makes clear. Practical arguments are but one among a number of different approaches to the development of reflective capacities in teaching. What distinguishes practical arguments from other approaches is that they are facilitative of a fairly specific form of reflective practice. This form is best described as *normative*, meaning that practical arguments are grounded in a particular view of what teaching is and what it is supposed to accomplish. This normative sense of what it means to educate is the first of two critical adjuncts to reflective practice.

In his justly praised work *Teacher in America*, Jacques Barzun (1945) says, "Education is indeed the dullest of subjects and I intend to say as little about it as I can" (p. 9). In so stating, Barzun sought to direct our attention away from the very big, highly contested notion of education to the more manageable notion of teaching. It was as laudable an effort nearly a half-century ago as it is today. Yet there are good reasons for attending to the concept of education, and one of these is making a distinction between an everyday and a normative sense of education. In its everyday sense, education is all that happens to us and all that we do that adds to our store of knowledge, understanding, and ability. This is the sense most likely subject to dismissal by Barzun.

In the normative sense, education involves those experiences and activities that must take place in order for us to lead what Socrates called the examined life. Few have captured this normative sense better than

Harvard philosopher Israel Scheffler (1976), who states that education encompasses

> the formation of habits of judgment and the development of character, the elevation of standards, the facilitation of understanding, the development of taste and discrimination, the stimulation of curiosity and wonder, the fostering of style and a sense of beauty, the growth of a thirst for new ideas and visions of the yet unknown. (p. 206)

The idea behind this normative sense of education is that if schooling is to be educative, in the normative sense of the term, then it must make a clear contribution to the intellectual and moral development of the learner, in ways quite like those Scheffler describes.

One of the most important purposes of engaging in the elicitation and reconstruction of practical arguments is to develop the capacity of the teacher to participate in the profound task of educating fellow human beings. To educate, in this normative sense, means that teachers are assisting students to become morally discerning in their conduct, intellectually sophisticated in their thinking, and worthy contributors to the advancement of the human race. Practical argument addresses this normative aspect by calling our attention to the moral and ethical grounds for the teacher's actions in the formulation of the initial premises of the practical argument. Recall that these premises address the objects of desire or goods to be gained from acting in a certain way. It is here that the teacher sets forth what it is that he seeks in acting as he did and how this goal or aim is grounded in moral ideas about advancing the education of the student. One of the important tasks of the Other in developing practical arguments is to introduce these normative conceptions of education as T and O work toward the mutual reconstruction of T's practical argument.

The second critical adjunct to reflective practice is accounting for what is known and commonly understood about the content area of one's instruction, as well as the methods one uses in instruction. This adjunct requires that the teacher, in the course of constructing and reconstructing practical arguments, brings to bear what knowledge is available on the topic of the practical argument. For example, RIS was initiated in an effort to assess the extent to which teachers took account of the research findings regarding the teaching of reading, and to ascertain how teachers might be assisted in making more extensive use of reading research. The concept of practical arguments appeared applicable to this endeavor because practical arguments call for attentiveness to new knowledge and understanding, while maintaining a reflective focus grounded in a normative sense of education.

A particular type of intermediate premise ensures the consideration of knowledge and understanding applicable to the goals and actions of the teacher. This intermediate premise is called an empirical premise (or premises, as there may be and often are more than one). An empirical premise makes a statement about the world that is subject to test through some form of controlled inquiry (scientific method is the best known form, though the teacher might use other, less sophisticated though quite reliable, means to check the validity of an empirical premise). Empirical premises encapsulate the teacher's claims about what knowledge and understanding undergird his practice, claims that the teacher himself is making or that he is calling forth from other sources (e.g., research or authoritative texts) to substantiate his action.

In the early practical argument work of RIS, and in my own work, it was found that in the course of elicitation teachers offered very few reasons for their actions that could properly be called empirical premises. That is, these teachers typically did not make knowledge claims in an effort to substantiate their practices. It was not then clear, and is still a subject for further study, whether the teachers simply did not possess a knowledge base for their practice; they possessed it but not in a form recognizable by the Others; or they possessed it but either thought it inappropriate or not worth mentioning to the Others. The issue of the knowledge available to and used by teachers remains a complex topic in the scholarly literature on teaching. Whatever the explanation, as the teachers and Others shifted from elicitation to reconstruction, the Others inquired about the knowledge claims undergirding the teachers' practice, offering alternatives to current practice that were suggested in the research literature, suggesting readings that would permit the teachers to explore the topic further, or indicating to the teachers ways they might test the knowledge claims that were often implied in the early phases of the elicitation.

The empirical premise of a practical argument creates for teacher and the Other an expectation that teaching practice will be based on evidence, when and where appropriate. This evidence may take the form of teachers' subjecting their own claims to test, or introducing the work of other teachers or researchers as substantiation. As in the case of a normative theory of education, it is the task of the Other to ensure that an inquiry into the empirical basis for practice takes place. Again, T may be the first to broach the subject, in which case O need only encourage its further consideration. However the matter arises, it is a critical adjunct to reflective practice and a vital element in the practical argument.

Though the empirical premise of the practical argument signals the need to consider one's own knowledge claims as well as such other knowledge and understanding that may bear on the practice at hand, consideration of this premise does not require the teacher to be engaged in practices that reflect or are based on such knowledge or understanding. That is, the teacher is entitled, with the provision of other good reasons, to set aside certain knowledge claims as inapplicable to his teaching, these students, or this setting (or some combination of these). What is critical to the success of the practical argument is that the teacher is aware of such knowledge claims as he brings to the argument, and is familiar with the knowledge claims advanced in relevant research and theory. What follows from this awareness is the teacher's best judgment about the soundness of these knowledge claims and their applicability in the particular context of this teacher.

In this section I have tried to show that reflection, standing by itself, is not sufficient to guide change in teaching practices. The reflection must be grounded in a normative theory of education, and it must take account of such knowledge and understanding as may relate to the teacher's instruction and the content of this instruction. These two elements are critical adjuncts to reflection, and both are fostered by consideration of the initial and intermediate empirical premises in practical argument. Lest you conclude that such considerations exhaust the concept of practical argument, it is time to take our last look at the concept of practical argument. Here the notion will be explored in detail, setting forth all the primary elements of a practical argument.

5. A DETAILED DESCRIPTION OF PRACTICAL ARGUMENT

Previous comments in this chapter have suggested that there is a definite structure to practical arguments. That is indeed the case. The structure to be described in this section may be thought of as an analytic framework to guide the discourse between teacher and Other as they attempt to gain insight on the teacher's practice, as well as pave the way for possible reconsideration of that practice. A complete practical argument includes premises that describe the end or valued outcome of the action, premises that provide meaning for the activities under scrutiny, premises that provide the evidence or empirical support for the action, and premises that clarify and acknowledge the situational realities that are the context for the action.[4] These premises are referred to as (1) value, (2) stipulative, (3) empirical, and (4) situational. Let us look briefly at each.

The *value premise* is a statement of the benefit or good to be derived from an action. The premise (or set of premises) may be phrased as a declarative statement (My goal is to help children become successful human beings), or as an imperative (Every child must learn to read). As T and O refine this premise, an effort is made to frame it within a normative sense of education. The value premise provides the occasion for introducing a normative view of education into the deliberations of T and O, and also provides a basis for T's further deliberation on the contribution of his action to the education (in the normative sense) of his students.

The *stipulative premise* is one that was developed in the course of RIS, as previous versions of the practical argument form did not provide for certain types of reasons teachers offered in explanation or support of their actions. The stipulative premise or set of premises incorporates the ways teachers make meaning out of their work. They are not expressive of sought-after outcomes, nor are they empirical in character; thus they are neither value nor empirical premises. For example, a teacher in the RIS study, in the early phase of an elicitation, claimed that reading is being able to accurately read aloud a passage of text. This claim has the form of a definition. It was an essential element in the practical argument if the teacher's actions were to be fully accounted for by the argument. It is not, however, a testable claim. Rather, it expressed the meaning the teacher gave to a student's being able to read. The stipulative premise takes its name from the fact that teachers stipulate a meaning for some of the activities in which they are involved.

The *empirical premise* has already been described. This is a statement or set of statements that makes a claim about the world, and is thus subject to scrutiny, usually in the form of a test of some kind. An example is the teacher's contention that students whose parents read to them when they are young will learn how to read faster than students whose parents do not read to them. This premise is testable, and has been the subject of research over the last several decades.

The *situational premise* is a statement or set of statements that describes the context in which the teacher's action takes place. This premise appears quite straightforward to many, and is sometimes considered the easiest to develop. However, it is often among the most difficult, given the difficulty of being an astute and powerful observer of one's own setting. Yet an appreciation of the situation in which one is engaged can be one of the most powerful sources of reflective understanding in teaching (Pendlebury, 1990, offers a very helpful analysis of the situational aspects of practical reasoning).

These are the four types of premises that one develops in the course of fleshing out a practical argument. They are not intended to serve as a model or template, wherein T and O adhere strictly to this form, or to this sequence of consideration. Indeed, as experience with practical argument elicitation and reconstruction shows, it takes a long time, often many hours of discussion over several weeks or months, to formulate a reasonably

coherent and complete practical argument. To impose some form of linear order or time line on this process defeats its purpose. Elicitation and
reconstruction are "messy," in that they happen according to the personalities of T and O, and within the relationship they build with one another.
As such, the framework described here is a guide that frames or sets up the
discussion between T and O, but does not dictate that discussion.

In the early, elicitation phase of practical argument, O is seeking to
have T set forth the reasons for acting as T did. In this phase, O raises
questions or makes inquiries that are designed to gain as much "purchase"
on T's reasoning as possible. In the course of the dialogue, O attempts—
without being overly directive—to place T's reasons within the framework
just described. In other words, O is on the lookout for reasons that fall
within the categories of value, stipulative, empirical, and situational, and
works with T in placing these reasons in a progression that is sensible to
both of them. As they move toward mutual reconstruction, they become
more evaluative of the argument. In this phase, O becomes the critical
friend mentioned in section 3 of this chapter (see Kroath, 1990).

The description of practical argument has been carried as far as possible, given the limitations of a chapter within a book. Many questions
and gaps remain, but trying to cover them here would require that this
chapter become the entire book. It is with such a handy excuse that I leave
the topic of the structure of practical argument to address the concluding
consideration of this chapter: What do practical arguments have to do with
staff development?

6. CONNECTING PRACTICAL ARGUMENT
TO STAFF DEVELOPMENT

Practical argument can be viewed as a potent form of staff development,
provided we accept a broader view of staff development than that typically employed by school personnel. For many school professionals, staff
development is seen as a mechanism for introducing a specific program
or curriculum into a grade level, school, or district. Or it is a way to introduce or extend teachers' skills with a particular set of teaching techniques
or instructional packages. It is seldom viewed as the acquisition of abilities or capacities that enable a teacher to teach himself. That is, staff development is not usually seen as something we do to inquire into our own
teaching, for the purpose of getting better at what one aspires to accomplish as a teacher.

This alternative form of staff development (Richardson, 1994, calls it
"practical inquiry") provides teachers with the means to examine their own

practices, to critically assess these practices and the consequences that follow from them, and to make choices about teaching differently or even becoming a different kind of teacher. It is to this form of staff development that practical argument applies, for as already pointed out, the purpose of engaging in practical argument is to become reflective, in a special way, about one's pedagogical actions.

If deployed with considerable understanding of its point and purpose, practical argument offers three different levels of impact on the development of teachers who are engaged in it. The first level, reflection, has already been explored. Thus it is only necessary to offer the reminder that reflection is the deliberative reconsideration of practice. It is an essential undertaking because there are so many pitfalls to using one's past and present experience as sources of knowledge about how to teach. But reflection alone is not sufficient to accomplish all that is called for in teaching for educative ends.

The critical adjuncts of a normative view of education and how one's own knowledge and the knowledge available to educators in general bear on practice are needed if our reflection is to open new avenues of inquiry and practice. When these adjuncts to reflection are present, practical argument offers a second level of development, the exploration and reconsideration of one's own beliefs as they affect one's practices. Each of us comes to the task of teaching with beliefs about who and what we are as teachers. As we teach, we add to or subtract from this store of beliefs, framing our conceptions of our work out of the experiences we have as teachers, as well as what we see and hear outside the classroom. These beliefs are often formed without much consideration; they may begin as impressions and, over time, solidify into major beliefs about teaching. As such, they may serve as impediments or enhancers to improvement.

Whether our beliefs impede or enhance our advancement as teachers often depends on the relationship between what we believe and what it is proposed that we consider. For example, a conventional staff-development activity seeks to have us adopt a program—let's call it Directed Discipline. As you listen to the tenets of Directed Discipline, you discover that you do not care for it. It seems rooted in an understanding of the classroom that you do not have, and it proposes solutions to matters that you believe are not problems. Metaphorically speaking, Directed Discipline does not "map onto" your existing set of beliefs about teaching. Over time your attitude toward Directed Discipline hardens, until you eventually dismiss it as irrelevant or inappropriate to your circumstances.

For the purposes of this chapter, your rejection of Directed Discipline is not itself problematic. It becomes a problem if you are unaware of your beliefs and how they are prompting your rejection of Directed Discipline.

It is essential that you (and others, as will be explained in a moment) are aware of your basic beliefs about teaching so that you can consider the possibility that your beliefs are not consistent with sound educational theory or current views of effective practice. In so stating, I do not seek to endorse Directed Discipline or anything like it. Rather, the essential point here is that you are aware of your beliefs and can hold them accountable to advances in theory and research.

No attempt to change teachers that I am aware of, short of brainwashing (which of course defeats the very idea of being engaged in education), is likely to succeed if it ignores or tramples on the basic beliefs teachers have about their work and how they may best carry it out. Assuming it is true, this contention requires careful consideration by administrators who would engage teachers in new programs, as well as by those who are themselves teachers of teachers. But it is not enough to argue that administrators and teachers of teachers must be aware of teachers' beliefs. It is also necessary that teachers themselves are aware. This awareness is aided to a considerable degree by the elicitation and mutual reconstruction of practical arguments.

There is a third level of impact, though it is not often viewed as an outcome to be sought by those who believe they have the best interests of teachers at heart. This third level is the growth of autonomy on the part of the teacher. It represents one of the most important and powerful possessions of the effective teacher. The sense of autonomy intended here is described by Dearden (1975), who argues that a person is autonomous

> to the degree that what he thinks and does in important areas of his life cannot be explained without reference to his own activity of mind. That is to say, the explanation of why he thinks and acts as he does in these areas must include a reference to his own choices, deliberations, decisions, reflections, judgments, plannings or reasonings. (p. 63)

When the RIS researchers discovered that, as teachers progressed through the Practical Argument Staff Development sessions, their reasons for their actions shifted from being more connected to external influences to being more connected to their internal beliefs and aspirations. This change illustrates Dearden's conception of autonomy. As the teachers grounded their actions with more internal reasons, they were referencing their own activities of mind. It is their choices, deliberations, and judgments that accounted for what they did, in contrast to the views of others.

In so stating, I do not mean to suggest that the views of Others, or the rules and policies established for teachers, should be ignored by teachers. Quite the contrary, they should be most carefully attended to. It is how they are attended to that is critical to determining whether the teacher is acting autonomously. If the rules are simply adhered to as if the agent were simply an automaton, there is a clear absence of autonomy. If, on the other hand, there is a conscious decision to obey the rule, on the basis that one understands it and consents to its need and value, then one has acted autonomously with respect to the rule. It should be understood, however, that the teacher may also choose to disobey the rule or requirement. In this event the autonomy of the teacher must be balanced against the larger welfare of the organization, as it is every time a citizen contravenes a regulation or policy, or even breaks a law, for what he or she regards as an ethical reason.

It is often quite easy to determine the difference between a person's simple adherence to a rule and a person's decision to obey a rule. When asked "Why did you do that?" the person responds, "That's the rule here." This answer does not tell you anything about the person's autonomy; the answer to the next question does: "Why are you following this rule?" Someone who has given the matter little or no thought will respond that she is following the rule because it is the rule, or that is the way things are done here, or there really is not any other way to do such things. The autonomous person will respond with reasons for following the rule.

Practical argument places great stress on the setting forth of reasons, which in turn presses the person engaged in it to think through why he does what the Other has asked about. As such, practical argument is a particularly useful device for promoting autonomy on the part of the teacher. It is designed to press the teacher to, as Dearden would say, reference "his own choices, deliberations, decisions, reflections, judgments, plannings, or reasonings." Recognizing that practical argument is a useful device for promoting autonomy, one might still ask what special value it has for teaching.

Autonomy is an essential quality of the educated person. Going back to the first critical adjunct of reflection, I argued that it was essential to set forth a normative view of education. This view places great emphasis on persons who are critical and creative in their intellectual endeavors as well as morally discerning and virtuous in their actions. Is it possible to imagine a person like this who is not autonomous, who is unable to explain "what he thinks and does in important areas of his life . . . without reference to his own activity of mind" (Dearden, 1975, p. 63)? Given its importance for becoming an educated person, how is it acquired by the young in the course of their schooling? The answer is that it is acquired by modeling those who are in possession of it. Thus a teacher who sets out to educate students, in the normative sense, must himself possess those traits and virtues that mark him as an educated person. An obligation of any activity that lays claim to developing a teacher ought, then, to further that person's capacities and dispositions as an educated person. Practical argument does this by positioning the teacher as an intentional agent, whose actions are understandable only with reference to his own habits of mind.

Here then are the three levels of impact: reflection, deliberative examination of one's beliefs, and the fostering of autonomy. Of course these are not automatic outcomes of "doing practical argument." Rather, the larger point or purpose of practical argument must be understood, especially by the Other at the outset of the practical argument activity. Teacher and Other must be willing to converse and explore as two persons interested in each other and in education. Practical argument is not something to be adhered to or followed. It is an approach to reflective teaching, grounded in a particular concept of what it means to educate fellow human beings and demanding consideration of what we claim to know about what we teach and how we teach it. Furthermore, it calls for an acute sense of situational appreciation, wherein one is able to grasp both the content and the texture of the situation in which one acts. As a guide to staff development, practical argument encourages us to critically examine the beliefs that affect our practice; it presses us to connect our actions to our own plans, deliberations, and decisions; and, it is hoped, it engenders an openness to reconsideration and change.

As you read further in this book, you will observe this orientation toward practical argument on the part of the researchers, in their conduct as researchers and in their role as Others to the teachers who participated in RIS. It is essential to note how they deployed the notion of practical argument in their work. As stated before, it is not a model, template, or program. It is a set of ideas about how to think along with practicing teachers in ways that honor their intelligence and their insights, while also providing a framework for engaging in a dialogue between teachers and their critical friends.

NOTES

1. The gender reference of singular pronouns has quite properly become a matter of concern in scholarly writing. The current compromises, "he or she," or "s/he," seem to disrupt the flow of text as they send the eye on a kind of steeplechase as it moves across the page. For the following analysis in which I am using a hypothetical teacher, the pronoun references to the teacher are masculine, while pronoun references to the staff developer (or "Other," a concept to be introduced in the next section) are feminine.

2. For a philosophical discussion of practical reasoning, see Audi (1989). For the relationship between practical reasoning and character development, see

Nussbaum (1986) and Sherman (1989). For an extended discussion of practical arguments in the context of education, including criticisms of this approach, see Fenstermacher (1986), the 1988 (*37*:4) issue of *Educational Theory*, and the 1993 (*25*:2) issue of the *Journal of Curriculum Studies*.

3. Although this step comes first in the actual development of practical argument, it was not the first step in the Reading Instruction Study. In RIS, the researchers first engaged in what they called belief interviews. These interviews provided a general understanding of the teachers' beliefs and practices, and served as a baseline for examining the effects of the Practical Argument Staff Development.

4. The precise structure of the practical argument is subject to change, given that it is based on work in progress. As more is learned about either of these, the form of practical argument is likely to evolve, as it certainly has over the last decade of my involvement with it.

REFERENCES

Audi, R. (1989). *Practical reasoning*. London: Routledge.

Barzun, J. (1945, 1954). *Teacher in America*. Garden City, NY: Doubleday Anchor Books.

Buchmann, M., & Schwille, J. (1983). Education: The overcoming of experience. *American Journal of Education, 92*(1), 30–51.

Clift, R. T., Houston, W. R., & Pugach, M. C. (Eds.). (1990). *Encouraging reflective practice in education*. New York: Teachers College Press.

Dearden, R. F. (1975). Autonomy and education. In R. F. Dearden, P. H. Hirst, & R. S. Peters (Eds.), *Education and reason* (pp. 58–75). London: Routledge and Kegan Paul.

Doyle, W. (1977). Paradigms for research on teacher effectiveness. In L. S. Shulman (Ed.), *Review of research in education: 5 (1977)* (pp. 163–198). Itaska, IL: F. E. Peacock.

Doyle, W. (n.d.). Classroom tasks: The core of learning from teaching. In M. S. Knapp & P. M. Shields (Eds.), *Better schooling for the children of poverty: Alternatives to conventional wisdom* (pp. 235–255). Berkeley: McCutcheon.

Doyle, W., & Carter, K. (1987). Choosing the means of instruction. In V. Richardson-Koehler (Ed.), *Educator's handbook: A research perspective* (pp. 188–206). New York: Longman.

Feiman-Nemser, S., & Buchmann, M. (1986). Pitfalls of experience in teacher education. In J. D. Raths & L. G. Katz (Eds.), *Advances in teacher education, volume 2* (pp. 61–73). Norwood, NJ: Ablex Publishing Corporation.

Fenstermacher, G. D. (1986). Philosophy of teaching: Three aspects. In M. Wittrock (Ed.), *Handbook of research on teaching* (3d ed., pp. 37–49). New York: Macmillan.

Green, T. F. (1976). Teacher competence as practical rationality. *Educational Theory, 26*(3), 249-258.

Kroath, F. (1990). The role of the critical friend in the development of teacher expertise. Paper presented at an international symposium on Research on Effective and Responsible Teaching, Université de Fribourg Suisse, Fribourg, Switzerland, 3–7 September.

Liston, D. P., & Zeichner, K. M. (1991). *Teacher education and the social conditions of schooling.* New York: Routledge.

Lortie, D. (1975). *Schoolteacher.* Chicago: University of Chicago Press.

Morgan, B. (1993). Practical rationality: A self-investigation. *Journal of Curriculum Studies, 25*(2), 115–124.

Nussbaum, M. (1986). *The fragility of goodness: Luck and ethics in Greek tragedy and philosophy.* Cambridge, England: Cambridge University Press.

Pendlebury, S. (1990). Practical arguments and situation appreciation in teaching. *Educational Theory, 40*(2), 171–179.

Richardson, V. (1994). Teacher inquiry as professional staff development. In S. Hollingsworth & H. Sockett (Eds.), *Teacher research and educational reform* (Ninety-third Yearbook of the National Society for the Study of Education), (pp. 186–203). Chicago: University of Chicago Press.

Russell, T., & Munby, H. (Eds.). (1992). *Teachers and teaching: From classroom to reflection.* London: Falmer Press.

Sarason, S. B. (1990). *The predictable failure of educational reform.* San Francisco: Jossey-Bass.

Scheffler, I. (1976). Basic mathematical skills: Some philosophical and practical remarks. *Teachers College Record, 78*(2), 205–212.

Schön, D. A. (1983). *The reflective practitioner: How professionals think in action.* New York: Basic Books.

Schön, D. A. (Ed.). (1991). *The reflective turn: Case studies in and on educational practice.* New York: Teachers College Press.

Sherman, N. (1989). *The fabric of character: Aristotle's theory of virtue.* Oxford, England: Clarendon Press.

3

Teaching Reading and Observing Teachers' Practices

DEBORAH L. TIDWELL AND JUDY N. MITCHELL

Learning to read is perhaps the most important part of children's elementary school learning. Certainly the ability to read provides access to other school learning opportunities in such subjects as science and social studies. Further, through the pleasurable activity of reading literature, children gain insights about themselves and society.

Because reading is so important, elementary teachers are heavily involved in the teaching of reading and the fostering of reading success among their students. School principals and curriculum directors also play supportive roles in offering staff development programs, which frequently address aspects related to reading comprehension (Samuels & Pearson, 1988).

Yet, even with all the attention, the complexities involved in learning to read are still poorly understood. Well-intentioned teachers seem to be doing all they can, but there are many students who are not learning at all, or learning at a substantially lower level than some of their peers. Teachers' practices may be the missing link to help us better understand how the reading process operates and how to facilitate students' learning.

The purpose of this chapter is to examine teachers' practices as they were observed during the Reading Instruction Study (RIS). Exploring teachers' practices may give us additional insights into improving teacher effectiveness, children's reading success, and the education of the reading teacher. We begin by presenting a context for the study of reading comprehension instructional practices. We want to explain why literacy is such an important focus for schools and society today. The importance of literacy relates to our subsequent discussion of teachers' practices for teaching reading comprehension and the need for literacy instruction.

THE IMPORTANCE OF READING

It is not surprising that many elementary school staff development programs focus on effective instructional approaches in reading and literacy education as compared with other subject-matter areas. In today's society, literacy has a tremendous impact on everyone's life, especially in the pursuit of a better quality of life. Successful participation as a member of a democracy, and of a complex information-processing society, requires one to engage in many forms of literate activity demanding synthesis, assessment, organization, and monitoring (Reder & Green, 1983; Stedman & Kaestle, 1987). This demand for literate activity also shapes the way in which a culture views reality, and the value and importance placed on each individual (Eisenstein, 1985; Winchester, 1985).

In a literacy-based society, valued individuals are those adept at literacy tasks, those who can communicate well through their writing and who can also understand and make sense of what others have written. This is especially true in the workplace, where the need for occupational literacy has invaded almost all aspects of work. The particular requirements of occupational literacy will vary according to the reading demands and literacy competency necessary for job performance (Diehl & Mikulecky, 1980; Heath, 1980; Mikulecky & Ehlinger, 1986). Most workers, however, must have some level of specific literacy skills in order to keep their jobs and continue to successfully perform their work (Guthrie, Schafer, & Hutchinson, 1991; Mikulecky & Winchester, 1983).

But difficulties in reading and other literate activities not only limit adult populations in terms of job options and success; these same literacy difficulties often prevent children and young adults from achieving success at the most basic levels, such as grade-level completion or high school graduation (Johnston, 1985; Kozol, 1985; Mann, 1986). It is clear that for children to reach their potential as students and future adults, literacy instruction must prepare them for the expectations and requirements of both school and workplace. The demand placed on schooling (and ultimately on teachers) is to provide an instructional environment in which learners are able to reach their literacy potential. This requires that teachers know a great deal about literacy. Research in reading and literacy suggests that learning to function in a literate society goes beyond mastering specific literacy skills to employing literacy actions (effective literate behaviors) such as comparing, interpreting, and creating (Heath, 1991). This more proactive view of the reader's role raises questions about the dynamics involved between the reader and the text, as well as the relationship between the reading instructor and the student. What do teachers do when they teach reading? How do they teach reading? Is their teaching based on theory? Where do they get their ideas? How do they know their teaching is effective? Do they teach specific skills for reading? What beliefs guide their choice of instruction?

THEORIES OF READING COMPREHENSION

To understand where we are today in reading comprehension instruction, we need to examine the history of reading theory and practice. In attempting to delineate the most pervasive reading theories, we chose to highlight those theories supported by research that have best informed instruction over the years. While there have been many theoretical propositions for how the mind works and how reading connects with the mind, there are three prevailing models of reading comprehension represented in the research: the skills-based model, the schema-driven model, and the interactive model.

The Skills-Based Model

Reading comprehension instruction studies began in the early 1900s when instruction focused on drill-based vocabulary study in isolation and in context (Robinson, Faraone, Hittleman, & Unruh, 1990). These early teacher-centered lessons reflected the belief that reading comprehension was a compilation of separate skills. Skills—such as blending sounds together to make a word—were seen as hierarchical in nature, and instructors were trained to teach each skill in isolation, allowing students opportunities for practice to attain mastery before moving on to the next skill. The reading materials used by students were vocabulary-controlled, chunked pieces that had minimal story structure cues, and were often composed of text that was disjointed or unrelated. Young learners were given lessons to prepare them for reading.

Basal readers, developed in the mid-century, provided what was often considered teacher-proof instruction. These reading series included scripted teacher's guides, stories with controlled vocabulary and formulaic text intended for children in specific grades to read, workbooks and supplemental sheets providing skills practice, and tests for ascertaining mastery. Reteaching unmastered skills was an integral part of the basal program. Reading was seen as the total sum of its parts (skills), and through learning each of the individual skills separately, it was thought, students should be able to integrate and transfer these skills to their other learning. This is not to say that reading theory was condensed into one theoretical stance. While reading instruction in the classroom continued as a skills-based system, some theorists and researchers were arguing early on for a focus on interpretation and genuine comprehension (Whipple, 1925); suggesting that reading was a thought-getting process steeped in understanding rather than recitation (Henry, 1946); and arguing that reading should include the experiences of children as an important part of meaning (Durrell, 1949)—a precursor to schema theory.

The Schema-Driven Model

Robinson et al. (1990) suggest that practices relating to schema theory were introduced in the educational research literature as early as 1918, though not formally recognized as such. The term *schema* first began to surface in the 1970s (Anderson, 1985; Bransford, 1985; Bransford & McCarrell, 1974). Schema theory posits that a reader's understanding of what is read relates to the organization of knowledge in a reader's mind. Knowledge is structured into large, complex, abstract units of organized information called schemata (Rumelhart, 1981). To make sense of a meaningful piece of text (an example might be a story about a wild bird), a reader must categorize or attach the understood message (life of a wild bird) to the appropriate schema (what I know about birds). Instruction based on this theory brings students' experiences into the presentation of lessons (in reading about wild birds, this might include asking students about their previous experiences with birds), and actively provides experiences to students to enhance or develop schemata (such as visiting a bird exhibit) to help the students make a schematic bridge to the text. Instructional programs that highlight activities connecting the known to the unknown, that relate what a student is doing with what a student already knows, are considered more child-centered than the skills model and suggest a grounding in schema theory. This theory of complex schemata encourages "a close interaction between the reader and the writer" (Robinson et al., 1990, p. 81).

The Interactive Model

In the interactive model of reading, interaction takes on a broader sense of encompassing the "operation of a set of parallel interacting processes" (Rumelhart, 1985, p. 736). In this model of reading, both sensory and nonsensory knowledge come together to help the reader make sense of the text. Interactive reading instruction highlights several different components of the reading process. In the example of reading about wild birds, the interactive model of instruction would include the use of the student's prior knowledge of birds, while highlighting the semantic (meaning), syntactic (sentence structure and grammar), and graphophonic (letter-sound) elements within the context of the story's structure. In this model, reading is far greater than the sum of its parts. Skills are taught within the context of the story and within the context of the student's knowledge. When reading is seen as a complex dynamic process, reading instruction is required to take into consideration the variables of text, reader purpose, task demands, and environment. This interactive process of constructing meaning is translated into student-centered instruction that highlights the importance of reader input (prior knowledge, previous experience, interest, a sense of control) and the value of quality literature. Students are encouraged to be thoughtful readers who are aware of their goals in reading and of various strategies for obtaining their goals (Lipson & Wixson, 1991).

Such child-centered instruction focuses on the active role of the learner in constructing meaning through beneficial and useful instruction (Harris & Pressley, 1991). Theories about reading have moved from a compartmentalized skills and disjointed text stance to a stance that looks more at the whole piece of literature and centers instruction at appropriate interest, content, and difficulty levels. Unlike the skills-based model in which the teacher is the locus of control, the role of the teacher varies in both the schema-driven model and the interactive model. Some situations during reading comprehension instruction require the teacher to be more facilitative, with the locus of control being student-centered with teacher-provided guidance. Other reading comprehension instruction is more explicit, involving teacher modeling, guided practice for students, consolidation, and independent practice for students, followed by opportunities for students to apply learning to new situations (Pearson & Dole, 1987).

THE CONNECTION BETWEEN THEORY AND PRACTICE

As the understanding of the reading process changes the way in which we talk about reading theory, this change impacts the type of research conducted on reading. Both the theory and the research about practice suggest ways in which instruction in the classroom could improve. These changes might include the following trends: from teacher-dominated classrooms to more student-centered classrooms, from skills in isolation to skills in context, from using formulaic text to using quality literature, and from recitation and cued skills response to instruction in strategies and processes. However, an examination of the research on instruction in reading comprehension shows discouraging results. While there is a vast amount of research on reading and the teaching of reading, results and implications of the research may not always be clear. For example, researchers have found that teachers spend very little time on actual instruction in reading comprehension (Durkin, 1978–79, 1984; Mason, 1983; Mason & Osborn, 1982; Wendler, Samuels, & Moore, 1989). Teachers often focus their instruction on skill-based worksheets and materials concerned with decoding and other reading skills at the word and sentence level, rather than practices that involve more extensive reading comprehension (Barr & Sadow, 1989; Durkin, 1984; Mason, 1983). In addition, the materials chosen and the amount of instructional time allotted are often determined by reading groups; poor readers are given less to read, and the focus of the reading is on decoding rather than comprehension (Allington, 1984). Yet some research does suggest that teachers are not only aware of specific reading comprehension practices, but also use the strategies in the classroom as part of comprehension instruction (Rich & Pressley, 1990; Shanklin, 1990). These conflicting results may be explained by the different ways in which comprehension instruction is operationalized and therefore examined in classrooms.

Another interesting dynamic in the reading instruction dilemma is the knowledge that teachers bring to their reading instruction. A significant number of teachers in our elementary classrooms have been there for many years; in 1983, teachers with 10 or more years' experience comprised two-thirds of the public school teaching force (Plisko & Stern, 1985), and this pattern seems to be holding. Therefore, the theoretical knowledge of many of our teachers may be dated. The reading courses these teachers took as preservice teacher education students did not reflect the changes in reading theory and research of the last 10 or more years. And it is not uncommon for teachers to maintain the fundamental perspectives and understandings about teaching and learning that they obtained during their preservice training (Tabachnick & Zeichner, 1984). The beliefs teachers hold about reading, learning, and teaching may not be easily changed through typical avenues such as scattered in-service programs, suggestions from supervisors, or tips for practice from publications or peers.

These dated theoretical understandings of reading and learning combined with the limited opportunities to actually engage in genuine reflection and discussion of teaching practices (Lortie, 1975) create a dilemma for public school teachers. Chances to think about their instructional practices in relation to the meaning and purpose behind such instruction are not available. There is also very little opportunity for teachers to determine/develop a common understanding among themselves concerning what reading is all about, and what that means in terms of their instructional choices. Any such efforts would also be frustrated by the fact that the very books, journal articles, and teacher manuals that might be of help do not consistently explain the connection between theory and practice (Beck, 1984; Tierney, 1984), and often discuss reading practice in contradictory ways.

There is also conflicting evidence as to whether, or how, teachers incorporate research into their teaching. Although some research suggests that teachers do not use research in their teaching (Berger, 1976; Florio-Ruane

& Dohanich, 1984; Vacca & Gove, 1982), this may be due to the manner in which the teachers were asked about their practices. These studies rely on teacher interviews or surveys; teachers may state that they do not use research in their classrooms, but may actually be using practices that have grown out of research. Teachers may reply negatively for several reasons: They may not be aware of the research, they may not feel that what they do in their classrooms really relates to research, or they may have learned their practices in ways they do not connect to research. In other words, teachers' responses to questions about their practices may have more to do with the ways questions are asked than with their reading instruction. In addition, research is often not accessible to classroom teachers, either because it appears in unfamiliar or obscure journals or because teachers lack experience in reading and interpreting research articles.

Another line of research about teachers' practices suggests that when teachers do use or adopt strategies/practices in their classrooms, it is because the assumptions in the practices match teachers' already established beliefs (Hollingsworth, 1989; Munby, 1984). If this is true, teachers may be trapped in their beliefs about reading comprehension practices because of their earlier experiences in preservice teacher training. If a new model of staff development were employed that gave teachers a greater opportunity to examine their own practices and other practices that have recently emerged in the research literature, would they change their practices? This was one of the questions addressed in the Reading Instruction Study.

OBSERVING READING PRACTICES: THE READING INSTRUCTION STUDY

The Reading Instruction Study was designed to explore the links between research and teachers' reading instructional practices. We wanted to know what teachers' practices were, and whether and how these practices might change during the staff development process. Therefore, at several points during the RIS, we wanted to be able to objectively measure the degree to which teachers were using research-based practices in their classrooms. We needed to devise ways of defining, gathering, describing, identifying, and analyzing these practices.

There were only two choices available to obtain this information: ask teachers directly about their reading comprehension practices, or observe teachers in their classrooms when they were teaching reading comprehension. The former involved questionnaires, surveys, or interviews, while the latter meant recording what teachers did as they taught reading comprehension to their students.

We decided to conduct classroom observations to determine what teachers were doing in their classrooms. While interviews were conducted, these were aimed at eliciting teacher beliefs about reading and reading comprehension rather than determining how they were teaching (see Chapter 5). Observations are more objective, accurate, and reliable than self-report data (Borg & Gall, 1983). Observations would permit us to gather data on teachers' practices objectively and systematically, whereas the very nature of self-report data emphasizes subjectivity and individuality. Further, by not relying on teachers' self-report of their practices, we would be able to eliminate a potential communication problem—that of relying on teachers to use a common language for labeling or naming reading comprehension instructional practices. Teachers might not be able to give their practices names, or they might give them names different from the ones we or others would use. With observation, although we would have to infer the practices, the language of identification would be our own, and we could employ outside criteria to help us label or name practices according to the patterns we found across different classrooms and teachers. We structured the classroom observation in three ways:

1. *Teacher-selected observation times*: We asked teachers to allow us to observe when they planned a reading comprehension lesson. We wanted the teachers to frame the content of their lesson according to their own norms for what reading comprehension meant to them. We did not suggest what they should teach; we only asked to observe a reading comprehension lesson.
2. *Length of observed lessons*: We wanted to observe complete reading comprehension lessons, regardless of length. This was a conscious choice over spending a specific amount of time in each classroom. We felt that we were more likely to observe a range of reading comprehension practices if we observed complete lessons. We realized that this would result in a range of observation times across teachers, rather than holding time constant across observations.
3. *Type of observations*: We selected two different options for gathering the observational data during two different phases of the study: baseline observational records and teacher videos. The purposes, methodology, and results of each of these observation types are discussed below.

Baseline Observational Records

During the 1987–1988 school year, we observed 38 intermediate classroom teachers from six elementary schools in two southwestern school districts during their instruction of reading comprehension. (One teacher was added to the sample in the fall of 1988.) The grade level and subject matter taught during observations are delineated in Table 3.1.

Observation Instruments. To record our observations, we designed three instruments. According to the classification system of Evertson & Green (1986), who present three types of systems that can be used in conjunction with conducting observations, the Pre-observation Instrument, the Timed Narrative Record, and the Follow-up Questionnaire are descriptive and narrative systems. Descriptive systems use symbols and transcriptions, while narrative systems employ anecdotal records in everyday syntax. Sample copies of the Pre-observation Instrument and Follow-up Questionnaire are found in the appendix at the end of this chapter.

The Pre-observation Instrument was used to obtain a description of the classroom layout and context of reading instruction, as well as materials to be used and the students involved in the lesson. The Timed Narrative Record was used to make written transcriptions of classroom events that occurred during the observation period. This instrument calls for the observer to record as accurately as possible what the teacher says during the lesson, and to record, in shorthand, the types of teacher and student actions that occur: for example, student response (SR), teacher writing on the board (TWB), student question (SQ), student's oral reading (SOR), or teacher roaming around the room (TRM). (See Figure 3.1 for a complete list of the shorthand used for the Timed Narrative Record.) Hand recording was chosen as a method of data collection less intrusive than audio or videotaping. This data-gathering technique is similar to one commonly

Table 3.1 Classes in Which Reading Instruction Was Observed

Grade	Reading	Language	Social Studies	Writing	Special Educ/LD	Science	Total
4	11	1					12
5	5	1	3	1		1	11
6	6	2	1				9
3-4			1				1
4-5	3						3
4-6						2	2
Totals	25	4	5	1	2	1	38

Figure 3.1   Observation Shorthand for Timed Narrative Record

M+	-	mangement through positive statements	SWP -	sweep (gather information about class)
M	-	managment - general instructions - procedural	SW -	students writing
			TB -	teacher refers to board/chart/etc.
M-	-	management through correction of behavior	TCW -	teacher checking work
1:1	-	teacher-student one-on-one	TGM -	teacher gets materials
S	-	teacher refers to a student by name	TOM -	teacher organizing/shuffling material
SOR	-	student oral reading	TOR -	teacher oral reading
SOT	-	students off task	TT -	teacher talk [questions, statements, responses (can't hear)]
SQ	-	student asks question		
SR	-	student responds to teacher question	TRM -	teacher roaming around group/room
SSR-B	-	students silently reading (basal)	TSR -	teacher silently reading
			TUM -	teacher uses manual (refers to)
SSR-O	-	students silently reading (other)	TWB -	teacher writes on board/chart/etc.
SWB	-	students working in workbook	... -	more but couldn't get all

used during classroom observations for clinical supervision (Goldhammer, Anderson, & Krajewski, 1980).

As part of the Timed Narrative Record, a running narrative was written for 10 minutes, followed by a two-minute visual "sweep"; during these sweeps the observer noted information about classroom management, the children not involved in the instruction, and other information about the classroom that provided a social context for instruction. Cycles of narrative and sweep were repeated throughout the remainder of the observation. Other reading studies (Ratekin, Simpson, Alvermann, & Dishner, 1985; Ysseldyke, Thurlow, Mecklenburge, & Graden, 1984) used similar procedures.

The observers completed the Follow-up Questionnaire after the observation, giving their impressions of the observation experience through responses to queries about classroom management issues, observer reactions, and teacher comments.

Four classroom observers, each with a background in classroom teaching, received training over a three-week period in the use of the three instruments and in the shorthand procedures. The observers conducted 76 classroom observations of lessons averaging 40 minutes in length, with a range of 13 minutes to 80 minutes.

Data Analysis. The research team then began the most arduous task of the study—analyzing the data. We had planned for the observation instruments to provide us with two things: rich descriptions of the context of reading comprehension instruction, and a careful, complete, and consistent record of reading comprehension practices. We had not realized the mountains of data we would generate.

Initially, we had intended to read through our transcripts and immediately identify and relate teachers' talk during reading comprehension lessons to the research-based practices we were identifying from our literature reviews and syntheses (see Chapter 4). We found, however, that correct labeling of practices was impossible, because the teaching practices were often embedded within other structures we had not yet teased out and identified. Also, since the literature review was ongoing, a complete list of practices and firm definitions of them were not available.

It took eight two-hour sessions for four coders to work through a handful of transcripts and gradually, through discussion and consensus, develop the process for analyzing the data. We needed to identify the context of the lesson and discover the instructional goals before we could attach codes to the practices. The process was complex and highly inferential; we needed considerable discussion to define our terms, apply them to the data, and reach a consistent degree of interrater agreement on our decisions.

Our transcripts were eventually coded and analyzed for lesson theme, focus, and practice (see Richardson & Anders, 1990, for a complete discussion). Lesson themes consisted of statements about the central purpose or goal of lessons; focuses signified an instructional genre or a category of instructional activity; and practices were defined as something observable, describable, and linked to a theory of reading (see Chapter 4) that occurred within the context of classroom reading instructional lessons. Practices were instructional approaches that teachers selected from their personal repertoires of teaching strategies to incorporate into lessons, as planned or unplanned events.

An example of a lesson theme, focus, and practice as described above comes from a transcript in which the teacher conducted a prereading lesson, involving several activities designed to prepare the students to read a story, such as defining vocabulary words, activating prior knowledge, and so forth. The lesson then ended. For this lesson, then, the lesson theme was prereading; the focus was prior knowledge; and the practice was a specific activity, captured on the transcript, the description of which matched brainstorming as identified in the literature.

The 76 lessons included 27 themes and 466 practices, incorporated within 15 focus areas. The complete array of Baseline Record practices according to lesson theme and focus is shown in Table 3.2.

When we examined the goal or context of the lessons through the themes, we found some surprising results. The most common theme across instruction was comprehending stories (49 percent of the practices), with the next most popular theme being comprehending expository text (11 percent). Overall, meaning-based comprehending themes involved 69 percent of the 446 practices (stories, expository text, poetry, cartoons, paragraphs, graphs, sharing books). Other themes involved the presentation of information, preparing for reading, task-related instruction, and oral reading instruction. These data suggest that teachers were indeed integrating reading comprehension instruction into their lessons. Especially important is the percentage of teachers using meaning-based comprehension themes (69 percent of the practices) in their instruction. Meaning-based instruction was also associated with the topics or focuses of the various themes. These topics represent the research-based focuses represented in the teachers' instruction. Teacher/text-generated questions constituted the most prevalent focus, accounting for 24 percent of the practices. This focus suggests that the teachers were very teacher-directed in their approach to instruction. The second most prevalent focus was vocabulary, at 19.7 percent of the practices, followed closely by background knowledge at 18 percent. Both these focus categories reflect activities commonly found in a directed-reading activity of a basal series. Modality focus, in which teachers highlighted different modes of instruction such as verbal, visual, and kinesthetic, represented 13.3 percent of the practices. Another 10.7 percent of the practices focused on issues of text characteristics. The remaining 11 focus categories constituted fewer than 10 percent of the total practices observed.

Within each focus, practices were identified as relating to specific discrete practices found in research literature. For example, the distribution of the 13 types of discrete practices listed under the focus "Prior Knowledge" according to lesson theme is shown in Table 3.3. Discussing was the most common practice, comprising 46 percent of the total practices under the prior-knowledge focus. Further support for the notion that teachers do teach comprehension is reflected in the prior-knowledge practices where comprehending stories was the dominant theme (59 percent).

These data appear to contradict other research findings that teachers do not use research-based practices in classrooms. Teachers in this study employed an average of 3.8 research-based practices per lesson. An examination of the lesson themes provides consistent support for the realization that teachers do indeed teach reading comprehension, and not as an

Table 3.2 Baseline Records: All Practices

THEME	Background Knowledge	Text Characteristics	Vocabulary	Independent Study Strategies	Imagery	Self-Monitoring/Metacognition	Teacher-/Text-Generated Questions	Self-Generated Questions	Modality	Evaluation/Feedback	Reading & Writing	Critical Reading	Integrate Text-Based Ideas	Attention/Selection	Memory & Retrieval	Total
Comprehending Cartoons	3	2					2		1							8
Comprehending Expository Text	8	6	11		3	1	9		7	2			1	2		50
Comprehending Graphs		1					1									2
Comprehending Paragraphs		1	1								1					3
Comprehending Poetry	1		1		1		5		4					1		13
Comprehending Stories	47	20	51		5	3	52	1	30	6	8		4	4		231
Distinguishing Fact & Fiction	2	1	1				3		2		1					10
Distinguishing Same & Different	1	1					1									3
Finding Main Idea/Details	3	3	1				7		4		1					19
Identifying Comprehension Strategies						1										1
Learning About an Author	1						1		1							3
Learning About Making Up Questions								1								1
Learning Cause/Effect		1														1
Learning Figurative Speech	1	2	5		1		4		4		2					19
Learning Parts of Speech			1													1
Learning Punctuation	1	2	1			1	2		2							9
Learning Syllabification		1	1				1	1								4
Learning Vocabulary	2	1	12					5	1							21
Previewing/Prereading	9	6	4			1	7	1	4		1		1	2		36
Prewriting	1	1				1			2							5
Reading Plays									1							1
Reading Students' Written Work	1						2		2		2					7
Sharing Books	1						1									2
Understanding Acronyms		1					1									2
Using Comprehension Skills	2		3					5			1					11
Using Encyclopedias							1									1
Writing Book Reports											2					2
Total	84	50	92	0	10	8	106	8	62	9	22	0	6	9	0	466

Table 3.3 Baseline Records: Prior Knowledge Practices

BACKGROUND KNOWLEDGE	Comprehending	Comprehending	Comprehending Graphs	Comprehending Poetry	Comprehending Stories	Distinguishing Fact and	Distinguishing Same &	Finding the Main	Learning About an	Learning Punctuation	Learning Figurative	Learning Vocabulary	Previewing/Prereading	Prewriting	Reading Students'	Sharing Books	Using Comprehension	Total
Providing BK Statements	1	1		1	5													8
Teaching/Using Analogies					2		1			1		1						5
Reading Multiple Texts (Same Topic)																		0
Advance Organizers																		0
Discussing	1	4			17			3					5		1		2	33
Brainstorming		2			2								1	1				6
Confronting Misconceptions					1													1
Previewing Stories					2													2
Predicting Characters' Actions					5											1		6
Reading Headings					1													1
Predicting Story Events	1				7													8
PREP																		0
Lecturing								1										1
	3	7	0	1	42	0	1	4	0	1	0	1	6	1	1	1	2	71

occasional addendum to lessons but as a dominant goal of their instruction. Teachers do use research-based practices, even if they themselves may not identify them as such. Indeed, what they do in their classrooms resembles what researchers recommend.

Changes in Practices

In a second investigation of this data, we were interested in answering two questions: (1) Again, what are the practices used during reading comprehension instruction? and (2) How do teachers' reading comprehension practices compare after a year's involvement in a practical-argument staff development process? To answer these questions we based our observations on videotaped classroom lessons. We changed to videotaping from narrative observations because we needed the videotapes for the staff development process.

Videotaped Observations. Five teachers who had been involved in the baseline study in the first year of the RIS project were observed in the second year. All five teachers taught at the same school site and were involved in the practical-argument staff development process. The staff development began in October and was completed in late April of the same school year. We videotaped the teachers in the fall, prior to participation in the staff development process, and again in the spring, toward the end of the staff development. The fall tapes were the same tapes used in the practical-argument staff development process. (For more information regarding the practical-argument process, see Chapters 2 and 6.) In addition to the videotape, we also took anecdotal notes of the materials used in the classroom and of specific lesson contexts not picked up through the video (such as teacher comments prior to taping that provided us with an explanation of the relation of the lesson to previous and future lessons). We also collected copies of materials used during the lesson. The average length of the lessons was similar to that of the lessons in the baseline data, averaging approximately 40 minutes.

We found both advantages and disadvantages in using videotape to observe teachers' practices. The biggest advantage was that videotaping freed us from having to document immediate perceptions of classroom activity. In addition, it gave us the luxury of viewing and reviewing the actions of teachers and students as often as we needed over an extended period of time. But this ability to view and review the tapes also constituted a disadvantage: an overwhelming abundance of documented details. A clear plan of action for analyzing helped to overcome what we called the "video detail anxiety."

Data Analysis. Two global considerations directed our decisions in analyzing the videotapes. First, how would the actions of the video be documented? To determine this we needed to answer several questions: What did we want to get out of the tapes? What amount of written documentation was needed? When, if ever, were exact transcriptions of dialogue necessary?

We developed a modified transcript that highlighted the key components of the lesson using descriptive language and documented the gist of the teacher's dialogue and actions, and the gist of the students' responses. Specific classroom features, such as chalkboard work and texts used, were also noted in the transcription. Specific statements made by the teacher or a student were highlighted with quotation marks when deemed pertinent to the understanding of the transcription. (See Figure 3.2 for an example of a modified transcription.)

The second global consideration involved determining how the video documents would be analyzed. We decided that since the overall purpose of the videotaped observations was to determine the reading comprehension practices used during instruction, we would be guided by our defini-

Figure 3.2 Example of a Modified Transcription

T: talks about assignment on board and the order of events. T then says story to be
      read is "really neat" "it's about a deaf girl" and tells Ss to read questions before
      rug so they know what they're reading for. T briefly describes work sheet to Ss
      then reminds Ss to read questions 1st before reading.
      Text: Houghton Mifflin Basal Series (1981)
      Board assignment:
      1) charts together skill lesson & practice together p.82. Go over questions from
         Tues., pg.80. Work sheet 19 - 20. Sheets 6B & 1.
      2) Redo together sheets 3B. Read 79 - 82. Workbook 20 -21, sheets 11-12.T:
         calls specific Ss by name to reading table. (Ss seem surprised to be called up).
T: returns comprehension check question answers from last Tues.- missing several
      Ss papers. Briefly asks Ss where papers are - Ss confused. T tells Ss it's the
      story about Tigger. T tells S to close her book (basal). T tells Ss she will go over
      questions & ask Ss to answer who did not turn in papers.
T: talks with student that's working on seat work.
SR: all sit and wait, with basals closed.
T: asks questions.
SR: mumbles correct answer.
T: says "right!" then "why?"

---

tion of practice as observable, describable, and identifiable (see Chapter
4). It was also decided that the transcriptions would guide the analysis,
but that the videotapes would be viewed again as an overview and confirmation of the transcribed practices. We used a categorizational methodology (Bogdan & Biklen, 1982) to analyze each transcript for the following elements: practices used, overall lesson elements, student involvement,
type of teacher-directed instruction, and materials used.

When we coded and analyzed the transcripts, categories emerged in
four areas: reading comprehension instruction practices, degree of teacher-
directed instruction, choice of text/use of text, and student interactions.

As we described the practices we observed in the videotapes, a clearer
image of what makes up a practice emerged. Besides being observable,
describable, and identifiable, practices also had a particular instructional
focus and related to a particular purpose, oftentimes incorporating more
than one task. We found the specific focus and related purpose by examining the teacher statements, the text and materials used, the sequence of
events, and the relationship of those events in a particular lesson. An
example of a practice focus and purpose is seen in one teacher's "Word
Find." This particular practice was used several times at the beginning of
her lesson and involved children's using dictionaries for word location,
with an emphasis on speed and accuracy. The focus of the practice was

vocabulary development. The purpose of the practice was to improve students' use of the dictionary to locate, pronounce, and define unknown words. The following is a detailed description of the steps in this practice.

WORD FIND

1. Target words written on board.
2. Students timed for locating words in dictionary.
3. Times recorded on board.
4. First to find word comes to board and divides word into syllables.
5. Students chorally say word.
6. Student at board reads definitions of the word to group.
7. Teacher rereads definitions.
8. Teacher asks students if anyone had similar experience.
9. Students provide examples from own experiences regarding word.
10. Teacher summarizes student responses.

Other investigated areas of practice included teacher- directed actions (from authoritative to facilitative), text choice and text use (from basal-based to literature), and levels of student interaction (from product to process) (see Tidwell & Schlegel, 1990, for a complete discussion).

These observations determined that teachers do indeed use practices related to reading comprehension, and that a practical-argument staff development process impacts the way in which teachers use practices in their instruction. This staff development process provided teachers with the opportunity to discuss their own rationales for instruction, combined with presentations and discussion of current research and theories of reading. We found it interesting that the number of practices used in instruction in the spring was fewer than the number presented in the fall. For example, one teacher used five practices in the fall, but only four practices in the spring. However, the quality of the practices shifted from a more skills-based product focus to a more process-oriented focus. This shift is apparent in Figure 3.3, which places teachers' approaches to reading instruction along three continua: authoritative teacher-centered instruction to facilitative student-centered instruction, use of basal readers to use of literature, and product-based lesson focus to process-based lesson focus. Each teacher's fall and spring approaches were placed on these continua. The most profound change was the switch from the use of basal materials to the use of literature. In addition, spring practices incorporated more of the students' prior knowledge and encouraged greater student interaction, represented in shifts toward process-based and facilitative instruction.

One teacher (Fd) remained consistent in her instructional approach to teaching reading comprehension. She used literature as her instructional

Figure 3.3 Teachers' Approaches to Reading Instruction

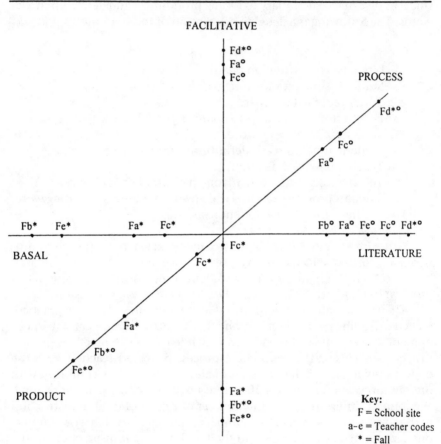

text and provided facilitative probes and prompts during instruction, encouraging high levels of student interaction. Her rationales for teaching also remained constant from fall to spring, with her beliefs grounded in an interactive child-centered understanding of reading, similar to the current research and theory discussed in the staff development program. Prior to staff development, she had already begun her own self-reflections into her teaching.

We found, overall, the changes in instruction were substantial where teacher actions differed across all three continua (e.g., Fa, Fc; see Figure 3.3): teaching style, use of text, and outcome focus of lesson. In the other teachers' instruction, we found that change did occur, but to a lesser degree. For two of the teachers (Fb, Fe), the change occurred in their choice of materials for instruction, with minimal change in their classroom interactions and lesson outcomes. For the teacher already grounded in current theory (Fd), her instruction changed in the quality of the student interactions, allowing students more internal locus of control for self-evaluation.

CONCLUSIONS: TEACHERS' USE OF RESEARCH-BASED PRACTICES

What is interesting about this analysis from a reading perspective is the number of research-based practices teachers use in their instruction. These results indicated that teachers use many of the practices suggested by scholarly research, and do indeed teach reading comprehension to their students.

From a staff development standpoint, the results are equally intriguing. Prior to involvement in the RIS staff development program, the teachers' predominant instructional choices (as observed in the initial observations) included focuses in teacher/text-generated questions, vocabulary, and background knowledge, with themes in comprehending, in presenting information, and in preparatory lesson elements. These choices coincided well with their fall instruction, as determined from the videotapes (teacher-directed, authoritative, basal-based, and product-oriented). However, after the staff development program, changes did occur across all teachers. Some teachers dramatically changed what and how they taught, and gave profoundly different justifications for why they taught in that manner. Others changed in smaller degrees.

Most important, however, is that teachers' beliefs and understanding (and therefore their instructional purposes, roles, and practices) *can* change, especially when provided with a staff development program that presents opportunities for teachers to examine their own beliefs and teaching, to provide practical arguments about their teaching, and to meet with other teachers to discuss their teaching. These changes, though varied in degree from visible but not substantive (Fe, Fb) to substantive (Fa, Fc), appear to signal an awareness in these teachers of alternative approaches to reading. While some changes appear merely cosmetic in nature, these "small" changes should not be minimalized. These teachers were involved in a staff development process that addressed teacher-held premises and corresponding actions in the classroom. The very act of changing the materials used in class suggests an examination of actions. The act of changing lesson outcomes, teaching style, and materials is evidence of a stronger impact: that the staff development process resulted in changes in beliefs and transformed teacher actions.

APPENDIX: Baseline Observation Instruments

Pre-observation Instrument

School:_____ Code:_____

Teacher:_____ Observer:_____ Date: _____

Start time:_____End time:_____

Describe the layout of the classroom and the general structure of the reading instruction (e.g. learning centers, ability groups with the teacher while others work independently, etc.). Include descriptions of centers when appropriate and general reactions to the classroom design.

_____

_____

_____

Materials used by the teacher-centered groups: (describe groups, name of group, number of students; indicate text name and page number)

1) _____

_____

2) _____

_____

3) _____

_____

4) _____

_____

Material used by remainder of class:

_____

_____

Observer Comments:

_____

_____

Follow-up Questionnaire

Reflect on the classroom experience immediately after the observational period; mark your responses on the checklist and make comments when appropriate.

1 = never   2 = seldom   3 = sometimes   4 = frequently   5 = always

1. Students in the instructional groups were on-task.

   1 2 3 4 5

2. The teacher spent the time on instructional activities rather than management and discipline.

   1 2 3 4 5

3. Students who were not in the instructional group were on-task.

   1 2 3 4 5

4. Students who were not in the instructional group interrupted the teacher to ask questions.

   1 2 3 4 5

5. The teacher spent time disciplining students outside the instructional group.

   1 2 3 4 5

6. There is a positive, warm relationship between the teacher and students.

   1 2 3 4 5

7. The students were enthusiastic.

   1 2 3 4 5

8. The students were motivated extrinsically.

   1 2 3 4 5

9. The teacher gave positive feedback.

   1 2 3 4 5

10. The teacher gave negative feedback.
    1 2 3 4 5

11. Any reactions to the lesson:

Observer Comments:

REFERENCES

Allington, R. L. (1984). Content coverage and contextual reading in reading groups. *Journal of Reading Behavior, 16*, 85–96.

Anderson, R. C. (1985). Role of the reader's schema in comprehension, learning, and memory. In H. Singer & R. B. Ruddell (Eds.), *Theoretical models and processes of reading* (3rd ed., pp. 372–384). Newark, DE: International Reading Association.

Barr, R., & Sadow, M. W. (1989). Influence of basal programs on fourth-grade reading instruction. *Reading Research Quarterly, 24*, 44–71.

Beck, I. L. (1984). Developing comprehension: The impact of the directed reading lesson. In R. C. Anderson, J. Osborn, & R. J. Tierney (Eds.), *Learning to read in American schools: Basal readers and content texts* (pp. 3–20). Hillsdale, NJ: Erlbaum.

Berger, A. (1976, August). *Implications of reading research on classroom teachers and administrators*. Paper presented at the Sixth World Congress on Reading, Singapore. (ERIC Document Reproduction Service No. ED 126-471)

Bogdan, R. C., & Biklen, S. K. (1982). *Qualitative research for education: An introduction to theory and methods*. Boston: Allyn and Bacon.

Borg, W. R., & Gall, M. D. (1983). *Educational research: An introduction*. Boston: Allyn and Bacon.

Bransford, J. D. (1985). Schema activation and schema acquisition: Comments on Richard C. Anderson's remarks. In H. Singer & R. B. Ruddell (Eds.), *Theoretical models and processes of reading* (3rd ed., pp. 385–397). Newark, DE: International Reading Association.

Bransford, J. D., & McCarrell, N. S. (1974). A sketch of a cognitive approach to comprehension. In W. B. Weimer & D. S. Palermo (Eds.), *Cognition and the symbolic processes* (pp. 189–229). Hillsdale, NJ: Erlbaum.

Diehl, W. A., & Mikulecky, L. (1980). The nature of literacy at work. *Journal of Reading, 24*, 221–227.

Durkin, D. (1978-1979). What classroom observations reveal about reading comprehension instruction. *Reading Research Quarterly, 14*, 482–533.

Durkin, D. (1984). Is there a match between what elementary teachers do and what basal reader manuals recommend? *The Reading Teacher, 37*, 734–744.

Durrell, D. (1949). Development of comprehension and interpretation. In N. B. Henry (Ed.), *Reading in the elementary school* (Forty-eighth Yearbook of the National Society for the Study of Education, Part 2) (pp. 193–204). Chicago: University of Chicago Press.

Eisenstein, E. (1985). On the printing press as an agent of change. In D. Olson, N. Torrance, & A. Hildyard (Eds.), *Literacy, language, and learning: The nature and consequences of reading and writing* (pp. 19–33). London: Cambridge University Press.

Evertson, C. M., & Green, J. L. (1986). Observation as inquiry and method. In M. Wittrock (Ed.), *Handbook of Research on Teaching* (3rd ed., pp. 162–213). New York: Macmillan.

Florio-Ruane, S., & Dohanich, J. B. (1984). Research currents: Communicating findings by teacher and researcher deliberations. *Language Arts, 61,* 724–730.

Goldhammer, R., Anderson, R. H., & Krajewski, R. J. (1980). *Clinical supervision: Special methods for the supervision of teachers.* New York: Holt, Rinehart & Winston.

Guthrie, J. R., Schafer, W. D., & Hutchinson, S. R. (1991). Relations of document literacy and prose literacy to occupational and societal characteristics of young black and white adults. *Reading Research Quarterly, 26,* 30–48.

Harris, K. R., & Pressley, M. (1991). The nature of cognitive strategy instruction: Interactive strategy construction. *Exceptional Children, 23,* 392–404.

Heath, S. B. (1980). The functions and uses of literacy. *Journal of Communication, 30,* 123–135.

Heath, S. B. (1991). The sense of being literate: Historical and cross-cultural features. In R. Barr, M. L. Kamil, P. Mosenthal, & P. D. Pearson (Eds.), *Handbook of reading research* (Vol. 2, pp. 3–25). New York: Longman.

Henry, N. B. (Ed.). (1946). *The measurement of understanding* (Forty-fifth Yearbook of the National Society for the Study of Education, Part 1). Chicago: University of Chicago Press.

Hollingsworth, S. (1989). Prior beliefs and cognitive change in learning to teach. *American Educational Research Journal, 26,* 160–190.

Johnston, P. (1985). Understanding reading disability: A case study approach. *Harvard Educational Review, 55,* 153–177.

Kozol, J. (1985). *Illiterate America.* Garden City, NY: Anchor/Doubleday.

Lipson, M. Y., & Wixson, K. K. (1991). *Assessment and instruction of reading disabilities: An interactive approach.* New York: Harper Collins.

Lortie, D. (1975). *Schoolteacher.* Chicago: University of Chicago Press.

Mann, D. (1986). Can we help the dropouts: Thinking about the undoable. *Teachers College Record, 87,* 307–321.

Mason, J. M. (1983). An examination of reading instruction in third and fourth grades. *Reading Teacher, 36,* 906–913.

Mason, J., & Osborn, J. (1982). *When do children begin "reading to learn"?: A survey of classroom reading instruction practices in grades two through five* (Tech. Rep. No. 261). Urbana-Champaign: University of Illinois, Center for the Study of Reading.

Mikulecky, L., & Ehlinger, J. (1986). The influence of metacognitive aspects of literacy on job performance of electronics technicians. *Journal of Reading Behavior, 18,* 41–62.

Mikulecky, L., & Winchester, D. (1983). Job literacy and job performance among nurses at varying employment levels. *Adult Education Quarterly, 34,* 1–15.

Munby, H. (1984). A qualitative study of teachers' beliefs and principles. *Journal of Research in Science Teaching, 21,* 27–38.

Pearson, P. D., & Dole, J. A. (1987). Explicit comprehension instruction: A review of research and a new conceptualization of instruction. *Elementary School Journal, 88*(2), 151–165.

Plisko, V. W., & Stern, J. D. (1985). *Condition of education.* Washington, DC: U.S. Department of Education.

Ratekin, N., Simpson, M. L., Alvermann, D. E., & Dishner, E. K. (1985). Why teachers resist content reading instruction. *Journal of the Sociology of Language, 42,* 9–39.

Reder, S., & Green, K. R. (1983). Contrasting pattern of literacy in an Alaskan fishing village. *International Journal of the Sociology of Language, 42,* 9–39.

Rich, S., & Pressley, M. (1990). Teacher acceptance of reading comprehension strategy instruction. *Elementary School Journal, 91*(1), 43–64.

Richardson, V., & Anders, P. (1990). Final report of the reading instruction study. Tucson: College of Education, University of Arizona. (ERIC Document Reproduction Service No. ED 324-655)

Robinson, H. A., Faraone, V., Hittleman, D. R., & Unruh, E. (1990). *Reading comprehension instruction, 1783–1987: A review of trends and research.* Newark, DE: International Reading Association.

Rumelhart, D. E. (1981). Schemata: The building blocks of cognition. In C. Anderson, R. Spiro, B. Bruce, & E. W. Brewer (Eds.), *Theoretical issues in reading comprehension* (pp. 33–58). Hillsdale, NJ: Erlbaum.

Rumelhart, D. E. (1985). Toward an interactive model of reading. In H. Singer & R. B. Ruddell (Eds.), *Theoretical models and processes of reading* (3rd ed., pp. 22–58). Newark, DE: International Reading Association.

Samuels, S. J., & Pearson, P. D. (1988). *Changing school reading programs: Principles and case studies.* Newark, DE: International Reading Association.

Shanklin, N. L. (1990). Improving the comprehension of at-risk readers: An ethnographic study of four Chapter One teachers, grades 4–6. *Journal of Reading, Writing, and Learning Disabilities International, 6*(2), 137–148.

Stedman, L. C., & Kaestle, C. F. (1987). Literacy and reading performance in the United States, from 1880 to present. *Reading Research Quarterly, 22,* 8–46.

Tabachnick, B., & Zeichner, K. (1984). The impact of the student teaching experience on the development of teacher perspectives. *Journal of Teacher Education, 21,* 165–167.

Tidwell, D. L., & Schlegel, M. (1990, December). *Teachers' reading comprehension practices: Impact of a staff development program on classroom instruction.* Paper presented at the annual meeting of the National Reading Conference, Miami.

Tierney, R. J. (1984). A synthesis of research on the use of instructional text: Some implications for the educational publishing industry in reading. In R. C. Anderson, J. Osborn, & R. J. Tierney (Eds.), *Learning to read in American schools: Basal readers and content texts* (pp. 287–296). Hillsdale, NJ: Erlbaum.

Vacca, R. T., & Gove, M. K. (1982). *Teacher reflections on the use and adaptation of instructional innovation presented during staff development.* Paper presented at the annual meeting of the American Educational Research Association, New York. (ERIC Document Reproduction Service No. ED 217-389)

Wendler, D., Samuels, S. J., & Moore, V. K. (1989). Comprehension instruction of award-winning teachers, teachers with master's degrees, and other teachers. *Reading Research Quarterly, 24,* 382–401.

Whipple, G. M. (Ed.). (1925). *Report of the national committee on reading* (Twenty-fourth Yearbook of the National Society for the Study of Education, Part 1). Bloomington, IL: Public School Publishing.

Winchester, I. (1985). Atlantans, Centurions, and the litron bomb. In D. Olson, N. Torrance, & A. Hildyard (Eds.), *Literacy, language, and learning: The nature and consequences of reading and writing.* London: Cambridge University Press.

Ysseldyke, J. E., Thurlow, M. L., Mecklenburge, C., & Graden, J. (1984). Opportunity to learn for regular and special education students during reading instruction. *Remedial and Special Education, 5*(1), 29–37.

4

Research-Based Practices as the Content of Staff Development

CAROL V. LLOYD AND PATRICIA L. ANDERS

Every spring semester Carol Lloyd, the first author of this chapter, teaches a graduate class in which current research in literacy is read and discussed. The students are teachers at the end of their masters degree program in reading education. Their comments during discussions of the research reveal their understandings of the functions of research and their frustrations. "I thought I was finally going to find out the right way to teach vocabulary." "I wanted to know for sure whether it's O.K. to have students read aloud." "Should I always set purposes before reading?" Implicit in these statements is the notion that research, especially those studies that investigate the efficacy of teaching practices, can and should be transferred into the everyday teaching practices of the classroom.

The implication that research should transfer to the classroom is also common in staff development programs. For example, an administrator might hear or read about a new strategy (or program), and design and offer an in-service day or staff development program to introduce teachers to the information. Often a researcher/teacher educator is invited as the "expert" who helps the faculty make this transfer (Kamil, 1984).

The process/product movement of the 1970s and 1980s is typical of attempts to transfer research-based findings to the school and classroom. Educational researchers sought to identify the teaching style, method, model, or strategies that best contributed to increased student achievement and improved attitudes (Gage, 1978). Hence, the goal of this movement was to develop a model or formula that could be followed by teachers and would result in specific student outcomes. In the reading field, this might best be demonstrated by the book *Becoming a Nation of Readers* (Anderson, Hiebert, Scott, & Wilkinson, 1985). A quote expresses this notion well: "America will become a nation of readers when verified practices of the best teachers in the best schools can be introduced throughout the country" (p. 120).

Research on reading comprehension can be traced back to 1884, but it was not a major focus of reading research until the 1960s (Venezsky,

1984). Research on the *instruction* of reading comprehension gained momentum in the 1970s and 1980s, as evidenced by the volume of citations in Tierney and Cunningham's review of research on the teaching of reading comprehension (1984). They cite over 260 studies and indicate that the number of studies they could have included was too numerous for their review to be exhaustive. In a subsequent review of reading comprehension instruction research, Pearson and Fielding (1991) also chose not to do a comprehensive review for the same reason. They characterized the conduct of comprehension instruction research in the few years before the writing of their manuscript as "frenetic in its pace" (p. 819). Most of the comprehension instruction research employs an experimental research paradigm (Tierney & Cunningham, 1984), asking which of two or more types of instruction result in better comprehension (Kamil, Langer, & Shanahan, 1985). In these studies, comprehension is typically measured by results on standardized or other objective tests.

Evidently, there is an abundance of instructional research to inform teaching practice. What is not obvious is the nature of the connection between the results of research and the use teachers may make of those results for teaching. The purpose of this chapter is to contemplate this connection.

APPLYING THE RESEARCH:
THE ROUTE FROM THEORY TO PRACTICE

Some imply that the connection should be direct; that is, if teachers would employ the practices research has shown to be effective, children would become readers (Anderson et al., 1985). Other educators decry this implication for its simplicity. Examples abound of research-based practices that result in less effective and even harmful effects (Samuels & Pearson, 1980). Nonetheless, the intersection of theory and practice has long been a topic of interest among educators, including Dewey (1929). He suggested that researchers and practitioners would benefit from an exchange of knowledge and experience: The practitioners would be liberated from "the bondage of habit which is always closing in on us, restricting our vision both of what is and of what the actual may become" (p. 210), and "the theorists would be liberated from the expectation that they carry all the burdens of knowledge" (p. 298).

This chapter describes the challenges we faced when attempting to connect research-based teaching practices with teachers in the Reading Instruction Study (RIS), a staff development program designed to be constructivist. We examine the assumption that teachers should use reading comprehension practices that research has shown to be effective. It is commonly assumed that "if teachers are exposed to carefully presented and understandable research findings, they will recognize the wisdom of the results and immediately employ them in their daily practice" (Tikunoff & Mergendoller, 1983, pp. 210–211). Tikunoff and Mergendoller do not agree with this quote; however, they report that it is a dominant assumption among research and policy communities.

Resources that present reading comprehension research are readily available to teachers. For example, teachers have access to numerous publications. In addition to scholarly and professional journals, books such as *Becoming a Nation of Readers* (Anderson et al., 1985) and *What Works* (1986) are widely distributed. Further, instructional research is an integral component of many preservice and graduate teacher education programs and is also presented at local and national teacher conferences. Why, then, do teachers consistently report *not* using research results in their teaching when they hear about them (Berger, 1976; Florio-Ruane & Dohanich, 1984; Vacca & Gove, 1982; Waxman et al., 1986)?

The RIS research team was confronted with this question as we prepared to create a staff development program that invited teachers to consider the veracity of the theories and practices we had garnered from our literature search. First, we elaborate on the kinds of reading comprehension research that have been conducted. Next, we describe the nature of teachers' reactions (in terms of both their language and their teaching behaviors) to the topic of teaching reading comprehension. Finally, we offer conjectures about the types of connections that are reasonable or possible between the recommendations of researchers and the realities of teaching.

OUR REVIEW OF RESEARCH-BASED PRACTICES

Since the focus of the project was on the barriers to teachers' use of research-based reading comprehension practices in the intermediate grades, we examined reading comprehension research that had either been conducted with intermediate-grade students or could be applied to this age group.

To identify the type of research we would consider appropriate for our study, the RIS team developed the following three criteria: "the paper must describe research; it must describe, suggest, and/or have tested a reading practice; and the stated purpose(s) of this practice must be to affect reading comprehension, and/or the effectiveness of the practice must be described through a measure of reading comprehension" (Lloyd, Tidwell, Anders, Batchelder, Bos, & Bradley, 1988, p. 1). Practices meeting these criteria were located through ERIC and through references made in syntheses and reviews of reading research. Near the conclusion of the search, three members of the research team grouped practices that had similar purposes. We found research that investigated 89 practices within 15 major categories of reading comprehension teaching practices appropriate for intermediate-grade students. The appendix at the end of this chapter shows these categories and the practices that were examined within each one.

Consistent with previous research reviews on this topic (Pearson & Fielding, 1991; Tierney & Cunningham, 1984), the published research we found was overwhelmingly quantitative. That is, most of the research was designed to compare how well different types of practices affected readers' comprehension through controlled studies that measured comprehension. Most often, the researched practices were designed by the researchers to verify a related theoretical assumption. The articles usually concluded with suggestions of practices to improve reading comprehension instruction.

To provide a sense of the diversity of the research-based reading comprehension practices, we describe a sample of what we found in a few of the categories. With the exception of vocabulary and imagery practices, all practices within each category were grounded in a common theoretical framework, namely an interactive model of comprehension (see Chapter 3). Since this model describes comprehension as the interaction between the reader and the text, the research looks at both reader and text variables. Typically, schema theory (see Chapter 3) is used to describe the reader's knowledge of content, skills, and strategies.

Background Knowledge Practices

The research that focused on background knowledge practices was designed to either develop the background knowledge readers would need or to help readers make the connections between their existing knowledge and text ideas.

Developing background knowledge may be as simple as assigning a text that is conceptually related to a second text. Crafton (1981) demonstrated that students' reading of the first text affected their comprehension of the second text by helping them organize what they remembered, understand more ideas, and understand the ideas better than if they had read only the second text.

The *story preview* (Graves, Cooke, & LaBerge, 1983; Graves & Palmer, 1981) is a more elaborate practice that not only develops background knowledge but also helps readers make connections between their existing knowledge and the story ideas. These purposes are accomplished through a series of questions and statements relating the story topic with students' experiences, a synopsis, character identification, and definitions of a few difficult words.

Sometimes the results of the research surprised us. For example, schema theory would suggest that asking students to predict upcoming story events would activate their related background knowledge and facilitate their engagement with the ideas. Interestingly, the research results are mixed. In a study with second- and fourth-graders of varying reading abilities, this practice was effective only for the younger and low-ability students (Hansen & Pearson, 1983). In a similar study with fifth-graders (Hansen & Ahlfors, 1982), teachers (rather than researchers) wrote the questions to encourage students to make predictions. In this instance the strategy did not affect students' comprehension.

Another surprise was the absence of research on commonly suggested and employed practices. For example, we did not find any research investigating the effects of *brainstorming* on comprehension. Brainstorming asks students to "think of everything they know" about an idea and is frequently used by teachers before students read stories or content area materials to help students relate new ideas to their background knowledge.

Imagery Practices

The role of imagery in reading comprehension is based on two compatible theories of comprehension. One of these is a *generative model of learning* (Wittrock, 1981), which describes how readers generate relationships between their existing knowledge and the ideas in the text. The second theory, *dual coding theory* (Paivio, 1986), describes how learners have not only a linguistic coding system to store ideas in memory, but also an imaginal coding system.

We found several studies that tested the efficacy of practices that encouraged students to develop images while they were reading. In these studies, researchers typically asked students to draw pictures or make up pictures in their heads of what was described in their reading. The results of these studies showed that directing students to create images either in their heads or on paper had inconsistent results. Sometimes these practices enhanced comprehension, but sometimes they did not (e.g., Gambrell & Bales, 1986; Linden & Wittrock, 1981; Pressley, 1976).

Self-Monitoring/Metacognitive Practices

Self-monitoring or metacognitive strategies are the strategies that readers use to be aware of their thinking and comprehension, and to make changes in their strategy use when comprehension is not occurring. They include the knowledge of reading skills and strategies and the ability to use them at appropriate times (Baker & Brown, 1984). Since a common characteristic of less successful readers is the inability to self-monitor, these students have been the focus of most of the instructional research in metacognition.

Some practices improved less successful readers' comprehension by teaching them one or two specific strategies. For example, teaching learning-disabled students to either make up questions about each paragraph after reading, underline two interesting words in each paragraph, or do a combination of the two improved their comprehension while having no effect on non–learning disabled students' comprehension (Chan & Cole, 1986). In another study (Garner, Hare, Alexander, Haynes, & Winograd, 1984), students were taught to look back in the text as a comprehension strategy. This enabled them to distinguish between questions that were text-based and opinion-based, and to look back at the text when trying to find text-based answers they had forgotten.

Other metacognitive research has investigated a comprehensive set of practices known as Informed Strategies for Learning (ISL) (Paris, Cross, & Lipson, 1984). Through a set of 20 modules, students learn how to develop plans for reading, strategies for determining and constructing meaning, how to critically evaluate their comprehension, and how to determine when comprehension breaks down and self-correct.

Questioning Practices

Questioning students about what they have read is a common practice often equated with teaching comprehension, though considered by others to be assessment rather than teaching (Durkin, 1978–1979). Though in classrooms these questions are typically generated by commercial materials used for both reading and content area instruction (see Pearson & Gallagher, 1983), research on questioning has investigated the effects of different types of questions, of questions asked before reading, and of strategies related to answering and generating questions.

Hansen (1981) demonstrated that young children's ability to make inferences could be improved through a three-step process. First, students were shown a visual model demonstrating the relationship between background knowledge and new ideas. Next, they were asked inferential questions that related a central story idea to their own experiences. Last, they were asked to hypothesize about upcoming story events.

Another strategy that improved students' ability to answer inference questions taught children why it is important to generate "think-type" questions, how to generate these types of questions, and how to determine what information in a text is important (Davey & McBride, 1986).

Vocabulary Practices

Word knowledge consistently correlates with reading comprehension (Davis, 1944; 1968). Theorists (Anderson & Freebody, 1981; Mezynski, 1983; Stahl & Fairbanks, 1986) explain the correlation in terms of four hypotheses: (1) the attribute hypothesis (readers who possess verbal agility have larger vocabularies), (2) the access hypothesis (those who rapidly and accurately decode words are more likely to comprehend), (3) the instrumental hypothesis (knowledge of word definitions contributes to reading comprehension), and (4) the knowledge hypothesis (the quality and quantity of a reader's interrelated and hierarchical structures of world knowledge are reflected in vocabulary knowledge).

Although students do learn words and their meanings when they are taught, research shows that instruction in definitions alone is less likely to affect reading comprehension than those practices that foster the interaction and elaboration of existing knowledge and the vocabulary. Thus, the relationship between vocabulary knowledge and reading comprehension is best explained by the knowledge hypothesis.

Graphic organizers such as *semantic maps* and *semantic feature analysis* ask students to use their background knowledge to predict the relationships between and among terms. These relationships are discussed and then depicted on a map or a matrix by the teacher or students. Students who participated in these strategies demonstrated better comprehension than those who engaged in other vocabulary strategies that did not encourage these types of interactions (Bos & Anders, 1993; Johnson, Toms-Bronowski, & Pittelman, 1982).

Beck and her colleagues (Beck, Perfetti, & McKeown, 1982; McKeown, Beck, Omanson, & Pople, 1985) developed rich and varied vocabulary instruction that demonstrated student gains in both reading comprehension and vocabulary. Beginning with sets of semantically related words, they provided instruction that included definitions but that emphasized the relationships of these words and their applications in varying contexts.

A researched practice that the knowledge hypothesis would predict to be effective but was not is a strategy called the *concept method*. This method is based on the work of Frayer, Frederick, and Klausmeier (1969) in conceptual development and understanding. Wixson (1986) compared the concept method with a dictionary method of learning five story-related vocabulary words with fifth-grade students. Those using the concept method participated in a discussion and worksheet in which students and the teacher identified critical attributes related to a particular word or concept. However, the two groups did not show any differences in their comprehension.

Text Characteristics Practices

Basic research on text characteristics has focused on attempts to discern the features of text that either contribute to or inhibit readers' comprehension. This basic research is then extended to instructional application by creating practices that address the way a text is written.

Three broad categories of practices are represented by these studies: those that teach students how to use the features of the text, those that teach students to focus on specific ideas in the text, and those that rewrite text to make it more understandable.

Focusing on Text Features. One practice that teaches students how to use text features is *story grammar instruction*. This practice assumes that if students know what the elements of a story are and can identify them, reading comprehension should improve. This assumption may be analogous to the theory that knowing parts of speech will improve students' compositions. Though there is a correlation between knowing grammar (either story or sentence) and reading and writing performance, it is not necessarily a causal relationship.

The effect on comprehension of teaching story grammar to students has been mixed. Some research has demonstrated increased gains for students who learn story grammar through direct instruction (Fitzgerald & Spiegel, 1983; Whaley & Spiegel, 1982), while other research has concluded that students already possess a sense of story by the fifth grade and that instruction is unnecessary (Dreher & Singer, 1980). When the structure of a story was used to generate questions, childrens' comprehension improved. This occurred when teachers asked the questions (Beck, Omanson, & McKeown, 1982) or when students generated their own questions (Nolte & Singer, 1985).

Focusing on Ideas. Reading practices that teach students to focus on specific ideas in the text are usually directed toward students' reading of informational text. They are based on the assumption that ideas are related hierarchically with main points and supporting details, or that ideas are related in rhetorical patterns that can be graphically organized to explicitly reveal those patterns.

An impressive body of research has emerged from this assumption regarding both the nature of main ideas and the kinds of instruction that result in improved reading comprehension (Bauman, 1983). The recommended research-based practices are linguistic (developing an outline) and pictorial (developing a graphic organizer). An effective linguistic-based practice asks students to create an outline that includes a summary statement of the main idea and supporting details for each paragraph. Afterward, they explain and justify their outlines through discussions with peers (Taylor, 1982). Teaching students to create a graphic organizer that represents the text-based ideas, and displays the relationship of the most important ideas (superordinate) to the less important (coordinate and subordinate) ideas, has been shown to enhance comprehension as well (Herber & Herber, 1993).

Another study of graphic organizer instruction was conducted by Alvermann, Boothby, and Wolfe (1984). Using social studies trade books, they taught students to construct semantic maps as they were reading. This was done using a conventional instructional model: First, the teacher displayed a map and discussed its creation; second, students were asked to fill in a partial map and their decisions were discussed and justified; and third, students were to construct maps independent of the teacher. One finding from this study was that map making was not adopted by the students as a study strategy until after 14 days of instruction. Hence, this and other research (Gordon, 1980; Tackett & Dewitz, 1981) suggests that students do not quickly adopt the creation of graphic organizers as a study strategy; rather, it seems that use of the graphic organizer develops through consistent and regular application. In addition, research has indicated that students must be actively engaged in the construction of the organizers if improved comprehension is to be achieved (Moore & Readance, 1984).

Rewriting Text. Some research has addressed the problem of poorly written, or inconsiderate, text by examining the effects of rewritten text on readers' comprehension. Typically, texts are rewritten to adhere to principles of considerateness. Considerate text is easier to comprehend because it is written with a structure that best matches its purpose (structure), has clear relationships between ideas (coherence), addresses one purpose at a time (unity), and matches the background of its readers (audience appropriateness) (Anderson & Armbruster, 1984).

Slater (1985) rewrote inconsiderate passages from social studies textbooks to be considerate. The fifth-grade students who read the rewritten passages were better able to comprehend the text than were the students who read the original passages. Beck, McKeown, Omanson, and Pople (1984) investigated the effects of rewriting basal reader stories to be more coherent. As in Slater's study, students who read the rewritten text had better comprehension than those who read the original stories.

STAFF DEVELOPMENT: BRINGING TOGETHER
TEACHERS AND RESEARCH

The RIS staff development program provided a context for the exploration of teachers' theories and related practices as well as literature-based theories and practices. The staff development process was based on Fenstermacher's (1986) and Greene's (1976) application of Aristotle's practical argument. (The theory of the practical argument is described in Chapter 2.) Essentially, the process calls for the staff developers and teachers to explain "why" a particular practice "works" or "doesn't work." The premises that justify a practice are identified as a practical argument. When premises are revealed, they are discussed in terms of alternative premises as derived from other teachers or from recent research.

The staff development program included both individual and group components. The individual component consisted of an interview about reading and reading instruction, a viewing and discussion by each teacher and two staff developers of a videotape when he or she was teaching reading comprehension, and two observations of the teacher during reading comprehension lessons. The interview and videotape elements were conducted at the beginning and the end of the staff development process. All interviews, discussions of videotapes, and classroom observations were transcribed and became data sources for analysis (see Chapter 3 for a description of the procedures and findings of the observations). The group component involved meetings at each school for teachers to discuss the instruction of reading comprehension. These meetings were videotaped and served as an additional source of data for analysis (for an explanation of the methods employed in data analysis, see Chapters 3 and 6). These descriptive analyses reveal the contrasts between reading comprehension practices supported by theory and research, and the actual beliefs and practices of teachers.

One way we made the research-based practices available to teachers was to provide them with a list of the practices we had found; the list is reproduced in the appendix at the end of this chapter. We added brief descriptions of each practice to this list, and distributed it at the second group staff development session. We provided teachers with an overview of how the list was created, what the categories meant, and a brief discussion of some of the practices. They were asked to read over the list and come to the next session prepared to discuss which practices they wanted to learn about. Then, as a group, we would set priorities based on this list and develop an agenda for our subsequent sessions.

This never happened. Teachers did not refer to the list during any of the staff development sessions, although the staff developers tried several times to use the list. Why did the teachers seem disinterested in the practices? What can we learn about the process of adopting and adapting research-based practices from our observations, staff development, and analyses?

We found at least three barriers to the use of research-based practices for these teachers: (1) The practices were decontextualized; (2) teachers' theoretical stances differed from the theoretical stance of the literature; and (3) teachers' real concerns were different from those addressed by the staff development goals.

Lack of Context

One reason teachers seemed disinterested in these practices might have been because the practices were decontextualized, making it difficult to connect the list with real life in the classroom. The list minimalized the complexity of teachers' thinking, and the challenges they faced, when talking about their thinking and practices. In fact, the handout probably encouraged the teachers to ask staff developers to decide which practices should be talked about, rather than choosing the practices themselves. For some time in both schools, the staff developers were treated as experts— "You tell us the practices we should use, you are the experts," the teachers would say. The staff developers resisted pressures to respond until the request for a practice emerged from the context of the conversation, so that the suggested practice could be situationally grounded. This resistance was apparently merited, because when information was presented that was less contextually based, teachers took on a "student" role and were not as likely to consider the practice within the context of their own teaching. In contrast, when practices were discussed within a constructive and supportive framework, and were grounded in a relevant context, teachers participated fully and enthusiastically (Richardson, 1992). It is ironic that we unwittingly contributed to this decontexualization by providing the list of practices.

Theoretical Contradictions

Initially, teachers used theoretical language about the reading process that we categorized as being skills-oriented. They proposed the following skills as being important for reading comprehension: good listening skills; reading at grade level; word attack skills, grammar skills, and dictionary skills; oral reading fluency skills; and being able to recall the sequence of a story. They contended that students needed to practice these skills at safe levels. These skills were also evident in the sorts of lessons teachers planned and the practices they used. As Richardson, Anders, Tidwell, and Lloyd reported (1991), "the relatively strong relationship between teachers' stated beliefs about the reading process and their classroom practices allows us to give credence to the beliefs as stated" (p. 578).

Teachers' initial theories help to explain why the research-based practices were of little interest: The theory and practices they believed in had little relationship to the theory and practices presented on the handout. The vast majority of practices described on the handout were based on the theory that reading comprehension is an interactive process. A majority of teachers within this sample neither held theories of reading that would accommodate these ways of thinking about reading nor demonstrated teaching practices within this framework (Lloyd, 1993; Richardson, Anders, Tidwell, & Lloyd, 1991).

At the conclusion of the staff development process, changes were evidenced in teachers' theoretical language and their reported reading comprehension practices. A follow-up study of these teachers three years after the staff development provides further indication of their shifts in theory and practice (Richardson, 1991). Therefore, it seems that the practices made available at the beginning of the staff development made no sense to the teachers because of the disparity between their theoretical stance and that of the research. Participating in the staff development process, however, gave them the opportunity to critically analyze their beliefs and provided a context for change.

Competing Concerns

Discussions about reading comprehension instruction, such as the relationships between reading and writing, literature study, and the nature of reading comprehension, were sprinkled throughout the staff development meetings. However, the most frequently discussed topic was that of assessment (Anders & Richardson, 1992).

The characterization of teachers' talk during these meetings also reveals the prominence of teachers' concerns about assessment, in comparison with the teaching of comprehension (Anders & Richardson, 1992). During talk about assessment, teachers were more likely to be actively involved and engaged in the topic. In contrast, during talk about instructional practices or reading comprehension, the participatory structure was more like a lecture by a staff developer or teacher.

CONNECTING RESEARCH AND PRACTICE

These findings suggest that the teaching of reading is a complex and dynamic endeavor, and challenge the assumption that research-based practices can and should be directly transferred to classroom practice. This assertion is based on the following considerations.

The typical experimental design of research studies makes it difficult, if not impossible, to suggest one-to-one correspondences between researched practices and what teachers should do in their classrooms. These types of studies typically ignore the complexities of the reading process (Tierney & Cunningham, 1984) and classroom instruction (Venezsky, 1984), by mandating control over variables that are rarely controllable in actual classroom teaching. As a result, the ecological validity of these studies is often quite limited.

The assumption that the results of reading comprehension research can be directly applied to classroom teaching presupposes that the knowledge a teacher should use to make instructional decisions is found in his or her "how to teach reading" schema. The teacher would merely need to activate that schema and choose from one of a few sets of manageable routines (Spiro, Vispoel, Schmitz, Samarapungavan, & Boerger, 1987), such as replicating a researched practice as instruction. We suggest that teaching is a dynamic process that requires the teacher to continually restructure the "how to teach reading" schema (Spiro et al., 1987) by arranging his or her knowledge of teaching reading in new ways. The contexts of classrooms change from day to day as new ideas are addressed, students come to school with different concerns than they had the day before, teachers try out new strategies, and students and teachers interact in ways that are often unpredictable.

Because most research studies are designed to look at the effects of practices (treatments) on groups rather than individuals, their results are based on an implicit assumption: that all members of a group are affected in a similar manner. This is often translated into classroom practices that ignore individual differences and the potential need for differential instruction.

The way in which the effects of a researched strategy are determined also affects its translation into classroom practice. Most studies use measures of comprehension that involve recall or recognition of specific text ideas. However, constructivist theories of learning suggest that readers construct their own understandings, which may derive from only some of the ideas in the text. Transactional theories (Rosenblatt, 1978) would suggest a different type of understanding, namely that readers' memories may not be of the text ideas, but of the "poem" they have created instead. Both of these perspectives suggest that readers may comprehend text in ways that are not assessed in current research.

The long-term effectiveness of a practice is a critical concern to teachers. Few of the studies we encountered addressed this issue. Usually, in the studies that did test long-term or transfer effects, none were found (e.g., Chan & Cole, 1986; Hansen, 1981). However, we do not believe that these few negative findings necessarily mean that the practice under investigation would not transfer over time and to new situations in certain circumstances. Perhaps if students had more guided opportunities with the ideas or the strategies than what subjects typically encounter during a research study, long-term effects would be seen.

Some findings from reading comprehension research may be too quickly translated to classroom practices. For example, research about young children's sense of story found that many young children have a schema for stories (Applebee, 1978). This finding has been translated into practices that teach children story grammar. However, what might be the essential experience is not directly learning about story grammar but reading and listening to stories. Another line of research informs us that there are practices that activate readers' background knowledge, and that this activation affects their comprehension. This finding is often translated into classroom practices that encourage readers to recall their related background knowledge and integrate it with the next ideas from the text. However, some research has found that these practices are likely to encourage readers to maintain their current perspective about a topic rather than acquire alternative understandings (Alvermann, Smith, & Readence, 1985).

Sometimes, a research-based practice would place unrealistic burdens on the teacher if he or she were to adopt it. For example, several of the researched practices we found required text to be rewritten to address concerns of vocabulary (Wittrock, Marks, & Doctorow, 1975) or poorly written (inconsiderate) text (Slater, 1985). Other practices required one-to-one instruction; for instance, teaching children to use a lookback strategy to find answers in the text (Garner et al., 1984). These results, however, could be used by teachers in other ways. Information about the nature and importance of well-written text might affect teachers' selection of materials for their classroom, or teachers might choose to adapt one-to-one strategies to group instruction.

We are not suggesting that there are no connections between researched reading comprehension practices and teaching. What we are suggesting is that teachers can use research results as a window into new perspectives and possibilities, but that it is the teacher's prerogative to create and adapt appropriate practices. The ways in which a teacher considers and implements recommended practices will be framed within his or her beliefs about teaching and reading.

APPENDIX: **Researched Reading Comprehension Practices**

---

1. Lesson Frameworks
   a. Guided Reading Procedure (GRP) with Prereading Chapter Survey and Class Discussion
   b. Directed Reading-Thinking Activity (DRTA)
   c. Directed Reading Activity (DRA)
   d. Experience-Text-Relationship (ETR)
   e. Revised Basal Lesson: Focus on Conceptual Vocabulary
   f. Revised Basal Lesson: Focus on Content Knowledge and Story Structure
   g. Revised Basal Lesson: Focus on Story Theme
   h. Revised Basal Lesson: Explicit Strategy Instruction
2. Background Knowledge
   a. Providing Background Knowledge Statements
   b. Teaching/Using Analogies
   c. Reading Conceptually Related Text
   d. Providing Advance Organizers
   e. Confronting Misconceptions
   f. Previewing Stories
   g. Reading Headings
   h. Predicting Story Events
   i. Providing Concrete Advanced Organizer
   j. Probing Background Knowledge
3. Text Characteristics
   a. Mapping Stories
   b. Mapping Expository Text Structure
   c. Teaching Lexical Ties
   d. Providing Pattern Guides
   e. Providing Cloze Exercises
   f. Using Sentence Anagrams
   g. Developing Structured Overviews (Graphic Organizers)
   h. Teaching Expository Text Structures
   i. Developing Structured Overview and Providing Cloze
   j. Re-ordering Information
   k. Identifying and Eliminating Extraneous Information
   l. Identifying Main Idea
   m. Creating Concept Relationship Matrix
   n. Mapping 5 Types of Text-Based Ideas (Links)
   o. Studying Map of Expository Text
   p. Completing Graphic Organizer Based on Text Structure

    q. Diagramming Relationships of Ideas (Idea-mapping)
    r. Revising Inconsiderate Text to be Considerate
4. Vocabulary
    a. Drilling Synonyms
    b. Decoding Drills
    c. Asking Questions to Determine Meaning from Context
    d. Using Familiar Content to Teach Word Meanings
    e. Developing Semantic Maps and Networks
    f. Reading Text with Explicit Context Cues
    g. Teaching Definitions
    h. Using Concept Method
    i. Discussing to Relate Words to Prior Knowledge
    j. Teaching the Concept of Definition
    k. Implementing Rich and Varied Vocabulary Instruction
5. Independent Study Strategies
    a. Teaching Survey, Question, Read, Recite, Review (SQ3R)
    b. Generating Summary of Each Paragraph
    c. Providing Study Guides
    d. Post-Questioning
6. Imagery
    a. Using Visual Imagery
    b. Drawing
    c. Providing Pictures
    d. Providing Mimetic Maps
7. Self-Monitoring/Metacognition
    a. Learning Strategies (Chicago Mastery Learning)
    b. Underlining Interesting Words
    c. Teaching Strategic Approach
    d. Using Informed Strategies for Learning (ISL)
    e. Using Reciprocal Teaching
    f. Teaching Inference Awareness
8. Teacher/Text Generated Questions
    a. Teaching Question/Answer Relationships (QAR)
    b. Questioning about Story Characters
    c. Asking Inferential Questions (post reading)
    d. Asking Reflective Questions
    e. Asking Interspersed Post Questions
    f. Teaching Text Look-Back Strategy
    g. Asking WH- Questions
9. Self-Generated Questions
    a. Asking Predictive Questions

     b. Listing Knowledge, Want to Know, Learned (KWL)
     c. Identifying Important Points
     d. Asking Higher-order Questions
     e. Asking Reciprocal Post Questions
     f. Asking Self Questions Plus Underlining
10. Modality
     a. Dramatizing Stories
     b. Reading Orally
     c. Reading Silently
11. Oral Reading Accuracy
     a. Not Correcting During Oral Reading
     b. Correcting During Oral Reading
12. Reading and Writing
     a. Summarizing
     b. Combining Sentences
     c. Asking Reflective Questions
     d. Writing After Listening to Stories
     e. Writing Creatively After Reading
13. Critical Reading
     a. Having Direct Instruction in Critical Reading
14. Attention/Selection
     a. Providing Purpose
     b. Providing Behavioral Objectives
     c. Providing Advance Organizer
15. Memory & Retrieval
     a. Providing Elaboration Training for Arbitrary Text

REFERENCES

Alvermann, D. E., Boothby, P. R., & Wolfe, J. (1984). The effect of graphic organizer instruction on fourth graders' comprehension of social studies text. *Journal of Social Studies Research, 8,* 13–21.

Alvermann, D. C., Smith, L. C., & Readence, J. E. (1985). Prior knowledge activation and the comprehension of compatible and incompatible text. *Reading Research Quarterly, 20,* 99–158.

Anders, P., & Richardson, V. (1992). Teacher as game-show host, bookkeeper, or judge? Challenges, contradictions, and consequences of accountability. *Teachers College Record, 94,* 382–396.

Anderson, R. C., & Freebody, P. (1981). Vocabulary knowledge. In J. T. Guthrie (Ed.), *Comprehension and teaching: Research reviews* (pp. 77–117). Newark, DE: International Reading Association.

Anderson, R. C., Hiebert, E. H., Scott, J. A., & Wilkinson, I. A. G. (1985). *Becoming a nation of readers: The report of the commission on reading.* Washington, DC: National Institute of Education.

Anderson, T. H., & Armbruster, B. B. (1984). Content area textbooks. In R. C. Anderson, J. Osborn, & R. J. Tierney (Eds.), *Learning to read in American schools* (pp. 193–226). Hillsdale, NJ: Erlbaum.

Applebee, A. N. (1978). *The child's concept of story: Ages two to seventeen.* Chicago: University of Chicago Press.

Baker, L., & Brown, A. L. (1984). Metacognitive skills and reading. In P. D. Pearson (Ed.), *Handbook of reading research* (pp. 353–394). New York: Longman.

Bauman, J. F. (1983). Children's ability to comprehend main ideas in content textbooks. *Reading World, 22,* 322–331.

Beck, I. L., McKeown, M. G., Omanson, R. C., & Pople, M. T. (1984). Improving the comprehensibility of stories: The effects of revisions that improve coherence. *Reading Research Quarterly, 19,* 263–277.

Beck, I. L., Omanson, R. C., & McKeown, M. G. (1982). An instructional redesign of reading lessons: Effects on comprehension. *Reading Research Quarterly, 17,* 462–481.

Beck, I. L., Perfetti, C. A., & McKeown, M. B. (1982). The effects of long-term vocabulary instruction on lexical access and reading comprehension. *Journal of Educational Psychology, 74,* 506–521.

Berger, A. (1976, August). *Implications of reading research on classroom teachers and administrators.* Paper presented at the Sixth World Congress on Reading, Singapore. (ERIC Document Reproduction Service No. ED 126-471)

Bos, C. S., & Anders, P. L. (1993). Using interactive teaching and learning strategies to promote text comprehension and content learning for students with learning disabilities. *International Journal of Disability, Development and Education, 30,* 129–137.

Chan, L. K. S., & Cole, P. G. (1986). The effects of comprehension monitoring training on the reading competence of learning disabled and regular class students. *Remedial and Special Education, 7,* 33–40.

Crafton, L. K. (1981). The reading process as a transactional learning experience. Unpublished Ph.D. dissertation, University of Indiana, Terre Haute.

Davey, B., & McBride, S. (1986). Effects of question-generation training on reading comprehension. *Journal of Educational Psychology, 78*, 256–262.

Davis, F. B. (1944). Fundamental factors in reading comprehension. *Psychometrika, 9*, 185–197.

Davis, F. B. (1968). Research in comprehension in reading. *Reading Research Quarterly, 3*, 499–545.

Dewey, J. (1929). *The quest for certainty*. New York: Minton Blach.

Dreher, M. J., & Singer, H. (1980). Story grammar instruction unnecessary for intermediate grade students. *Reading Teacher, 34*, 261–268.

Durkin, D. (1978–1979). What classroom observation reveals about reading comprehension instruction. *Reading Research Quarterly, 14*, 481–533.

Fenstermacher, G. D. (1986). A philosophy of research on teaching: Three aspects. In M. C. Wittrock (Ed.), *Handbook of research on teaching* (3rd ed.) (pp. 37–49). New York: Macmillan.

Fitzgerald, J., & Spiegel, D. L. (1983). Enhancing children's reading comprehension through instruction in narrative structure. *Journal of Reading Behavior, 15*, 19–36.

Florio-Ruane, S., & Dohanich, J. B. (1984). Research currents: Communicating findings by teacher and researcher deliberations. *Language Arts, 61*, 724–730.

Frayer, D., Fredrick, W. C., & Klausmeier, H. J. (1969). *A schema for testing the level of concept mastery* (Working Paper No. 16). Madison: Wisconsin Research and Development Center for Cognitive Learning.

Gage, N. L. (1978). *The scientific basis of the art of teaching*. New York: Teachers College Press.

Gambrell, L. B., & Bales, R. J. (1986). Mental imagery and the comprehension monitoring performance of 4th and 5th grade poor readers. *Reading Research Quarterly, 21*, 454–464.

Garner, R., Hare, V. C., Alexander, P., Haynes, J., & Winograd, P. (1984). Inducing use of a text look-back strategy among unsuccessful readers. *American Educational Research Journal, 21*, 789–798.

Gordon, C. J. (1980). The effects of instruction in metacomprehension and inferencing on children's comprehension abilities. Unpublished doctoral dissertation, University of Minnesota.

Graves, M. F., Cooke, C. L., & LaBerge, M. J. (1983). Effects of previewing difficult short stories on low ability junior high school students' comprehension, recall, and attitudes. *Reading Research Quarterly, 18*, 262–276.

Graves, M. F., & Palmer, R. J. (1981). Validating previewing as a method of improving fifth and sixth grade students' comprehension of short stories. *Michigan Reading Journal, 15*, 1–3.

Greene, T. (1976). Teacher competence as practical rationality. *Educational Theory, 26*, 240–258.

Hansen, J. (1981). The effects of inference training and practice on young children's reading comprehension. *Reading Research Quarterly, 16*, 391–417.

Hansen, J., & Ahlfors, G. (1982). Instruction in inferential comprehension: An extension and a summary. In J. A. Niles & L. A. Harris (Eds.), *New inquiries in reading research and instruction* (Thirty-first Yearbook of the National Reading Conference, pp. 54–59). Rochester, NY: National Reading Conference.

Hansen, J., & Pearson, P. D. (1983). An instructional study: Improving the inferential comprehension of good and poor fourth-grade readers. *Journal of Educational Psychology, 75,* 821–829.

Herber, H., & Herber, J. (1993). *Reading in the content areas.* Boston: Allyn and Bacon.

Johnson, D. D., Toms-Bronowski, S., & Pittelman, S. D. (1982). *An investigation of the effectiveness of semantic mapping and semantic feature analysis with intermediate grade level children* (Program Report no. 83-3). Madison, WI: Wisconsin Center for Education Research.

Kamil, M. L. (1984). Current traditions of reading research. In P. D. Pearson (Ed.), *Handbook of reading research* (pp. 39–62). New York: Longman.

Kamil, M. L., Langer, J. A., & Shanahan, T. (1985). *Understanding reading and writing research.* Boston: Allyn and Bacon.

Linden, M., & Wittrock, M. C. (1981). The teaching of reading comprehension according to the model of generative learning. *Reading Research Quarterly, 17,* 44–57.

Lloyd, C. V. (1993). A descriptive analysis of prereading story comprehension lessons. *Journal of Classroom Interaction, 28,* 27–33.

Lloyd, C. V., Tidwell, D., Anders, P. L., Batchelder, A., Bos, C. S., & Bradley, J. (1988, April). *Research-based comprehension instruction practices.* Paper presented at the annual meeting of the American Educational Research Association, New Orleans.

McKeown, M. G., Beck, I. L., Omanson, R. C., & Pople, M. T. (1985). Some effects of the nature and frequency of vocabulary instruction on the knowledge and use of words. *Reading Research Quarterly, 20,* 522–535.

Mezynski, K. (1983). Issues concerning the acquisition of knowledge: Effects of vocabulary training on reading comprehension. *Review of Educational Research, 53,* 253–279.

Moore, D. W., & Readence, J. E. (1984). A quantitative and qualitative review of graphic organizer research. *The Journal of Educational Research, 78,* 11–17.

Nolte, R., & Singer, H. (1985). Active comprehension: Teaching a process of reading comprehension and its effects on achievement. *Reading Teacher, 39,* 24–31.

Paivio, A. (1986). *Mental representation: A dual coding approach.* New York: Oxford University Press.

Paris, S. G., Cross, D. R., & Lipson, M. Y. (1984). Informed strategies for learning: A program to improve children's reading awareness and comprehension. *Journal of Educational Psychology, 76,* 1239–1252.

Pearson, P. D., & Fielding, L. (1991). Comprehension instruction. In R. Barr, M. L. Kamil, P. B. Mosenthal, & P. D. Pearson (Eds.), *Handbook of reading research* (Vol. II, pp. 815–860). New York: Longman.

Pearson, P. D., & Gallagher, M. C. (1983). The instruction of reading comprehension. *Contemporary Educational Psychology, 8,* 317–344.

Pressley, G. M. (1976). Mental imagery helps eight-year-olds remember what they read. *Journal of Educational Psychology, 68,* 355–359.

Richardson, V. (1991). *A study of long-term changes in teachers' beliefs and practices* (Proposal to OERI, U.S. Department of Education). Tucson: College of Education, University of Arizona.

Richardson, V. (1992). The agenda-setting dilemma in a constructivist staff development process. *Teaching and Teacher Education, 8,* 287–300.

Richardson, V., Anders, P., Tidwell, D., & Lloyd, C. (1991). The relationship between teachers' beliefs and practices in reading comprehension instruction. *American Educational Research Journal, 28,* 559–586.

Rosenblatt, L. (1978). *The reader, the text, the poem: The transactional theory of the literary work.* Carbondale: Southern Illinois University Press.

Samuels, J. S., & Pearson, P. D. (1980). Caution: Using research in applied settings. *Reading Research Quarterly, 15,* 1–5.

Slater, W. H. (1985). Revising inconsiderate elementary school expository text: Effects on comprehension and recall. In J. A. Niles & R. V. Lalik (Eds.), *Issues in literacy: A research perspective* (Thirty-fourth Yearbook of the National Reading Conference, pp. 186–193). Rochester, NY: National Reading Conference.

Spiro, R. J., Vispoel, W. P., Schmitz, J. G., Samarapungavan, A., & Boerger, A. E. (1987). Knowledge acquisition for application: Cognitive flexibility and transfer in complex content domains. In B. K. Britton & S. M. Glynn (Eds.), *Executive control processes in reading.* Hillsdale, NJ: Erlbaum.

Stahl, S. A., & Fairbanks, M. M. (1986). The effects of vocabulary instruction: A model-based meta-analysis. *Review of Educational Research, 56,* 72–110.

Tackett, S. A., & Dewitz, P. (1981, December). *Teaching story grammar for which students for how long.* Paper presented at the National Reading Conference, Dallas.

Taylor, B. M. (1982). Text structure and children's comprehension and memory for expository material. *Journal of Educational Psychology, 74,* 323–340.

Tierney, R. J., & Cunningham, J. W. (1984). Research on teaching reading comprehension. In P. D. Pearson (Ed.), *Handbook of reading research* (pp. 609–655). New York: Longman.

Tikunoff, W., & Mergendoller, J. R. (1983). Inquiring as a means to professional growth: The teacher as researcher. In G. Griffin (Ed.), *Staff development* (Eighty-second Yearbook of the NSSE, pp. 210–227). Chicago: University of Chicago Press.

Vacca, R. T., & Gove, M. K. (1982, April). *Teacher reflections on the use and adaptation of instructional innovation presented during staff development.* Paper presented at the annual meeting of the American Educational Research Association, New York. (ERIC Document Reproduction Service No. ED 217-389)

Venezsky, R. L. (1984). The history of reading research. In P. D. Pearson (Ed.), *Handbook of reading research* (pp. 3–38). New York: Longman.

Waxman, H. C., et al. (1986). *Using research knowledge to improve teacher education: Teachers' perceptions of the value of educational research.* (ERIC Document Reproduction Service No. ED 267-031)

Whaley, J. F., & Spiegel, D. L. (1982, April). *Improving children's reading comprehension through instruction in schematic aspects of narratives.* Paper presented at the annual meeting of the American Educational Research Association, New York.

What works. (1986). Washington, DC: U.S. Department of Education.

Wittrock, M. C. (1981). Reading comprehension. In F. J. Pirozzolo & M. C. Wittrock (Eds.), *Neuropsychological and cognitive processes in reading.* New York: Academic Press.

Wittrock, M. C., Marks, C., & Doctorow, M. (1975). Reading as a generative process. *Journal of Educational Psychology, 67,* 484–489.

Wixson, K. (1986). Vocabulary instruction and children's comprehension of basal stories. *Reading Research Quarterly, 21,* 317–329.

5

The Consideration of Teachers' Beliefs

VIRGINIA RICHARDSON

Current interest in teachers' thinking has been spurred in large part by the more general cognitive revolution and the movement away from behaviorism. For several years, research on teachers' classroom actions has focused on the complexity of decision-making (Shavelson, 1983), and on cognition (Carter, 1990), situated knowledge (Leinhardt, 1988), practical knowledge and reasoning (Elbaz, 1983), and other thought processes. This has led to a consideration of teachers' beliefs and their relationship to teaching practices. While beliefs have, over the years, received considerable attention in anthropology (e.g., Goodenough, 1963), social psychology (e.g., Rokeach, 1968), and philosophy (Green, 1971), empirical studies of teachers' beliefs and the relationships between these beliefs and their classroom actions have only recently received the attention they deserve (see Nespor, 1987, and Pajares, 1992, for reviews of teacher belief studies).

The results of these studies have led to the sense that teacher beliefs are an important consideration in understanding classroom practices, and therefore in conducting staff development programs designed to alter teachers' practices. If beliefs are related to practices, and more particularly, if beliefs drive practices, staff development that focuses solely on teaching practices may not be successful in effecting change, unless the teachers' beliefs and the theories underlying the practices are also explored.

There are three current conceptions of the typical pattern of events in the teacher-change process. The first, posited by Guskey (1986) and Fullan (1985), suggests that teachers change their beliefs *after* they change their practices and are able to see that these new practices positively affect their classroom and students. The second, represented in a case study in the Reading Instruction Study (RIS) (Richardson, Anders, Tidwell, & Lloyd, 1991), suggests that changes in beliefs *precede* changes in practices. The third, which will be developed in this chapter, suggests that the process of changing beliefs and practices is interactive; that is, depending on the types of changes and the teachers themselves, the change process may begin either with changes in beliefs or changes in practice.

WHAT ARE BELIEFS AND WHY ARE THEY IMPORTANT?

Within Green's (1971) and Fenstermacher's (1978) philosophical conceptualization of teaching and teacher education, it is clear that beliefs play a central role. Beliefs are an individual's understandings of the world and the way it works or should work, may be consciously or unconsciously held, and guide one's actions. The teacher or teacher educator is responsible for helping students explicate and examine their beliefs and belief sets, alter and/or add to them.

Anthropologists and social psychologists have also contributed to our understanding of beliefs. Goodenough (1963) describes beliefs as propositions that are held as true, and are "accepted as guides for assessing the future, are cited in support of decisions, or are referred to in passing judgment on the behavior of others" (p. 151). Rokeach (1968) defines beliefs from the viewpoint of the observer: Beliefs, which may be conscious or unconscious, may be inferred from behavior—what a person does or says. Beliefs, he states, are propositions that may begin with the phrase: "I believe that . . ." (p. ix).

Green's (1971) philosophical exposition on teacher beliefs has had a considerable influence on my own thinking, particularly concerning the potential for holding contradictory beliefs, and for ways in which beliefs change. While he focused on the role of the teacher, his view of beliefs in teaching are applicable to teacher education and staff development. According to Green, we hold beliefs in clusters, and each cluster within a belief system may be protected from other clusters; there is little cross-fertilization among them. As long as the incompatible beliefs are never set side by side and examined for inconsistency, the incompatibility may remain.

Such incompatibility may be seen in the example of a teacher who believes that when students read out loud accurately, they are not necessarily comprehending the passage; that reading silently contributes more to comprehension than reading out loud. At the same time, he or she may see a need to ask students to read out loud because he or she believes that this is the only way to ensure that the students are actually reading. These two beliefs may be held within different clusters—one related to learning to read, and one related to classroom management. Since they are held in different clusters, the teacher may not have considered these two beliefs together nor confronted the contradictions.

Green (1971) describes teaching as being concerned with the formation of beliefs, both what we believe and how we believe it. He states:

> Teaching has to do, in part at least, with the formation of beliefs, and that means that it has to do not simply with *what* we shall believe, but with *how*

we shall believe it. Teaching is an activity which has to do, among other things, with the modification and formation of belief systems. (p. 48)

One goal of teaching, for Green, is to help students form belief systems that consist of a large proportion of evidential beliefs, or beliefs based on evidence and reason. Green also suggests that teaching should aim at minimizing the number of core beliefs and belief clusters and maximizing relations among the clusters. Thus Green is looking at teaching as helping students reduce conflict among beliefs and increase the number of evidential beliefs, as well as providing opportunities for students to assess the evidence and thereby alter and/or add to the beliefs that are already present.

This concept of the purposes of teaching in relation to beliefs has also been employed in the consideration of teacher education. Fenstermacher (1978) argues that one goal of teacher education is to help teachers transform tacit or unexamined beliefs about teaching, learning, and the curriculum into objectively reasonable, or evidentiary beliefs. The process through which this can happen in teacher education or staff development is similar to Green's view of how teachers should work with students—that is, the focus of the change program is on helping teachers identify and assess their beliefs in relationship to their classroom actions.

Beliefs and Knowledge

I have found that many scholars and teachers feel uncomfortable using the term *beliefs* in discussions of formal education. For some, their conception of beliefs relates more to metaphysical beliefs—"I believe in God"—than to propositions that have an empirical or value basis—"I believe that kids whose parents read to them when they are young learn to read more quickly than those whose parents don't read to them," or "It is my goal to ensure that students in my class feel supported and welcome." For these people, it is inappropriate to consider beliefs in formal education. Others feel more comfortable talking about teachers' knowledge than teachers' beliefs, because the domain of "knowledge" seems scientific, and therefore more befitting the profession of teaching.

Indeed, in the traditional philosophical literature, knowledge depends on a "truth condition" that is outside the individual with the particular thought (Green, 1971; Leher, 1990). Knowledge is not, then, viewed by philosophers as a psychological concept. A proposition is knowledge if there is rigorous evidence for the premise, and the procedures for developing the argument as well as the conclusions are agreed on by a community of scholars, scientists, or other professionals. By contrast, when a proposition is held, psychologically, by an individual, and drives his or her actions, it is a belief. Beliefs do not require a truth condition. In fact, many beliefs, such as the notion that the holocaust was a hoax, are simply not true. If the belief is derived from knowledge, it is an evidential belief.

Such a differentiation between knowledge and beliefs is not evident, however, in much of the research on teaching and learning literature (see Fenstermacher, 1994, for a summary). This may be explained by the fact that a considerable proportion of the literature treats knowledge as an outcome of a psychological process. And there are many different forms of knowledge in this literature. For example, Alexander, Shallert and Hare (1991) described 26 terms that are used in the literature on literacy to denote different types of knowledge. These include procedural knowledge, content knowledge, and syntactic knowledge. They equate knowledge with belief: "*Knowledge* encompasses all that a person knows or believes to be true, whether or not it is verified as true in some sort of objective or external way" (p. 317).

Kagan (1990) also made the decision to use the terms *beliefs* and *knowledge* interchangeably in her analysis of methodological issues inherent in studying teachers' beliefs and knowledge. "I do so in light of mounting evidence that much of what a teacher knows of his or her craft appears to be defined in highly subjective terms" (p. 421). The following terms are also often used interchangeably: beliefs, attitudes, world views, perceptions, ideologies, theories, and values.

There is considerable similarity between the terms *knowledge* and *beliefs* in the concept of teachers' personal practical knowledge. Personal practical knowledge is a term used by Clandinin and Connelly (1986; also, Clandinin, 1985; Connelly & Clandinin, 1986) as an account of how the teacher knows or understands a classroom situation. This knowledge is gained through experience, and is thought of as embodied within the whole person, not just his or her mind (see also Hollingsworth, Dybdahl, & Minarik, 1993, on relational knowing). It is this latter quality, the embodiment of knowledge, that differentiates between personal practical knowledge and beliefs. Embodied knowledge is more than cognitive, and relates to the way in which we physically interact with the environment (Johnson, 1987). As Carter (1990) points out, this conception of understanding does not separate knowledge from the knower. It is personalized and idiosyncratic, often tacit, and for Schön (1983) emerges during action.

The term *belief*, as used in this chapter, is derived from Green (1971) and other philosophers and anthropologists. It is a psychological concept that differs from knowledge, which implies some type of validation process external to the individual. However, the conception of beliefs in this chapter encompasses the psychological concepts of knowledge found in much of the research on teaching literature, particularly knowledge that is subjective and personal.

THE RELATIONSHIP BETWEEN BELIEFS AND PRACTICES

As noted above, beliefs would be an important consideration in staff development programs if they could be assessed and understood by the participants, and if they were related directly to classroom practices. Many definitions of beliefs do imply that they drive actions (see Rokeach, 1968); however, the nature of the relationship is only now beginning to be understood.

While there is a considerable body of literature on beliefs in mathematics education (see Thompson, 1992, for a summary), the work in reading is only now beginning to expand. And there is still lack of agreement on the relationship between beliefs and practices within the literature. Some researchers conclude that teachers' beliefs in reading do not match their practices; others suggest that nonreading beliefs, such as those related to classroom management, are stronger than reading beliefs and therefore drive classroom practices.

Harste and Burke (1977) felt that their research-in-progress supported the conclusion that "despite atheoretical statements, teachers are theoretical in their instructional approach to reading" (p. 32). Deford (1985) developed a multiple-choice instrument (TORP) designed to differentiate among teachers on the basis of their theoretical orientation toward reading (phonics, skills, or whole language), and validated it by predicting a sample of teachers' theoretical orientations on the basis of classroom observation. She found a strong relationship between the TORP scores and the predictions.

On the other hand, after a three-year study of teachers' instructional decisions, Duffy (1981) concluded that teachers' theoretically based conceptions are not related to their teaching of reading practices. Hoffman and Kugle (1982), using the TORP measure, also found a lack of correlation between teachers' theoretical orientations and specific classroom behaviors that were assumed to accompany specific theoretical orientations.

Several researchers have attempted to understand this contradiction by adding additional variables to their studies to explain the lack of a perfect relationship between beliefs and practices. For example, O'Brien and

Norton (1991) conducted case studies of 10 elementary school teachers who were obtaining an M.A. degree in reading. They found that many factors—including the graduate course work the teachers were taking, institutional constraints such as mandates related to ability grouping, the textbooks they were using, their beliefs about teaching and learning, and their theoretical perspectives on reading and language—seemed to affect the decisions they made in their classrooms. They concluded the following:

- Beliefs about reading combine pedagogical and theoretical elements.
- Teachers' complex systems of beliefs help to diminish the constraints on their teaching caused by materials—such as basal texts—and by institutional elements.
- Success with a new practice is important if the teacher is to incorporate the theory underlying the practice into his/her belief system.

Roehler, Duffy, Herrmann, Conley, and Johnson (1988) abandoned their concept of beliefs, which they considered to be too static, and concluded that *knowledge structures* rather than beliefs drive teachers' classroom actions. Knowledge structures are fluid and unique to individuals, and relate to the ways in which concepts are stored or are related to each other. Roehler et al. found that an individual's knowledge structure varies depending on the situational context. They hypothesized that expert teachers are more effective than less expert teachers because their knowledge structures are more coherent and integrated, making it easier for them to access knowledge and make decisions more quickly. In a case study of preservice students, Johnson (1987) found that students whose knowledge structures were coherent and integrated taught coherent and integrated lessons, whereas students whose knowledge structures contained few integrated elements taught lessons that were less coherent and integrated.

The Roehler et al. (1988) notion of knowledge structures is very similar to Green's (1971) conception of belief clusters. Green suggests that teaching should, in part, be aimed at decreasing the number of clusters and core beliefs, and maximizing the logic of the way the beliefs are ordered in the clusters. These prescriptions are similar to the criteria of coherence and integration as promoted by Roehler et al. (1988).

What accounts for the contradictions in the literature? Are teacher beliefs related to classroom actions or not? The next section will discuss several measurement and design issues that could have led to these contradictory results.

Measurement Issues

Many of the instruments used in earlier belief studies in reading were multiple-choice measures of theoretical orientations derived from the scholarly literature. Hoffman and Kugle (1982) hypothesized that the finding in their study of a lack of relationship between beliefs and practices could be explained by the lack of validity of such an instrument:

> It would be easy to conclude that for most teachers there is no strong relationship between teacher beliefs and teacher behaviors. It would be more reasonable based on the findings from the focused interviews, however, to bring to question the notion that we can validly assess beliefs through a paper-and-pencil type task. (p. 6)

This measurement problem may also help to explain the contradictory relationship documented in the general teaching literature between teachers' reports of behaviors and beliefs, and actual observations of their classroom practices. Hook and Rosenshine (1979) reviewed this literature and found a low correlation between teacher reports and observer ratings of many different teacher behaviors. However, if the responses were grouped into more global dimensions or general styles (such as open versus traditional), groups of teachers with similar styles were found to behave differently from other groups with different styles. Most of these studies also used multiple-choice questionnaires to determine beliefs and self-reported practices.

One problem with multiple-choice questionnaires in assessing teachers' beliefs is that the categories of beliefs or theories must be predetermined by the researcher. Thus, many of the reading-belief questionnaires were developed using theories found in the scholarly literature. Perhaps teachers' beliefs and theories do not mesh with those in the literature. Also, it may be that teachers' beliefs about reading are combined with what scholars would consider to be nonreading beliefs such as classroom management. The multiple-choice measure would force teachers to respond in nonnatural categories.

Recall, for example, the O'Brien and Norton (1991) study, which used open-ended interview techniques to determine teachers' beliefs and theories. They found that teacher beliefs about reading seemed to be a mixture of pedagogical and theoretical reading notions. These teachers' beliefs encompassed much more than the reading theories in the literature, and would not have been adequately explored in the typical multiple-choice belief questionnaire.

There is another school of thought that suggests that since teachers are not consciously aware of many of their beliefs, the only way to examine beliefs is to observe the teachers in action (see Thompson, 1991). There is an assumption in these studies that beliefs drive actions, and therefore should be interpretable from observations of actions. Without disparaging this approach—since I do think that an understanding of teachers' beliefs is enhanced by classroom observation,—it is important to develop separate measures for beliefs and actions if one is looking at the relationship between them.

One approach to examining beliefs that has been used successfully in another field is the anthropological belief interview. This involves open-ended conversations in which the interviewer becomes the student of the interviewee's language and thinking. It was this way of examining teachers' beliefs that was used in the RIS.

BELIEFS AND PRACTICES IN THE READING INSTRUCTION STUDY

In order to study the relationship between teachers' beliefs and their practices in reading comprehension, we used data that were collected primarily at the beginning of the process before the formal staff development began (Richardson et al., 1991). We conducted extensive belief interviews with 39 grade 4, 5, and 6 teachers in five schools. In addition, each teacher's instruction of reading comprehension was observed, and a subset of the teachers was videotaped. The interviews were analyzed, and, on the basis of the analysis, predictions were made about specific aspects of each teacher's reading comprehension instruction. The observations were analyzed using the same categories to describe the teachers' reading instruction as those that had been used in the analysis of the belief interviews. (The two authors who conducted and analyzed a teacher's interview did not participate in the same teacher's observation, and vice versa.) The relationship between the predictions made from the beliefs and the observed practices was quite strong; but before describing the findings further, I will describe the nature of the belief interview.

The Interview

The belief interview was designed to elicit teachers' beliefs inductively (see also Eisenhart, Shrum, Harding, & Cuthbert, 1988; Munby, 1984; Smith & Shepard, 1988). We used an adaptation of the heuristic elicitation technique, developed by anthropologists to determine belief systems in groups of people (Metzger, 1973). This process leads to an understanding that is shared by interviewer and interviewee (Mishler, 1986). Within this framework, beliefs consist of a set of assertions held by informants and realized in the natural language as declarative sentences. This technique uses open-ended questions to construct the informants' propositions about reading and learning to read and closed-ended questions to establish the interviewers' understanding of the response. For example, after a teacher responds to a open-ended question such as "What contributes to a student's learning to read?" the interviewer may check out his or her understanding of the answer with a question that calls for a yes or no answer: "Are you saying, then, that parents are the main influence on a student's learning to read?"

Teachers were asked about their notions of reading comprehension and how students learn to read in general, and then asked to identify and describe one of their problem readers, an excellent reader, and one below average. The first set of questions was designed to elicit what Goodenough (1971) described as their "declared" or public beliefs, given by a person in public behavior and speech, cited in argument, or used to justify actions to others. The second set was designed to elicit more "private" beliefs—those that may come closer to their beliefs-in-action. We also asked the teachers about their own backgrounds, and their classrooms, schools, and fellow teachers. (See the appendix at the end of this chapter for a copy of the interview protocol.)

The Analysis

These were extensive interviews, lasting from 45 minutes to two hours. The interviews were transcribed, and chunks of dialogue were coded using Glaser and Strauss's (1967) constant comparative method to develop the coding categories. The qualitative analysis methods were selected to allow the teachers' theories to emerge from careful and open-minded reading of the transcripts, rather than to impose a set of formal constructs extracted from the literature on reading comprehension. We analyzed the same interview in two different ways:

Theoretical Orientation. In examining the transcripts, we found that the teachers described the teaching and learning of reading comprehension along two dimensions. The first dimension, called "Teaching Reading/Learning to Read," moved along a continuum from a word-and-skills approach to a literature approach. That is, placement of a teacher at one end of the continuum suggested that the teacher viewed teaching and learning reading as a set of skills that revolved around recognition and attribution of meanings to individual words. Placement of a teacher at the other end indicated that the teacher believed that people learn to read by reading; according to this view, teaching consists of putting students in contact with interesting literature. Teachers could be placed anywhere along the continuum.

The second dimension, called "Reading/Purpose of Reading," reflected the teachers' sense of where the meaning resides. At one end of this dimension, the meaning is located in the text, and it is the reader's purpose to figure out exactly what the authors meant. At the other end, meaning is constructed from an interaction between the reader and the text. The latter, constructivist concept of reading suggests that readers interpret texts according to their own prior knowledge and understandings.

In order to determine the teachers' overall theoretical orientations, each teacher was placed in one of four quadrants formed from the intersection of the two dimensions. Figure 5.1 shows the placement of each of the teachers. Quadrant I is similar to a word-and-skills approach, in which the subskills of reading must be learned before the meaning of the text can be determined, and the purpose of reading is to determine what the author meant. Quadrant II is a structuralist approach to literature, in which learning to read is accomplished by reading, and the purpose is to determine what the author meant. Quadrant III represents the whole language philosophy in which authentic literature is used as a vehicle through which students construct meaning. Quadrant IV indicates why such an inductive approach to determining teachers' beliefs is important. It does not represent an extant theory in the literature. In this quadrant, a skills approach leads to the construction of meaning in students. The few teachers in this quadrant had taught in schools with students from cultural orientations very different from their own. One teacher, for example, had taught on the Navajo reservation. She had learned that the same word meant very different things to people from different cultures, and therefore developed an interpretive concept of reading. However, she still believed in the skills approach to teaching reading.

Individual Belief Statements. We also extracted teachers' individual premises about reading and reading comprehension, and their statements about their classroom practices. After analyzing these statements, we made predictions about the following classroom practices:

- Did the teacher use basal readers in teaching reading comprehension and, if so, did he or she use them in a flexible or inflexible manner?
- Did the teacher take the students' background knowledge into account in their reading comprehension instruction?

Figure 5.1 Teachers' Theories of Reading

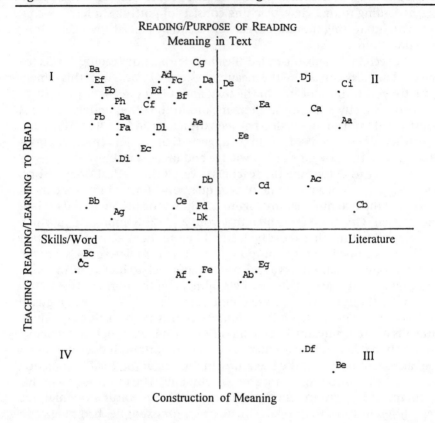

READING/PURPOSE OF READING
Meaning in Text

Skills/Word

Literature

TEACHING READING/LEARNING TO READ

Construction of Meaning

A–E = School site
a–l = Teacher codes
I–IV = Quadrant

- Did the teacher ask students to read orally or silently? If orally, did he or she interrupt students if they misread at the word level?
- Did the teacher teach vocabulary in or out of context?

We found that we were able to predict these practices from the belief interviews quite successfully. This suggested to us that the interview technique we used was useful in revealing the teachers' beliefs that turned out to be related to their classroom practices. The strong relationship between beliefs and practices in this study gave credence to the teachers' beliefs as elicited, and to the way in which they were elicited.

We also, however, examined situations in the data in which the beliefs did not match practices. In a case study of Susan, we were able to show, from an analysis of her initial interview, that her public beliefs (Quadrant III, Whole Language) were quite different from her private beliefs or beliefs-in-action (Quadrant I, Skills Approach). Her public beliefs were also quite different from her observed practices, which also placed her in a skills approach. However, at the beginning of the next school year, without any intervention on our part, her practices were beginning to resemble her Quadrant III public beliefs. This suggested to us that in Susan's case, changes in belief were preceding changes in practice. And this leads us to the next section, which examines the issue of the importance of beliefs in staff development.

BELIEFS AND STAFF DEVELOPMENT

Our study and others like it provide convincing evidence that teachers' beliefs are related to their classroom practices. However, these results do not make it clear how to design staff development programs with the goal of altering teachers' practices. How do beliefs interact with practices during a change process? And what does this interaction suggest for staff development? Fortunately, as will be examined in depth in Chapter 8, we were able to observe teachers who were going through the process of change during our staff development process.

Our experiences indicate that staff developers should become knowledgeable about the beliefs that the participants hold, and their current practices. The process should involve discussing these teacher-held beliefs and practices, and relating them to the practices and underlying theories that staff developers are discussing. We saw several instances of teachers trying to use a practice, such as activating students' background knowledge, but the attempts were weak and ineffectual. These teachers, when interviewed, did not express an understanding of the theory that supports the practice. We also talked with teachers who were developing different ways of thinking about the teaching of reading, but did not know of the practices that would allow them to act on those beliefs. Which should come first, changes in beliefs or in practices?

Guskey's (1986) model of teacher change suggests that changes in teacher belief follow changes in practice. Only when teachers see positive results of different behaviors in terms of student learning do they begin to change their beliefs. O'Brien and Norton's (1991) study supports this view of change. However, our case study of Susan, as described above, counters Guskey's model because Susan was changing her beliefs before changing her practices.

Rich (1990) attempted to explain such contradictions through a concept called "goal orientation." She conducted a study of teachers' beliefs and how they affected teachers' decisions to adopt and implement cooperative learning in their classrooms. She concluded that "teachers' orientations toward the goals of schooling and their beliefs regarding the process of knowledge acquisition may have profound impact on decisions made consciously or unconsciously regarding the adoption and implementation of innovations like cooperative learning" (p. 88). She also suggested that Guskey's (1986) argument that belief change follows change in behavior holds only when there is congruence between teachers' goal orientations and their perceptions of the purposes of the innovation being advocated. It may be that Susan's goals for reading instruction no longer matched those that she perceived to be inherent in the skills approach; in which case, according to Rich (1990), belief change would precede behavior change.

Perhaps, in the long run, we are dealing with a change process that can begin with change in either beliefs *or* practices, depending on the particular teachers and the type of change. On the other hand, Baird, Fensham, Gunstone, Penna, and White (1991) present an alternative thesis. In a four-year study of teaching, learning, and change, they found that the change process involved an interaction among action, observation, evaluation, and reflection. It may not be important to determine which comes first in the change process. What is important is the notion that changes in beliefs, ways of thinking, and classroom actions all come into play in the teacher-change process. Thus, it is a fluid process. At any point in time, beliefs may not be congruent with practices. This may be a consequence of the interactive process and may suggest that teachers whose beliefs do not match their practices, as in the case of Susan, are undergoing a major change in beliefs and/or practices.

This interactive view suggests that staff development that focuses only on theory or only on behaviors may not bring about substantial change. Genuine changes will come about when teachers think very differently about what is going on in their classrooms, and are provided with the practices to match their different ways of thinking. Providing practices without theory may lead to misimplementation or no implementation at all, unless the teachers' beliefs are congruent with the theories underlying the practice being advocated. On the other hand, staff development programs in which theory is discussed with a goal of changing beliefs, without suggesting practices that embody those theories, may lead to frustration.

An implication of these conclusions is that staff development programs should weave together, in an interactive, dialogical manner, three forms of knowledge and beliefs. The first is teachers' beliefs or practical knowledge about the teaching and learning process, and discussions of their practices. Teachers' knowledge of practice, gained from experience and other sources, is seldom articulated and therefore often not examined. Such knowledge, even while tacit, interacts with and frames new sources of knowledge that may be a part of the content of the staff development process. The articulation of these beliefs and descriptions of their practices allows teachers to examine them in relation to theories and practices stemming from current research. The second form of knowledge is the formal theoretical frameworks and empirical understandings as derived from current research and scholarship. And the third form is alternative classroom practices that instantiate both teachers' beliefs and research knowledge. These forms of knowledge should be perused in an interactive, iterative, and dialogical process, allowing teachers to examine their own beliefs and practices, consider new ways of thinking about teaching, and experiment with new practices. This approach provides the flexibility for different styles of change and does not force teachers into a model of change that may be inappropriate.

APPENDIX: Teacher Belief Interview Protocol

Background

Number of years teaching—grade levels—types of kids.

Preservice education. Where? Special program? Reading program? Student teaching. Where? When? How did Cooperating Teacher teach reading? Any innovative instruction in his/her class? (Probe: Quality of student teaching experience)

Reading and Learning to Read

When a student enters into Grade, what should that student be able to do in terms of reading? (Probe: Their conviction, not what the "program" expects)

What can a really good reader do? (difference between good and poor reader qualitative or quantitative?) When that student leaves Grade, what can she do? So how has that student learned to read up to Grade?

What accounts for the differences between a good and poor reader? (Probe: Parents? Genetic? Good teaching? Learning style?)

Is it possible for a teacher or other person to help a poor reader become a good reader?

How do you define reading comprehension? What is included in that?

Reading Instruction

Could you describe the way you teach reading comprehension? (Probe: Typical day— do they read out loud?)

Objective: Vocabulary? Remembering ideas? Memorizing facts? Questioning students: Why? What is a good response? What is a poor response? What is a creative response?

Where did you learn to teach it that way?

Have you ever had in-service/graduate courses on how to teach it?

Have you ever tried something different? Why? What happened? Have you ever wanted to do something different?

Grouping: On what basis? Why? (Probe: Do you change the groups? Why?)

Have you ever tried to teach the whole group? Under what conditions would you do so? Do you do different things in the different groups? Why?

What indicates to you that a lesson is going poorly?

How is teaching reading different from teaching math? From teaching science or social studies? From teaching writing? (Probe: More/less difficult? Less clarity about objectives?)

Do you ever feel like you are getting behind in reading?

The Students

Describe the students in your class. Do they have a pretty good chance of making it through school?

Describe a student who is having great difficulty in reading. (Probe: Cause, what is teacher doing about it?)

Describe a student who is just slightly behind— not terrific, but not a real problem. (Probe on same.)

Describe a student who is really doing well. (Probe on same.)

The School

Do you feel that there is a characteristic way of teaching reading comprehension in this school?

Do you know what the other teachers are doing? I mean sort of? How do you know?

Do you ever observe in other classrooms?

Do you exchange materials, ideas, methods, or communicate with other teachers? Specialists?

Personal Reading

What types of things do you read now? (When you have a chance?)

REFERENCES

Alexander, P. A., Shallert, D. L., & Hare, V. C. (1991). Coming to terms: How researchers in learning and literacy talk about knowledge. *Review of Educational Research, 61*(3), 265–286.

Baird, J. R., Fensham, P. J., Gunstone, R. F., Penna, C., & White, R. T. (1991). *Challenge: A focus for improving teaching and learning.* Paper presented at the annual meeting of the American Educational Research Association, Chicago.

Carter, K. (1990). Teachers' knowledge and learning to teach. In W. R. Houston (Ed.). *Handbook of research on teacher education* (pp. 291–310). New York: Macmillan.

Clandinin, D. J. (1985). *Classroom practice: Teacher images in action.* London: Falmer.

Clandinin, D. J., & Connelly, F. M. (1986). Rhythms in teaching: The narrative study of teachers' practical knowledge of classrooms. *Teaching and Teacher Education, 2*(4), 377–387.

Connelly, F. M., & Clandinin, D. J. (1986). On narrative method, personal philosophy, and narrative unities in the story of teaching. *Journal of Research in Science Teaching, 14*, 147–157.

Deford, D. (1985). Validating the construct of theoretical orientation in reading instruction. *Reading Instruction Quarterly, 20*, 351–367.

Duffy, G. (1981). *Theory to practice: How does it work in real classrooms?* (Research Series #98). East Lansing, MI: Institute for Research on Teaching, College of Education.

Eisenhart, M., Shrum, J., Harding, J., & Cuthbert, A. (1988). Teacher beliefs: Definitions, findings, and directions. *Educational Policy, 2*, 51–70.

Elbaz, F. (1983). *Teacher thinking: A study of practical knowledge.* New York: Nichols Publishing.

Fenstermacher, G. D. (1978). A philosophical consideration of recent research on teacher effectiveness. In L. Shulman (Ed.), *Review of research in education, No. 6* (pp. 157–185). Itasca, IL: F. E. Peacock.

Fenstermacher, G. D. (1994). The knower and the known in teacher knowledge literature. In L. Darling-Hammond (Ed.), *Review of research in education, 20* (pp. 3–56). Washington, DC: American Educational Research Association.

Fullan, M. (1985). Change processes and strategies at the local level. *Elementary School Journal, 85*, 391–421.

Glaser, B., & Strauss, A. (1967). *The discovery of grounded theory: Strategies for qualitative research.* Chicago: Aldine.

Goodenough, W. H. (1963). *Cooperation in change.* New York: Russell Sage Foundation.

Goodenough, W. H. (1971). *Culture, language, and society* (Addison-Wesley module in anthropology, No. 7). New York: Addison-Wesley.

Green, T. (1971). *The activities of teaching.* New York: McGraw-Hill.

Guskey, T. R. (1986). Staff development and the process of teacher change. *Educational Researcher, 15*, 5–12.

Harste, J., & Burke, C. (1977). A new hypothesis for reading teacher research: Both the teaching and learning of reading are theoretically based. In P. D. Pearson (Ed.), *Reading: Theory, research and practice* (Twenty-Sixth Yearbook of the National Reading Conference) (pp. 32–40). Clemson, SC: The National Reading Conference, Inc.

Hoffman, J. V., & Kugle, C. (1982). A study of theoretical orientation to reading and its relationship to teacher verbal feedback during reading instruction. *Journal of Classroom Interaction, 18,* 2–7.

Hollingsworth, S., Dybdahl, M., & Minarik, L. T. (1993). By chart and chance and passion: The importance of relational knowing in learning to teach. *Curriculum Inquiry, 23*(1), 5–35.

Hook, C. M., & Rosenshine, B. U. (1979). Accuracy of teacher reports of their classroom behavior. *Review of Educational Research, 49,* 1–12.

Johnson, M. (1987). *The body and the mind: The bodily basis of meaning, imagination, and mind.* Chicago: University of Chicago Press.

Kagan, D. (1990). Ways of evaluating teacher cognition: Inferences concerning the Goldilocks principle. *Review of Educational Research, 60*(3), 419–469.

Leher, K. (1990). *Theory of knowledge.* San Francisco: Westview Press.

Leinhardt, G. (1988). Situated knowledge and expertise in teaching. In J. Calderhead (Ed.), *Teachers' professional learning* (pp. 146–168). Philadelphia: Falmer.

Metzger, D. (1973). Semantic procedures for the study of belief systems. In H. Siverts (Ed.), *Drinking patterns in highland Chipas* (pp. 37–47). Bergen, Norway: Norwegian Research Council for Science, Universitetsforlaget.

Mishler, E. (1986). *Research interviewing: Context and narrative.* Cambridge, MA: Harvard University Press.

Munby, H. (1984). A qualitative study of teachers' beliefs and principles. *Journal of Research in Science Teaching, 21,* 27–38.

Nespor, J. (1987). The role of beliefs in the practice of teaching. *Journal of Curriculum Studies, 19,* 317–328.

O'Brien, K., & Norton, R. (1991). Beliefs, practices and constraints: Influences on teacher decision-making processes. *Teacher Education Quarterly, 18*(1), 29–38.

Pajares, M. F. (1992). Teachers' beliefs and educational research: Cleaning up a messy construct. *Review of Educational Research, 62*(3), 307–332.

Rich, Y. (1990). Ideological impediments to instructional innovation: The case of cooperative learning. *Teaching and Teacher Education, 6*(1), 81–91.

Richardson, V., Anders, P., Tidwell, D., & Lloyd, C. (1991). The relationship between teachers' beliefs and practices in reading comprehension instruction. *American Educational Research Journal, 28*(3), 559–586.

Roehler, L., Duffy, G., Herrmann, B. A., Conley, M., & Johnson, J. (1988). Knowledge structures as evidence on the "Personal": Bridging the gap from thought to practice. *Journal of Curriculum Studies, 20*(2), 159–165.

Rokeach, M. (1968). *Beliefs, attitudes, and values: A theory of organization and change.* San Francisco: Jossey-Bass.

Schön, D. A. (1983). *The reflective practitioner: How professionals think in action.* New York: Basic Books.

Shavelson, R. (1983). Review of research on teachers' pedagogical judgments, plans and decisions. *Elementary School Journal, 83,* 392–413.

Smith, M. L., & Shepard, L. (1988). Kindergarten readiness and retention: A qualitative study of teachers' beliefs and practices. *American Educational Research Journal, 25,* 307–333.

Thompson, A. (1992). Teachers' beliefs and conceptions: A synthesis of the research. In D. Grouws (Ed.), *Handbook of research on mathematics education* (pp. 127–146). New York: Macmillan.

6

The Practical-Argument
Staff Development Process

VIRGINIA RICHARDSON AND MARY LYNN HAMILTON

Staff development has been defined by Griffin (1983) as any formal and systematic attempt to "alter the professional practices, beliefs and understanding of school persons toward an articulated end" (p. 2). Fenstermacher and Berliner (1985) state the goal of staff development in a manner compatible with Griffin: "to advance the knowledge, skills and understandings of teachers in ways that lead to changes in their thinking and classroom behavior" (p. 283). While staff development and professional development are often used interchangeably, Stevenson (1987) points to two major differences. Professional development refers to the continuing development of the individual teacher, usually undertaken voluntarily, whereas staff development usually refers to a systematic and formal group process: one in which a group of teachers are asked or required to get together for purposes of developing and/or advancing the goals of the institution. Despite these differences, staff development processes, as Edelfelt (1984) suggested, may meet both institutional and individual professional development goals. In this chapter, we will be referring to staff development as both individual and group processes designed systematically to examine and change practices.

Unfortunately, the history of staff development in schools has not always been bright (Guskey, 1986). Citing incompetent design (Corey, 1957; Davies, 1967), ineffectual programs (Howey & Vaughan, 1983) and minimal long-term change (Goldenberg & Gallimore, 1991), scholars have outlined the inadequacies of staff development available to teachers. Indeed, staff development programs have often been recognized as failures. Yet, when there are calls for reform, whether through the restructuring of schools or through changes within the teaching profession, staff development is the most frequently identified means of achieving the desired goals.

The purpose of this chapter is to examine new ways of thinking about and implementing staff development, and to present an example of one particular innovation: the Practical Argument Staff Development (PASD) process. Two interrelated conceptual issues are involved in these new approaches to staff development: the content itself, and the ownership of the process and content. Proponents of the newer staff development programs are struggling to ensure that the content of staff development includes and is driven, in part, by participants' personal practical knowledge, beliefs, and concerns. Further, they seek to create an atmosphere in which the participants and staff developers collaborate in setting the agenda and deciding on how it will be enacted. The questions to be addressed in this chapter are: What does such a staff development process look like? And, how can staff developers facilitate the introduction of new content, while recognizing and respecting teachers' existing knowledge?

STAFF DEVELOPMENT OWNERSHIP: THREE MODELS

As mentioned above, staff development is defined as a set of processes that are either imposed on a group of teachers or are initiated by an individual teacher. Sparks and Loucks-Horsley (1990), in their summary of the staff development research literature, dubbed the latter "Individually Guided Staff Development." Cole and Thiessen (1991) divided all forms of staff development into two types: those conducted *by* teachers within one school, and those conducted *for* teachers within and across schools. In this chapter, three forms of staff development will be described, with the divisions determined by who sets the agenda as well as who controls the process and content.

    1. *Externally Driven*: This kind of program remains the traditional form of staff development implemented in most school settings. These programs, often mandating teacher participation, are designed and implemented by individuals or groups from outside the school or school district, and take place over several hours or, less frequently, several days. Sometimes, however, staff development programs are considerably longer. For example, the Schenley High School project in the Pittsburgh, Pennsylvania, school district required all high school teachers, in all subject matter areas, to attend the model high school and staff development facility over almost one semester. The purpose was to enable teachers to learn a particular lesson model as well as to acquire observation and supervision skills (Wallace, 1985). Many times, this type of process is accompanied by coaching, in which an individual, often a teacher, works with the teacher who is implementing a new practice to provide feedback on how well the practice is being implemented (Joyce & Showers, 1981).

2. *Teacher-initiated*: This is an umbrella term to denote individually determined professional growth. Examples of the kinds of activities involved vary widely and include taking courses at a local university, participating in a study group either within a school or within a district, networking on computer bulletin boards, and other types of networking activities such as those related to Foxfire (Smith, Wigginton, Hocking, & Jones, 1991).

3. *Collaborative*: This type of program represents a partnership between two individuals or groups, one of whom participates in staff development while the other facilitates it. This category also includes organizational development (Deal & Derr, 1980), collaborative teacher centers (Dawson & Finlay, 1990; Devaney & Thorn, 1975), and professional development schools (Stallings & Kowalski, 1990).

STAFF DEVELOPMENT CONTENT

Traditional staff development programs use imported content, usually in the form of new curricula, methods, or instructional programs. In these staff development programs, it is assumed that the change being promoted is good, and that if teachers are not now using the new procedures, they should adjust their instructional programs in directions suggested by the staff developer. In the early implementation literature, the success of the dissemination process, often handled through staff development, was determined by the degree to which the new practices adopted by the teachers matched the original practice being promoted (Berman & McLaughlin, 1975). More recently, it has been acknowledged that teachers, schools, and school districts may adapt a new practice depending on contextual demands (McLaughlin, 1987).

The view of staff development content as a practice or set of practices that someone outside the classroom thinks the teacher ought to adopt is usually present in the externally driven programs described above. However, it may also be a characteristic of collaborative projects in which a particular approach to teaching is being examined. Elliott (1976) describes such a collaborative approach in the constructivist science program founded by Lawrence Stenhouse, the founder of modernization research. The content of the program included discussions of a constructivist approach toward the teaching of science; however, the staff developers worked collaboratively with the teacher participants in examining what such an approach would look like when implemented in the classroom.

Prior Knowledge and Beliefs as Content

On the other hand, a number of staff development programs have recently been created from new understandings of how and why teachers change and use new practices in their classrooms. These programs are usually cognitively framed to encourage teachers to examine their own beliefs and understandings, reexamine their premises about teaching and learning, and modify their practices. Thus, within such a group process, the content of staff development is, in part, an articulation and sharing of the beliefs, practical knowledge, and practices of the teachers who are participating. The content is, therefore, not fixed ahead of time, and the practices that are eventually experimented with by the teachers may vary from one group to the next.

The conceptual framework for many of these programs relates to various theories of constructivist learning (see Chapter 4). These theories suggest that one's previous beliefs and knowledge are important in the construction of new understandings: that "learning" is an active process in which students construct and reconstruct concepts, premises, and theories. In translating this learning theory into instructional theory, the teacher is more of a guide than an imparter of facts and skills. In order to develop a constructivist environment, the teacher must also become a student: a student of students' beliefs and understandings, as well as a student of the content being discussed. The teacher and students become inquirers by posing problems, designing experiments, hypothesizing, observing, and reaching viable conclusions. A significant literature is being developed on this theoretical framework and its instructional implications (see, for example, Cobb, 1986; Duckworth, 1987; Fosnot, 1989; Glassersfeld, 1987; Lester & Onore, 1990), and is only recently being explored in staff development processes.

One of the first staff development programs designed and written about within a constructivist framework was Bamberger and Duckworth's year-long staff development project undertaken in Cambridge, Massachusetts (Bamberger, Duckworth, & Lampert, 1981). The purpose was to help teachers examine and develop their own theories of certain science concepts, such as a ball rolling down an inclined plane and the movement of the moon in relation to the earth. The staff developers hypothesized that if teachers could develop an awareness of their own processes of theory construction, they would alter their instructional programs for their students in a constructivist direction. While many of the teachers had taught these science constructs and processes within their classrooms, they had neither developed nor articulated their own deep theories to account for the phenomena.

Since that time, there have been a number of additional attempts at constructivist staff development projects, in science, mathematics, literacy, and higher-order thinking skills (see, for example Au, 1990; Baird, 1992; Bamberger, 1991; Carpenter, Fennema, Peterson, Chiang, & Loef, 1989; Peterman, 1991; Senger, 1992; Taylor, 1991; Tobin & Jakubowski, 1990). We will be describing one of these below (Anders & Richardson, 1991; Richardson & Anders, 1990). But first, we will briefly summarize the research on staff development.

STAFF DEVELOPMENT RESEARCH

Externally Driven

Early research on externally driven staff development programs suggested that teachers generally do not like such programs, and the evaluations of these programs demonstrated few well-documented results (Howey & Vaughan, 1983).

Exceptions to the conclusion concerning lack of results were the second phases of large-scale process/product studies. The first phase of these studies was correlational, designed to uncover relationships between certain teacher behaviors (processes) and student learning as measured by standardized tests (product). In the second phase of these studies, staff development programs were implemented as "treatments" in experimental studies to test the relationships between teacher behaviors and student achievement that were revealed in correlational studies (for example, Emmer, Sanford, Evertson, Clements, & Martin, 1981; Good & Grouws, 1979; Stallings, Needels, & Stayrook, 1983). These studies, summarized by Gage (1985), suggested that the staff development programs in all but one of the studies led to changes in teacher behaviors and student achievement. Griffin, Barnes, O'Neal, Edwards, Defino, and Hukill (1984) also worked, successfully, with the process/product findings in training staff developers in the findings, and in ways of introducing them to teachers in their districts and schools.

The process/product staff development studies differed from many previous studies of externally driven staff development programs in terms of the sophistication of the research design. They involved observation in the participating teachers' classrooms prior to, following, and sometimes during the process, and an examination of pre and post student scores on achievement tests. In the case of the Stallings et al.'s (1983) project, teachers were apprised of the results of their observations as a part of the staff development process. Further, the staff development programs used as

treatments in the studies were longer than the one-shot processes represented in many of the earlier studies.

The coaching studies conducted by Showers, Joyce, and colleagues
also provided long-term staff development programs and thorough research designs (Joyce, Murphy, Showers, & Murphy, 1989). These coaching programs, which focus on student achievement, promotion of collegiality, and development of site-based materials and peer-coaching, were
well documented and demonstrated success in changing teacher behaviors.

Analyses of this literature in combination with research on implementation and effective schools have led to a number of lists of characteristics
of successful staff development programs (for example, Griffin, 1986;
Griffin, Lieberman, & Jacullo-Noto, 1983; Loucks-Horsley, Harding,
Arbuckle, Murray, Dubea, & Williams, 1987; Ward, 1985). Some common
elements of these lists are:

1. The program should be context-specific; the school is seen as the
   important unit of change.
2. Teachers and administrators in the school should be involved in
   all aspects of the process.
3. The process should take place over an extended period of time.
4. The content should incorporate current knowledge obtained
   through well-designed research.

Teacher-initiated

Unfortunately, little scholarship exists on teacher-initiated professional development. What we do have are the results of teacher research
projects that are presented at such conferences as the National Council of
Teachers of English, as well as in various publications directed toward other
teachers and teacher educators. Heinemann Education Books, for example,
publishes works by teachers for teachers (e.g., Bissex & Bullock, 1987;
Newkirk & Atwell, 1988). Further, the Foxfire teacher networks have been
studied and written about in a number of publications (e.g., Smith, Wigginton, Hocking, & Jones, 1991) as has the Boston Women's Teachers'
Group (Freedman, Jackson, & Boles, 1983).

McDonald's (1986) description of a process in which a group of high
school teachers met together to study their practical knowledge is one of
several published articles about such activities. He concluded that academic
theory helped to elevate the voices of the teachers, but pointed out that
this may have been enhanced by the fact that he and several members of

the group split their time between the school and the university. By and large, however, professional development initiated by individuals and groups of teachers is a neglected area of research.

Collaborative

The collaborative staff development projects that have received the greatest attention in research are collaborative action research programs. Tikunoff, Ward, and Griffin (1979) conducted extensive research on their collaborative model that involved a researcher, a staff developer, and a group of teachers within a school; together, they identified a problem in the school, conducted research on it, and implemented a staff development program to deal with the problem. They found that the process led to considerable changes in teachers' practices, and that the research was considered by a number of experts to be of high quality. This study was followed by another in the New York City area, in which school context issues were examined (Griffin, Lieberman, & Jacullo-Noto, 1983).

In addition to spurring changes in professional practices, a number of studies suggest that collaborative action research affects teachers' personal growth and thinking. For example, Groarke, Ovens, and Hargreaves (1986) found that teachers in action research projects became more flexible in their thinking, and a summary of the literature by Noffke and Zeichner (1987) suggests that teachers increased their disposition toward reflection and their awareness of their beliefs.

Oja and Smulyan's (1989) analysis of the literature led to the following necessary conditions for successful collaborative action research:

1. Clear and specific goals should be carefully negotiated at the beginning of the process, and frequent interactions among participants maintained throughout the process.
2. Strong leadership by someone who can model democratic processes is essential. However, there may be a tension between leadership and democracy.
3. Action research should proceed through recursive cycles of planning, execution, and fact-finding.
4. The school environment should be one with a collegial atmosphere, in which teachers are free to identify problems and experiment with solutions. However, collaborative projects can be conducted without such support, with individuals or with small groups who work with collaborators in their own classrooms.

A COLLABORATIVE PROGRAM: THE PASD PROCESS

The Practical Argument Staff Development (PASD) program accommodated both individual teachers and groups of teachers in each school, and was designed to help teachers examine and possibly change beliefs about and practices in the teaching of reading comprehension. While the teaching of reading comprehension was the focus for this staff development program, the staff development processes were designed to be implemented with a focus on any discipline. In fact, the school-based aspect of the program was intended to develop the teachers' processes of reflection and the use of practical arguments, with the hope that these processes would be carried over to other content areas.

The Participants

The staff development program took place in five schools, and involved both university and school faculties. The university team included four persons within each school: the two staff developers—one with expertise in reading comprehension and the other in teaching and teacher education—and two research associates.

In each of the schools, grades 4, 5, and 6 teachers were involved, and often the learning disabilities (LD) teachers and/or the curriculum specialist were involved as well. Considerable data were collected on the staff development processes in two of the schools, Jones and Sumpter, and it is to these schools that we will refer when describing the research results. Jones School participants included seven teachers (three females and four males), one of whom was the LD teacher. The Jones principal attended sessions when her schedule permitted. At Sumpter, five female teachers, one of whom was the LD teacher, participated. In addition, the curriculum specialist participated, but the principal did not. The years of experience for the participants ranged from 1–16 years at Jones, and 8–32 years at Sumpter.

The Program Design

The first step in designing the program involved the development of the individual practical-argument process for teacher change; and the second step entailed developing a way of working with school faculties to discuss premises and practices, experiment with new ones, and share results. The development of the practical-argument process followed examples set by Fenstermacher (1986, pp. 44–45). We then adapted this process for our work with groups of teachers.

As elaborated by Fenstermacher in Chapter 2 of this book, a practical argument is a device used to assist teachers in examining their beliefs and possibly reconstructing them. These beliefs consist of four types of premises: value, situational, empirical, and stipulative. Together, these arguments represent an intention for action, although it is not expected that teachers will be consciously thinking in practical arguments when acting (Fenstermacher, 1987; Fenstermacher & Richardson, 1993). A second person is required to listen to the teachers, talk with them, and help them lay out their arguments. First, a videotaped lesson from each teacher's classroom was used to elicit information from the teachers about what they do in their classrooms. The listener asked questions designed to help teachers articulate information and ideas that, until then, may have been tacit. The process then moved to reconstruction, in which the participants (both teachers and staff developers) assessed the practical arguments, and introduced new premises and practices for consideration.

In more traditional group settings, the teachers were asked about issues important to them. Their responses became a group practical argument of sorts, and a chance for the teachers, as a group, to explore changes in their classrooms.

The Individual Component. One element of the practical-argument process involved the videotaping of teachers performing an activity or a task. Although the topic of the videotaping—the teaching of reading comprehension—was chosen by the staff developers, the teachers were asked to choose the time and instructional activity to be videotaped. Thus, some teachers were videotaped teaching reading using basal texts, some in social studies classes, and others teaching a skills lesson.

The teachers' interpretation of the staff developers' requests, as well as the lessons themselves, became substance for the individual sessions. The viewing partners helped the teachers lay out their practical arguments while viewing the tape. Meichenbaum and Butler (1980) suggested that such a process is useful because both verbal and nonverbal cues are available.

The staff developers intended the sessions to be as informal as possible. To that end, they arranged for them to occur at the convenience of the teacher—before, during, or after school. Prior to the session, the teachers were asked to view the videotape by themselves, although they sometimes did not do so.

The staff developers had not established a prescribed way to undertake these practical-argument sessions prior to the project. However, a certain format developed. Initially, they described the purpose of the meeting, which was to discuss the tapes in some detail, exploring what was done and why, with the hope of establishing areas the teachers wanted to improve. The project operated on the notion that teachers wanted to be the best teachers they could possibly be, and, therefore, were looking for improvement strategies.

It was explained to the teachers at the start of these individual sessions that they or the staff developers could stop the tape whenever they wanted to discuss what occurred. The videotape was shown, and the viewed classroom actions were discussed. In particular, teachers were often asked to describe their rationale for instruction, and to respond to questions about performance. This discussion yielded practical arguments for actions in teaching reading comprehension. Sessions culminated as individual teachers identified areas of practice that they would explore in theory and practice. Follow-up was provided by the research associate assigned to the school.

The Group Component. The second component of the PASD process involved group meetings with all of the intermediate-grade teachers in the designated schools. In these meetings, teachers talked about the practices they used during the reading comprehension instruction in general, and reflected in a group setting on these practices. The staff developers served as catalysts for these discussions, and also as models for reflection. Further, they provided some of the information that teachers used for both reflection and implementation, including their knowledge of theories of reading comprehension and examples of practices that were supported by those theories. The group sessions had components more typical of a traditional staff development atmosphere, including sitting in circles, focused discussions, and agendas based on topics that the teachers identified as important to them.

INTERACTIONS THROUGHOUT THE PROCESS

The purpose of this section is not to indicate how the teachers changed in beliefs and practices, or the effects of the staff development process on the teachers' students. These will be described in the next two chapters. This section will attempt to describe the flow of the process, and particularly the nature of the conversation as the process unfolded. Fortunately, data collected during the study provided us with the opportunity to conduct both discourse and topic analyses. Each group staff development session was videotaped, and the individual practical-argument sessions were audiotaped and transcribed. The data-collection methodology and analyses are described thoroughly in Hamilton (1989), Richardson (1992), Richardson and Anders (1990), and Richardson and Valdez (1991).

Hamilton (1989) described the three stages of conversation in the PASD process. In the "Introductory" stage, the teachers got to know each other. They did not ask many questions, and they politely listened to the conversation. The "Breakthrough" occurred when a person or persons moved through a line of thinking or a way of doing things to a new way of thinking about the topic. In the third, or "Empowerment," stage, teachers claimed ownership of the staff development itself, and the conversation began to be dominated by the teachers. The appendix summarizes the conversations in Sumpter elementary school within each session, and within each of the three stages.

Hamilton (1989) also found differences between the two schools in terms of the point at which each arrived at the empowerment stage. These differences are described in Chapter 7 of this book, as are the explanations of the effects of school context on the staff development process. The differences between schools are also apparent in Table 6.1, in which the percentage of talk time by teachers and staff developers is portrayed.

The types of talk have been described as SDT, or staff developer talk, SDTT, or staff-developer-initiated teacher talk (when, for example, the teachers were asked what had gone on in their classrooms that week); TTT, or teacher-initiated teacher talk; and DISC, or discussion. The movement toward teacher talk and discussion is clear in both schools, but occurred more quickly at Sumpter than at Jones.

We also found that some methods of introducing new practices were more conducive to discussions of theory and practice than others. An analysis of the data indicated five ways in which practices were introduced:

1. *Sharing:* One participant (teacher or staff developer) is reminded by the discussion of something he or she does or has done in the past, and talks about it with the rest of the participants. It usually is described in a personal, at times hesitant, manner.
2. *Show and Tell:* A participant does something during the week, and *prepares* to talk about it at the session. Often the participant will bring some materials to back it up—students' work or charts, for example.
3. *Lecture 1:* A participant gives a prepared presentation, planned for in advance of the session, about an activity extracted from the literature or from observation. It is presented in a depersonalized manner, and generally is not described as something the participant does or did.
4. *Lecture 2:* A participant gives a presentation about a practice that grows out of a discussion. It is not prepared in advance of the session, but, like Lecture 1, is presented in a depersonalized manner.

Table 6.1 Percentage of Talk Time by Teachers and Staff Developers

SD Session Number*	JONES				SUMPTER			
	SDT	SDTT	TTT	DISC	SDT	SDTT	TTT	DISC
1	66%	7%	1%	25%	67%	18%	0%	15%
2	22	36	5	37	15	10	13	62
3	23	29	7	41	30	12	16	35
4	61	9	5	25	40	8	27	25
5	28	7	13	51	27	2	17	55
6	9	11	26	54	15	3	25	57
7	27	15	12	44	14	0	12	74
8	23	10	25	42	13	0	14	72
9	9	4	6	80				
10	15	5	5	75				

SDT = Staff Developer Talk   SDTT = Staff-Developer-Initiated Teacher Talk
DISC = Discussion   TTT = Teacher-Iniated Teacher Talk

* There were fewer sessions at Sumpter than at Jones. The Jones sessions were two hours, each; the Sumpter sessions were three hours each.

5. *A New Suggestion*: The participants introduce into the discussion a "new" practice that emerges out of the conversation itself, a practice that could be tried by the participants.

In analyzing the participants' responses to the five modes of presenting practices, some differences emerged. They are summarized in Table 6.2. When sharing a practice was embedded within a conversation, the interest shown was intense, with participants "leaning into" the conversation. For both Lectures 1 and 2, the teachers would lean back, and some would begin to take notes, although the interest shown was higher in Lecture 2 than in Lecture 1. Also, there was much more animated discussion following Lecture 2 than Lecture 1. Questions following Lecture 1 would, by and large, be related to classroom management. The Lecture 2 follow-up consisted of discussions that revolved around theory and practice—the why's of a practice. The conversations following Lecture 2 presentations were lengthier and involved more participants.

We concluded that Lecture 2 was the mode of presentation that best met our goal of introducing alternative practices and their theoretical bases, and stimulating interest and discussion. A Lecture 2 presentation, however, could not be planned because it grew out of the conversation. This implies that the staff developer must have considerable knowledge of the content in order to spontaneously present the material.

The Agenda-Building Dilemma

Oja and Smulyan (1989) suggest that one important aspect of a successful collaborative process relates to leadership. The leader must set an example of the collaborative process, dispersing power and sharing control (also, Baird, 1992; Hord, 1981). They also suggest that there may be a delicate balance between leadership and democracy to be negotiated during the course of the process.

This problem relates to the agenda-building dilemma, which can be described with reference to the PASD process. It had been decided prior to staff development that the content would relate to reading comprehension instruction. The staff developers, however, were seen as "experts" by the teachers in formal reading comprehension scholarship. The agenda-building dilemma, then, relates to the dual and sometimes competing goals of (1) introducing participants to a particular content and (2) creating an empowering and emancipatory environment that requires that the participants own the content and process. The achievement of both goals simul-

Table 6.2 Classroom Practices: Styles of Presentation

Presentation Style	Theory/Research Embedding	Interest Level/ Style	Follow-up Discourse
Sharing	Low	High: Leaning forward	Some discussion
Show and Tell	Low	Polite	Some Polite Questions
Lecture 1	High	Medium High: leaning back, taking notes	"How to" questions (Management)
Lecture 2	Medium High	High: Sometimes taking notes	Considerable discussion, questions
"New" Suggestions	Low	Polite	Little

taneously seems to be particularly difficult when teachers expect staff development to be externally driven and the staff developers to be the experts. The second goal requires that power be shared equally by the participants, and that each participant contribute expertise. However, with content that is seen to reside in the staff developers, the goal of shared power may be difficult to reach.

We found the delicate balance somewhat difficult to establish in the PASD process, particularly in one school. The teachers were used to staff development processes in which an expert would provide information on how to do something new in the classroom—whether it is cooperative learning, the implementation of a new curriculum, or hands-on mathematics activities. In such in-service programs, it is not necessary for the participants to talk about their practices or beliefs. They may make private judgments about the potential impact of the program and accept it or not.

The PASD process was asking the participants to do something very different: something that broke the individualism norm described by Lortie (1975) as an element in the ethos of school faculties. This norm implies little reliance on others for sources of knowledge or experience except during the first two years (Fuchs, 1969). We were asking the teachers both to talk about their classroom practices and beliefs in front of their fellow teachers, and to take responsibility for and control of the content of the process. As described above, this process led to some tension in one of the schools between the teachers and the staff developers. This tension emerged and was resolved in one session, after which the participants reached the empowerment stage.

As suggested in Table 6.1 above, however, the staff development process did move toward a constructivist atmosphere in which all participants shared control of the agenda and process. The higher percentage of discussion time in the later sessions and the number of practices shared by the teachers attests to this change. In addition, the topics of conversation moved well beyond those originally defined by the staff developers. But we did experience the tensions between leadership and democracy described by Oja and Smulyan (1989). The delicate balance was maintained, ultimately; however, it was more difficult to do so in one school than in the other. We now turn to a discussion of the outside collaborator in the role of leader and democratizer. In this project, the outside collaborators were the staff developers.

The Role of the Facilitator or "Other"

The role of the person who facilitates a collaborative staff development process has only recently been examined. In this chapter, we call this person the "Other." This concept was developed within the framework of the elicitation and reconstruction of teachers' practical arguments (see Chapter 2), which was one aspect of the PASD process. However, it may also be considered an appropriate concept in examining the facilitator in the group process.

Oja and Smulyan (1989) have examined the role of the outside university researcher in action research projects. They suggest that the person(s) in this role performs a number of functions: acts as the essential facilitator of the dialogue process and method; brings a variety of resources to the project; acts as a sounding board for the teachers in trying out their ideas and talking about them; organizes the distributions of data and other materials. While action research differs somewhat from the process examined in the Reading Instruction Study, these functions are certainly appropriate in describing the role of the Other in the PASD process.

The role of the Other in the practical-argument process has been examined in both the individual practical-argument sessions and in the group process. Vasquez-Levy (1993) describes the role in this manner:

> the role should be perceived as that of an advocate assisting teachers to examine their beliefs, to acquire or to develop further their *strong sense of knowing*, beliefs supported by truth and evidence to ground their practice. (p. 26)

Morgan (1993) suggests that the role of the Other in a practical-argument process may be taken by the teacher, and presents a case study of her own process. However, she found the process difficult. Kroath (1990) developed the notion of the "critical friend" in action research projects. He suggested that the role "consists in destabilizing and deconstructing rigidly held convictions and taken-for-granted views of one's own teaching practice, thus enabling the teacher to gain new perspectives on his/her classroom reality" (p. 5).

The Other as teacher-learner is a strong theme in descriptions of the outside facilitator in group processes. Bamberger (1991) portrayed her role in facilitating teachers' reflective conversations:

> So as the conversation unfolds, I am playing a double role; mutual participant, freely joining in with the others in making my spontaneous associations and views known; and also watchful listener, looking for moments to grab on-the-wing so as to provoke, probe, prod, and reinforce germinating ideas. (p. 51)

Elliott (1988) also focuses on the teacher-learner role, and suggests that the Other should inquire, publicly, into his or her own role.

A recent review of the literature on the Other concluded that certain characteristics of manner, beliefs, ethics, knowledge, and skills are essential to the successful facilitation of a collaborative process (Richardson & Fenstermacher, 1992).

Manner and Ethics. Freire (1983) suggests that because it is necessary when facilitating a group process to set up an initial teacher-learner dichotomy, a "self-effacing" stance on the part of the Other is necessary. This manner suggests that the Other is both teacher and learner. The Other must also have a genuine intellectual interest in and curiosity about the topics of conversation, and a personal interest in how the teachers think about teaching. The teachers' practical knowledge must be valued, and the climate must be open, trusting, and nonjudgmental (see Vasquez-Levy, 1993). This manner is enhanced if the caring ethic (Noddings, 1986) enters into the feelings of the Other in facilitating the dialogue.

Knowledge and Skills. Examination of the PASD process, as well as Vasquez-Levy's (1993) study, points to the need for "finger tip" theoretical and research knowledge to bring into the conversation. The facilitators had to move with the conversation. They could not prepare material in advance unless the teachers had asked them to do so in a previous session. A deep and broad understanding of the theoretical and research knowledge was required in order to bring it forward at appropriate times. Elliott (1988) and Kroath (1990) also talk about the broad knowledge of research methodology required by the facilitator of an action research project.

In an analysis of the PASD process, it appeared that one of the most important skills of the Other relates to questioning. Questioning seems to accomplish two functions: The first is that the Other learns about the thinking and premises of the teacher; the second is that it moves the conversation along. However, questions must be asked in a manner that does not threaten the participants or dominate the direction of the conversation.

The Other must also be willing to reflect and to conduct inquiry on the process as it is unfolding. The staff developer who publicly reflects and inquires into the process may contribute to the success of the process, but is also modeling an inquiring approach to teaching.

CONCLUSION

The Practical Argument Staff Development program offers a different perspective on the ownership of process and content, as well as on the role of the staff developer. This new way of thinking and practice regarding staff development, driven by participants' personal practical knowledge, beliefs, and interests, engages the teachers as partners in the process and content selection. In support of the partnership, the staff developer encourages this process, becoming a facilitator of the process and a participant in the teaching and learning process. While this type of collaborative staff development is challenging, there is good evidence, much of which emerged from the RIS project and will be discussed in subsequent chapters, that it produces long-standing change for the participants.

In conclusion, the following characteristics describe the nature of the Practical Argument Staff Development process:

1. It is based on the notion that teachers' beliefs and understandings are important contributors to their classroom practices, and should become, in part, the content of staff development. This requires that a highly trusting atmosphere be created, to allow the participants to share their beliefs about teaching and learning with others.
2. The goal is not to lead toward the implementation of a particular method or curriculum. Instead, the goal is related to helping the participants understand their own beliefs and practices, consider alternative premises and practices, and experiment with new ones. This new perspective, and the change it fosters, should not cease with the completion of the staff development process, but continue throughout the teachers' professional life.
3. The group process involves the sharing of expertise and encourages the development of new understandings and practices. The teachers have embedded knowledge of their context, teaching, and subject matter that may be shared with others; and the staff developers have knowledge of current research and theory about the teaching of particular subject matter.
4. During the course of the process, the interaction between staff developers and teachers moves away from domination by the staff developers toward teacher control of the process and content.
5. The process is long-term—at least one semester—for both the group and individual components. The group component may work better in a place other than the school itself.
6. The staff developer, or Other, must be knowledgeable about current research and practice in instruction; however, he or she must not be seen as the only expert. A democratic process must be facilitated that allows the teachers to recognize and value their own expertise.

Appendix: Description of PASD Sessions at Sumpter

This staff-development program, which occurred once a month, actually took place at a staff developer's home. This location was selected because it was accessible and because the teachers felt it was imperative to meet off campus both for their well-being and for their comfort in revealing sources.

Introductory Stage

Session 1: This first session began with a description of the project and reassurances to the teachers that the staff developers wanted to figure out the areas that the teachers wanted to cover. The teachers seemed fascinated to hear each other talk. Prior to these meetings, there was little cohesiveness among the faculty and they now seemed to be thrilled by the new discoveries of their colleagues. Although apparently just getting to know each other, the teachers engaged in an exploration of practices and appeared committed to using the staff development program to gain as much information as possible.

Breakthrough Stage

Session 2: Assessment was a major focus. First, they looked at the activities students did when studying comprehension strategies. The teachers defined reading comprehension, explored the purpose of skills, and looked at ways to evaluate reading. Then the issue shifted to assessment and the problems related to it. During this session the teachers became seriously engaged in an exploration of practices. They spoke their mind about the basal readers, skills, and the purposes of reading comprehension. They also explored the issues of accountability and assessment. It was also during this session that the curriculum specialist became simply a participant rather than an administrator. When the staff developers challenged her statements and modeled challenging her direction, the teachers no longer acquiesced to her control. As they took control of the meeting, the breakthrough stage began.

Session 3: The breakthrough stage carried over into session 3. The initial discussion centered on the disruption of classes during reading. The teachers felt that they too often had school interruptions. Next, they discussed their focuses and prior knowledge; other reading research issues were also discussed. Several teachers followed up by stating the importance of developing shared knowledge among teachers and students. Many of the topics discussed involved "do you" questions. The teachers were almost desperate to find out what their colleagues had done. When a teacher brought up a subject, the others seemed compelled to discuss it and offer suggestions. They discussed journals, book reports, and formula answers. The topic then turned, as usual, to assessment, focusing on the power of parent involvement and testing criteria. The teachers each had their experience to relate, yet the similarities were strong. Along with these similarities, there was a discussion of the "power of the test-makers" and how often teachers gave the power of knowing students over to the standardized-test people. Finally during this session, a videotape of a teacher was viewed. The teacher was observed working successfully with students in groups. A discussion ensued that looked at the "traditional ways of teaching," as well as other aspects of teaching.

Session 4: The teachers began to talk more. Although staff developer 2 initially provided an agenda, the teachers monitored it. They also requested classroom modeling done by project staff. An initial discussion for this session observed the differences between the use of the basal text and literature books. They all talked about their concerns and purposes for using the texts that they used. Other issues of practice were discussed, including the use of vocabulary, writing, evaluation of students, and how to reach students. Staff developer 2 suggested that a teacher's knowledge of the history of the classroom propelled the students more rapidly along the path of knowing.

Session 5: The discussion began with an exploration of Jane's use of concept analysis and how it worked. The staff developers developed her practical argument as she proceeded, and the teachers listened and discussed ways of using concept analysis in their classrooms. Next, they discussed the district gifted program at length and speculated on why that sort of process versus outcomes teaching was not done throughout the district. From there the discussion turned to grading and how to approach it. Several teachers addressed the importance of recognizing prior knowledge and what the students knew as they entered the classroom. They also condemned the school reward system, because it set up a bad self-esteem problem. Further, several teachers expressed fear that the principal would not support them if the parents challenged their grading, and also discussed grading alternatives. One final discussion centered on an exploration of modeling done in Sarah's classroom. The research associate explained why she thought it worked/did not work as well as the participation of the students. Sarah followed up with her concerns about certain students.

Session 6: After a brief discussion of a concern by two participants, the teachers explored the use of literature versus basal approach to reading in the classroom. There were questions about comprehension checks, variations in students' questions, the suffocation of creativity, providing feedback, and grading. They also discussed the videotape of a research associate modeling brainstorming in Sarah's classroom. First, the research associate discussed her experience, and then Sarah discussed hers. The session ended with an assignment. Each teacher was to go to his or her students and ask them what they thought reading was, so that the teachers could begin to elaborate on those ideas.

Empowerment Stage

Session 7: The discussion revolved around literature. Andrea talked about the use of novels in her classroom, as did Deloris. The curriculum specialist talked about the literature-based basal programs and their potential value. Andrea then raised the issue of authenticity between a basal text and a literature selection. Jane brought up a question of skills. They discussed the value of outlining to help students explore their lives. Outlining could help organize students' thinking as well as organize students' views of reading. As they discussed this, the topic turned to reading and making sense of the text. During a break in the meeting the teachers planned the next session. It would be a literature group, so that they could experience a discussion group. They selected book choices, dates, topics, and strategies and were quite excited. After addressing the issue of a good reading practice, the discussion moved into a look at students' views of reading. Many students had a different view of reading. As the discussion proceeded, teachers revealed their own learning-to-read process. Interestingly, there appeared to be a connection between personal process and the ways teachers taught reading. The teachers also made connections between their own processes and students' processes. This led to an insightful discussion of different students and their needs. The shift from breakthrough to empowerment was subtle. The teachers did not simply take over. Rather, they eased into the empowerment stage and suddenly seemed to be directing the action. The level of excitement and interest seemed to rise in this process.

Session 8: The final session began with a recounting of teacher activities. Four of the five teachers were working with novels. Their students were quite happy with that, and the teachers were pleased as well. A literature group discussion followed, revolving around their book selection. They discussed the book, its important issues, and then ways to use it with their students. Given the different interpretations in the room, it was certainly a testimony to the interactivity between text and reader. There was also a focus on the importance of prior knowledge. All the teachers contributed, and they appeared pleased by the discussion. A final discussion turned to assessment and how students might be graded when literature was used. Each teacher offered suggestions. The key for most of the teachers was that they were professionals, and whatever decisions they made about assessment should be appreciated in that light. As the meeting closed, the teachers talked about its success. They had revealed a lot about themselves, but were grateful for it, realizing the importance of knowing their own beliefs. The themes for the Sumpter School sessions varied. Specifically, the struggle over what best served the students—literature or basal—appeared to be a focal point. The teachers were also interested in the practices and strategies used by their colleagues. This contact starved faculty seemed glad for any tidbit of attention given to them and were willing to make the best of it. It appeared they wanted to make every moment count.

REFERENCES

Anders, P., & Richardson, V. (1991). Research currents: Staff development that empowers teachers' reflection and enhances instruction. *Language Arts, 68*(4), 316–321.

Au, K. (1990). Changes in teacher's views of interactive comprehension instruction. In L. Moll (Ed.), *Vygotsky and education* (pp. 271–286). New York: Cambridge University Press.

Baird, J. R. (1992). Collaborative reflection, systematic enquiry, better teaching. In T. Russell & H. Munby (Eds.), *Teachers and teaching: From classroom to reflection* (pp. 33–48). Philadelphia: Falmer.

Bamberger, J. (1991). The laboratory for making things: Developing multiple representations of knowledge. In D. Schön (Ed.), *The reflective turn* (pp. 37–62). New York: Teachers College Press.

Bamberger, J., Duckworth, E., & Lampert, M. (1981). *Final report: An experiment in teacher development.* Cambridge: Massachusetts Institute of Technology.

Berman, P., & McLaughlin, M. (1975). *Federal programs supporting educational change* (Vol. 5, Executive Summary, R-1589/4-HEW). Santa Monica, CA: Rand Corporation.

Bissex, G., & Bullock, R. (1987). *Seeing for ourselves.* Portsmouth, NH: Heinemann Educational Books.

Carpenter, T., Fennema, E., Peterson, P., Chiang, C., & Loef, L. (1989). Using knowledge of children's mathematics thinking in classroom teaching: An experimental study. *American Educational Research Journal, 26,* 499–532.

Cobb, P. (1986). Making mathematics: Children's learning and the constructivist tradition. *Teachers College Record, 56,* 301–306.

Cole, A., & Thiessen, D. (1991). *Inservice education of teachers INSET: An interpretive review.* Toronto, Canada: Ontario Institute for Studies in Education.

Corey, S. (1957). Introduction. In N. B. Henry (Ed.), *Inservice education* (Fifty-sixth yearbook of the National Society for the Study of Education, pp. 1–12). Chicago: University of Chicago Press.

Davies, D. (1967). Notes and working papers prepared for the Senate Subcommittee on Education. Cited in L. Rubin (Ed.), *Improving inservice education: Proposals and procedures for change* (p. 38). Boston: Allyn and Bacon.

Dawson, A., & Finlay, F. (1990). Bringing teacher education to remote Northern Canadian Centres: The AHCOTE story. In H. Schwartz (Ed.), *Collaboration: Building common agendas* (pp. 32–33). Washington, DC: Clearing House on Teacher Education and American Association of Colleges for Teacher Education.

Deal, T., & Derr, C. (1980). Toward a contingency theory of organizational change in education: Structure, process and symbolism. In C. Benson, M. Kirst, S. Abromowitz, W. Hartman, & L. Stoll (Eds.), *Educational finance and organization: Research perspectives for the future.* Washington, DC: National Institute of Education, U.S. Department of Education.

Devaney, K., & Thorn, L. (1975). *Exploring teachers' centers.* San Francisco: Far West Laboratory for Educational Research and Development.

Duckworth, E. (1987). *"The having of wonderful ideas" and other essays on teaching and learning*. New York: Teachers College Press.

Edelfelt, R. (1984). *Inservice education: Moving from professional development to school improvement*. Washington, DC: American Association of Colleges for Teacher Education.

Elliott, J. (1976). Developing hypotheses from teachers' practical constructs: An account of the work of the Ford Teaching Project. *Interchange, 7*, 2–22.

Elliott, J. (1988). Educational research and outsider-insider relations. *Qualitative Studies in Education, 1*(2), 155–166.

Emmer, E., Sanford, J., Evertson, C., Clements, B., & Martin, J. (1981). *The classroom management improvement study: An experiment in elementary school classrooms*. Austin: Research and Development Center for Teacher Education, University of Texas. (ERIC Document Reproduction Service No. ED 178-460)

Fenstermacher, G. D. (1986). Philosophy of research on teaching: Three aspects. In M. Wittrock (Ed.), *Handbook of research on teaching* (3rd ed., pp. 37–49). New York: Macmillan.

Fenstermacher, G. D. (1987). Prologue to my critics. *Educational Theory, 37*(4), 357–360.

Fenstermacher, G. D, & Berliner, D. (1985). Determining the value of staff development. *Elementary School Journal, 85*(3), 281–314.

Fenstermacher, G. D, & Richardson, V. (1993). The elicitation and reconstruction of practical arguments in teaching. *Journal of Curriculum Studies, 25*(2), 101–114.

Fosnot, C. (1989). *Enquiring teachers, enquiring learners: A constructivist approach to teaching*. New York: Teachers College Press.

Freedman, S., Jackson, J., & Boles, K. (1983). Teaching: An imperilled "profession." In L. Shulman & G. Sykes (Eds.), *Handbook of teaching and policy* (pp. 261–299). New York: Longman.

Freire, P. (1983). *Education for the critical consciousness*. New York: Continuum.

Fuchs, E. (1969). *Teachers' talk: Views from inside city schools*. New York: Doubleday.

Gage, N. (1985). *Hard gains in the soft sciences: The case of pedagogy*. Bloomington, IN: Phi Delta Kappa.

Glassersfeld, E. von (1987). *The construction of knowledge*. Seaside, CA: The Systems Inquiry Series, Intersystems Publication.

Goldenberg, C., & Gallimore, R. (1991). Changing teaching takes more than a one-shot workshop. *Educational Leadership, 49*(3), 69–72.

Good, T., & Grouws, D. A. (1979). The Missouri mathematics effectiveness project: An experimental study of fourth-grade classrooms. *Journal of Educational Psychology, 71*, 355–362.

Griffin, G. (1983). Introduction: The work of staff development. In G. Griffin (Ed.), *Staff development* (Eighty-second Yearbook of the National Society for the Study of Education) (pp. 1–12). Chicago: University of Chicago Press.

Griffin, G. (1986). Clinical teacher education. In J. Hoffman & S. Edwards (Eds.), *Reality and reform in clinical teacher education* (pp. 1–24). New York: Random House.

Griffin, G., Barnes, S., O'Neal, S., Edwards, S., Defino, M., & Hukill, H. (1984).

Changing teacher practice: Final report of an experimental study, Report No. 9052.
   Austin: Research and Development Center for Teacher Education, University of Texas.

Griffin, G., Lieberman, A., & Jacullo-Noto, J. (1983). *Interactive research and development on schooling: Executive summary of final report.* Austin: Research and
   Development Center for Teacher Education, University of Texas.

Groarke, J., Ovens, P., & Hargreaves, M. (1986). Towards a more open classroom.
   In D. Hustler, T. Cassidy, & T. Cuff (Eds.), *Action research in classrooms and
   schools.* London: Allen & Unwin.

Guskey, T. (1986). Staff development and the process of teacher change. *Educational Researcher, 15*(5), 5–15.

Hamilton, M. (1989). *The practical argument staff development process, school culture and their effects on teachers' beliefs and classroom practice.* Unpublished
   doctoral dissertation, College of Education, University of Arizona, Tucson.

Hord, S. (1981). *Working together: Cooperation or collaboration?* Austin: Research
   and Development Center for Teacher Education, University of Texas.

Howey, K., & Vaughan, J. (1983). Current patterns of staff development. In
   G. Griffin (Ed.), *Staff development* (Eighty-second Yearbook of the National
   Society for the Study of Education) (pp. 92–117). Chicago: University of Chi-
   cago Press.

Joyce, B., Murphy, C., Showers, B., & Murphy, J. (1989). School renewal as cultural change. *Educational Leadership, 47*, 70–77.

Joyce, B., & Showers, B. (1981). Transfer of training: The contribution of coaching. *Journal of Education, 163*(2), 163–172.

Kroath, F. (1990). *The role of the critical friend in the development of teacher expertise.* Paper presented at an international symposium on Research on Effective and Responsible Teaching, Université de Fribourg Suisse, Fribourg, Switzerland.

Lester, N., & Onore, C. (1990). *Learning change.* Portsmouth, NH: Boynton/Cook.

Lortie, D. (1975). *Schoolteacher.* Chicago: University of Chicago Press.

Loucks-Horsley, S., Harding, C., Arbuckle, M., Murray, L., Dubea, C., & Williams, M. (1987). *Continuing to learn: A guidebook for teacher development.*
   Andover: Regional Laboratory for Educational Improvement of the North-
   east and Islands/National Staff Development Council.

McDonald, J. P. (1986). Raising the teacher's voice and the ironic role of theory.
   Harvard Educational Review, 56(4), 355–378.

McLaughlin, M. (1987). Learning from experience: Lessons from policy implementation. *Educational Evaluation and Policy Analysis, 9*, 171–178.

Meichenbaum, D., & Butler, L. (1980). Cognitive ethnology: Assessing the streams
   of cognition and emotion. In K. Blankstein, P. Piner, & J. Polivy (Eds.), *Advances in the study of communication and affect: Assessment and modification
   of emotional behavior* (Vol. 2, pp. 139–164). New York: Plenum.

Morgan, B. (1993). Practical rationality: A self investigation. *Journal of Curriculum Studies, 25*(2), 115–124.

Newkirk, N., & Atwell, N. (1988). *Understanding writing* (2nd ed.). Portsmouth,
   NH: Heinemann Educational Books.

Noddings, N. (1986). Fidelity in teaching, teacher education, and research for teaching. *Harvard Educational Review, 56,* 496–510.

Noffke, S., & Zeichner, K. (1987). *Action research and teacher thinking: The first phase of the AR project at the University of Wisconsin, Madison.* Paper presented at the annual meeting of the American Educational Research Association, Washington, DC.

Oja, S., & Smulyan, L. (1989). *Collaborative action research: A developmental approach.* Philadelphia: Falmer.

Peterman, F. (1991). *A teacher's changing beliefs about learning and teaching.* Unpublished doctoral dissertation, University of Arizona, Tucson.

Richardson, V. (1992). The agenda-setting dilemma in a constructivist staff development process. *Teaching and Teacher Education, 8*(3), 287–300.

Richardson, V., & Anders, P. (1990). *Final report of the reading instruction study.* Tucson: College of Education, University of Arizona. (ERIC Document Reproduction Service No. ED 324-655)

Richardson, V., & Fenstermacher, G. D. (1992, April). *The role of the "other" in teacher change.* Paper presented at the annual meeting of the American Educational Research Association, San Francisco.

Richardson, V., & Valdez, A. (1991, April). *Changes in teachers' beliefs about and theories of reading comprehension.* Paper presented at the annual meeting of the American Educational Research Association, Chicago.

Senger, B. (1992). *Personalized staff development: The effect of reflective dialogue on the beliefs, values, and practices of three elementary mathematics teachers.* Unpublished doctoral dissertation, University of Arizona, Tucson.

Smith, H., Wigginton, E., Hocking, K., & Jones, R. E. (1991). Foxfire teacher networks. In A. Lieberman & L. Miller (Eds.), *Staff development for education in the 90's* (pp. 193–220). New York: Teachers College Press.

Sparks, D., & Loucks-Horsley, S. (1990). Models of staff development. In R. Houston (Ed.), *Handbook of research on teacher education* (pp. 234–250). New York: Macmillan.

Stallings, J., & Kowalski, T. (1990). Research on professional development schools. In R. Houston (Ed.), *Handbook of research on teacher education* (pp. 251–263). New York: Macmillan.

Stallings, J., Needels, M., & Stayrook, N. (1983). *How to change the process of teaching basic reading skills in secondary schools: Phase II and Phase III.* Menlo Park, CA: SRI International.

Stevenson, R. (1987). Staff development for effective secondary schools: A synthesis of research. *Teaching and Teacher Education, 3*(3), 233–248.

Taylor, P. (1991, April). *Collaborating to reconstruct teaching: The influence of researcher beliefs.* Paper presented at the annual meeting of the American Educational Research Association, Chicago.

Tikunoff, W., Ward, B., & Griffin, G. (1979). *Interactive research and development on teaching study: Final report.* San Francisco: Far West Laboratory for Educational Research and Development.

Tobin, K., & Jakubowski, E. (1990). *Cooperative teacher project: Final report.* Tallahassee: Florida State University.

Vasquez-Levy, D. (1993). The use of practical arguments in clarifying and chang-
    ing practical reasoning and classroom practices: Two cases. *Journal of Cur-
    riculum Studies, 25*(2), 125–144.
Wallace, R. (1985). The Schenley High School Teacher Center. In S. Hord, S. O'Neal,
    & M. Smith (Eds.), *Beyond the looking glass* (pp. 333–336). Austin: The Re-
    search and Development Center for Teacher Education, University of Texas.
Ward, B. (1985). Teacher development: The challenge of the future. In S. Hord,
    S. O'Neal, & M. Smith (Eds.), *Beyond the looking glass* (pp. 283–312). Austin:
    The Research and Development Center for Teacher Education, University of
    Texas.

7
Schools as Contexts:
A Complex Relationship

PEGGY PLACIER AND MARY LYNN HAMILTON

Although much research on staff development emphasizes its failures (Guskey, 1986), researchers are beginning to claim some understanding of the conditions under which staff development is likely to succeed. Some conclude that the effects of staff development are dependent on much more than design or content (Griffin & Barnes, 1986; Howey & Vaughan, 1983; Lieberman & Miller, 1984). The social context must be taken into account. In fact, Little (1981) has gone so far as to claim that the school organization is not merely the "context" of staff development but the "heart of the matter" (p. 4).

> Researchers who study school improvement tend to agree on this point. Political theorist Blase (1987a) has warned that rational orientations to school improvement, which focus on attitudes and beliefs of individuals and small groups, or formal school structures, without attention to the politics of a given situation, may result in failure (p. 30).

Cultural theorists warn of the power of cultural norms, what Deal calls the "less rational" aspects of schools, which can either impede or facilitate change (Deal, 1984; Sarason, 1982).

Staff developers have begun to heed these warnings. For example, the original proposal for the Reading Instruction Study (RIS) stated:

> Programs designed to change teaching of reading practices that ignore the context in which teachers operate may be doomed to failure (Richardson & Anders, 1986, p. 14).

To avoid such doom, the RIS investigators decided that an assessment of the political and cultural characteristics of participating schools would be essential, and assigned one component of the project to this assessment.

This chapter synthesizes the literature on school context and staff development, drawing illustrative examples from two schools in the RIS study. Surprisingly, the investigators' observations of the two school contexts were not good predictors of the outcomes of the staff development process. At the school that seemed a very unpromising context for staff development, the teachers responded quite positively. The opposite was true for the seemingly more welcoming school. In our conclusions, we will discuss why our prophecies for the two schools were unfulfilled, and make recommendations for further investigation of the complex relationship between school context and staff development.

TEACHER BELIEFS AND SCHOOL CONTEXT

In Chapter 5, Richardson frames the RIS study in terms of changes in teacher beliefs. This framework emphasizes the individualistic element of teaching. Indeed, there is support for viewing both teaching and teacher change as processes conducted in isolation (Goodlad, 1983; Lieberman & Miller, 1984; Little, 1987; Lortie, 1975). As Johnson (1990) puts it, "For teachers, learning and growth are personal rather than institutional responsibilities, occurring largely at the margins of their work" (p. 249). Moreover, in this staff development process, change was voluntary. Teachers were not obligated or pressured to adopt certain beliefs and practices, as is the case for the majority of staff development programs. If the direction and extent of teacher change depend largely on individual, voluntary decisions, how might the school context affect such decisions?

A teacher's beliefs, however, are not constructed in isolation, but in contexts such as the family, the classroom (both as student and teacher), and the teachers' lounge. American teachers share certain beliefs as a result of their socialization in teacher education programs, membership in a common profession, and central role in the culture of the American school (Bowers & Flinders, 1990; Deal, 1984; Feiman-Nemser & Floden, 1986; Hamilton, 1989; Lortie, 1975; Page, 1988).

The staff development process associated with the RIS project, in fact, invited the social construction of teacher beliefs. It was designed around regular meetings of participating teachers from each school. The direction of the meetings was not predetermined, and varied with the interests of each group. The outcomes of this group process were uncontrollable, influenced as they were by interpersonal dynamics (both among teachers and between teachers and staff developers), and the politics and culture of each school. To present teacher change in this context as entirely individualistic would be an oversimplification of the staff development process.

The staff developers also recognized that the social context of a school or district could constrain rather than enhance teachers' freedom to act on their beliefs. Even if staff development changed a teacher's beliefs, this change might not manifest itself in practice; or the effects might be short-lived, because the political or cultural pressures of the school reasserted themselves. The purpose of studying the context was to identify social conditions in schools that might limit teachers' abilities to transform their beliefs into practice.

THE EFFECTS OF SCHOOL CONTEXT: WHAT THE RESEARCH SHOWS

We have synthesized the literature on context effects into four conditions, presented in the form of questions that a prospective staff developer should ask about a school. For each condition, a discussion of prior research is presented; then, the findings related to that condition for the two elementary schools in the RIS study, Jones and Sumpter, are reported. The names of the schools and of the teachers have been changed to preserve their anonymity. The appendix at the end of this chapter contains a brief explanation of the design and methodology of the context component (see also Richardson & Anders, 1990). Based on these findings, we became convinced that Jones, although not the "perfect context," came much closer to meeting the conditions for successful staff development than did Sumpter.

Teachers' Assessment of Working Conditions

Condition #1: Do teachers in this school experience positive working conditions, or is their work so stressful that it inhibits their motivation to participate in staff development and/or to improve their practice?
Little (1982) states that successful staff development "calls for a stability that may be in short supply, especially in urban districts" (p. 339). High-stress working conditions in some schools may encourage teachers to seek control and routine, rather than change and experimentation (Blase, 1991b). Sources of teacher stress include lack of time (Blase, 1986), negative supervisory behavior, discouragement about student learning, and role ambiguity (Bacharach, Bauer, & Shedd, 1986). Interpersonal conflict is another source of stress. Studies of the micropolitics of schools (Ball, 1987; Blase, 1991a) indicate that conflict, whether overt or covert, is a fact of life in schools.
Teachers lower their expectations for their own performance and for student achievement under stressful conditions (Blase, 1986; Frymier, 1987; Johnson, 1990). They may be skeptical of innovations that depend on "ideal" conditions or resources that do not exist in their school (Firestone & Herriott, 1981). Staff developers, therefore, must consider physical conditions and resources, teachers' duties and schedules, and the micropolitics

of the school as potential barriers to teacher change (Anderson, 1991; Blase, 1991a, 1991b; Corcoran, Kohli, & White, 1988; Greenfield, 1991; Lieberman & Miller, 1984). To succeed, staff development must be perceived as a positive opportunity, not an additional burden or a stimulus for conflict.

Finding #1: Jones School appeared to be a less stressful place to work than Sumpter School.

Jones School was an attractive school, built within the last two years, with a quiet, relaxed atmosphere. The student population, about half Anglo and half Hispanic, lived in the immediate suburban neighborhood. Teacher-student interactions were positive, and discipline was not a preoccupation. The teachers and principal expressed mutual admiration. Lack of time seemed to be the major source of teacher stress. After the first meeting of teachers and staff developers, the principal complained that the staff developers took too long to explain the project. The teachers had three meetings that week, and she had promised this one would be brief. In fact, the teachers had so many meetings that it was difficult for them to agree on a time for the staff development sessions. Despite this, the classroom observer found them generally cooperative and enthusiastic about participating.

Sumpter School was located in a declining neighborhood. The building was old and in need of renovation; the principal called the oldest section a "dungeon." The classroom observer felt that people at Sumpter were "not very friendly." There was obvious strain between the principal and teachers. Class sizes were larger than at Jones, and project assistants observed negative teacher-student interactions in some classrooms. The principal complained of time spent on discipline. Due to busing in of both low-income Hispanic and affluent Anglo children for desegregation, the student population was complex. The primary grade population was 35 percent Hispanic and black and the rest Anglo and a very small percentage of children of other ethnicities; the intermediate grades were 10–12 percent Hispanic and black and the rest Anglo. In the first four grades, the principal blamed discipline problems on student diversity, and felt pressured by affluent parents to maintain the school's "image." Given such working conditions, it was not surprising that the Sumpter teachers expressed some resistance to participating in the project. Their initial reactions set up the expectation that they would be a "difficult" group with whom to work.

Teachers' Sense of Autonomy

Condition #2: Do teachers in this school have autonomy to change their practices in reading instruction, or do they feel constrained by forces beyond their control?

Meyer and Rowan (1978) once argued that school systems are "loosely coupled"—that is, given the structure of schooling, it is very difficult for one level to supervise the activities at the next lower level. Thus, top-down control over teaching is nearly impossible. The coupling, however, appears to be tightening (Anderson, 1991). Many recent reforms employ coercive strategies or mandates that limit teacher discretion over instruction practices (Frymier, 1987; Gallagher, Goodvis, & Pearson, 1988; Hargreaves, 1991; Johnson, 1990). For instance, teachers' choices may be limited by centrally adopted reading textbooks or standardized tests that embody a particular view of reading (Shannon, 1989). Facing political pressure for accountability and higher student achievement, administrators may in turn pressure teachers to link their practices to district and/or state criteria or tests (Apple & Teitelbaum, 1985; Corcoran et al., 1988; Fraatz, 1987; Frymier, 1987; Johnson, 1990).

The micropolitics of school relationships may also limit teacher autonomy. According to Anderson (1991), "the control versus autonomy battle is fought out in subtle and not-so-subtle ways daily among principals, teachers, parents and students in school" (p. 120). Some principals nurture teacher autonomy, some simply leave teachers alone, and others intervene to promote their own preferences or to enforce top-down mandates (Bifano, 1988; Johnson, 1990; Leithwood & Montgomery, 1982).

Much interpretation of the limits placed on teacher autonomy has been critical. However, Murphy (1988) actually claims that in "effective" school districts there are *more* clearcut expectations, and greater control over instruction. Hallinger and Murphy (1985) further claim that principals of effective schools exercise more bureaucratic control over teaching. The trade-offs for teachers in such schools are more frequent interaction, incentives and recognition, and a reduction in uncertainty. According to this view, teachers in some systems or schools may be less autonomous, but also feel more positive about their work, if they develop a shared belief that what they are doing works, and if they are rewarded for it.

Finding #2: Teachers in both schools reported a high degree of autonomy on the school context questionnaire, but teachers at Jones described themselves as somewhat less constrained than those at Sumpter.

At Jones School, some teachers espoused a basal reader system, and others what they called a "whole language" approach. Their self-perception was that their practices were quite different; the observers saw more similarities than differences. One teacher said that the principal fostered freedom of choice, rather than forcing the teachers to adopt her own whole language philosophy. Some in the basal reader group said that they felt constrained by parents, who preferred the more familiar basal/workbook approach.

The principal both supported teacher autonomy and wanted to move teachers in the whole language direction. She said she would not force her position on teachers; she preferred a "give-and-take" approach. However, she did exert her influence by selecting topics for teacher in-service that reinforced her position. She told teachers to ignore achievement test scores, but thought some were "suspicious" of that message and taught to the test. In her opinion, this showed that teachers limited their own autonomy. Even when they had choices, too many relied on the textbook manual or the way they had been taught. One respondent said that teachers were "victims of the system . . . and it's a bunch of baloney."

Sumpter teachers at first mentioned few outside constraints on their teaching. Several claimed that the major constraint on their work was the poor quality of students' home lives. One commented that the principal "wanted" her to teach from textbooks, and another discussed the pressure of achievement tests. As time for the test approached, we heard more anxious talk about preparing for the test, and about how the principal, parents, and district would react if test scores dropped. At staff development sessions, teachers complained that limited time, isolation, and pressure from the principal kept them from sharing and implementing innovations.

The principal said that when he arrived three years earlier, he had a mandate from the district to "come in here and . . . hit them over the head with a two-by-four if I had to . . . because the school was festering." Despite this, he said he had been cautious about being directive with teachers; from his point of view, they were autonomous. However, there was a real contrast in this principal's position on achievement tests. He thought that test scores influenced teachers "a great deal [because] there's always a fear that your scores are going to be published and that you're going to be held to close scrutiny." Although Sumpter's scores were far above the district average, this fact did not relieve the pressure. If scores dropped, affluent parents in particular would complain to the principal and the district. Whereas the Jones principal would buffer teachers from such complaints, the Sumpter principal would not.

Support from School Culture

Condition #3: If a teacher at this school has both the motivation and the freedom to change his or her practices, does the school culture support and sustain these changes?

According to Deal (1984), the relationship between school culture and innovation is ambiguous, because "attitudes, beliefs, skills and norms are the catalysts for new directions," but also "form powerful barriers or offer resistance in support of the status quo" (p. 125). Failure to understand the resistant aspects of school culture has impeded many attempts at educational innovations (Hamilton, 1989; Popkewitz, Tabachnick, & Wehlage, 1982; Romberg & Price, 1983; Sarason, 1982).

Nevertheless, certain cultural norms have been shown to foster teacher change. Huberman and Miles (1984) found that more change occurred in schools with norms of collaboration, cohesive relationships, and tolerance for diversity. Rosenholtz, Bassler, and Hoover-Dempsey (1986) identified four factors—principal-teacher collegiality, effective evaluation practices, teacher coordination and collaboration, and effective and consistent management of student behavior by teachers—as aspects of school culture that contributed to teachers' learning. In another study, teachers identified a climate of confidence, trust, security, and collegiality, as well as positive, nonthreatening teacher-principal relationships, as the factors that nurtured their professional growth (Schwille & Melnick, 1987).

Teacher-principal relationships emerge in these studies as crucial to what Barth (1986) has called the "ethos of the workplace." The principal as cultural leader is a popular image in administrative theory (Deal, 1984; Owens, 1987; Schein, 1986). A principal leads through cultural style by calling forth shared values and powerful symbols, rather than enforcing bureaucratic rules. However, a principal may invoke culture to either encourage or discourage teacher change. Democratic, collegial principals reverse the trend toward teachers' deprofessionalization and nurture teacher innovation (Barth, 1986). But a principal is just as likely to invoke cultural traditions to reinforce authority and control (Anderson, 1991).

Teacher collaboration and collegiality, rather than teacher autonomy, have also emerged as characteristics of schools that nurture teacher innovation. The paradox of teacher autonomy is that while it is a necessary condition for teacher change, it can also be a barrier. Autonomy has a negative side—isolation—that tends to foster caution and conservatism, rather than change (Johnson, 1990; Little, 1981; Lortie, 1975; Whiteside, 1978). Isolation "deprives teachers of the stimulation of working with peers and the close support they need to improve through their careers" (Bird & Little, 1986, p. 495). Moreover, teacher isolation may mean that open discussion of teaching practices comes to feel threatening (Little, 1990). According to Little (1987), "A long-standing element of the culture of teaching is the maxim: You don't interfere with another teacher's teaching" (p. 16).

With the dual-sided nature of autonomy in mind, we see that recent work promotes teacher collegiality as an alternative, but Little (1990) argues that it is not so simple.

The assumed link between increased collegial contact and improvement-oriented change does not seem to be warranted: Closely bound groups are instruments both for promoting change and for conserving the present. (p. 509)

In one study, Blase (1987b) found that teacher collegiality meant pressure on individuals to conform to the majority's position, which may have worked *against* innovation. According to Little (1987), "An emphasis on cooperation may place a premium on coherence and uniformity at the expense of individual inventiveness and independent initiative" (p. 513).

In fact, teacher collaboration and collegiality may "intensify norms unfavorable to students" (Little, 1990, p. 524). King (1983) and Page (1988) hold that teachers in a school often share an image of their students that influences their instructional practices and their receptivity to change (i.e., a practice will or will not work with *our* students). Further, Barr (1985) has suggested that teachers adapt their reading instruction to match their perceptions of student ability (i.e., *our* students are (in)capable of learning to read in this way).

Finding #3: The culture at Jones appeared to be somewhat more conducive to teachers' professional development than that at Sumpter.

Principal-teacher Relationships. At Jones School, the classroom observer described the principal as "highly visible" and a "dynamic individual who has a good relationship with teachers." The principal described her style in democratic terms, and said her staff was "cooperative" and "growing." Her critical comments about some teachers revealed a deep dissatisfaction with their teaching, but none of the teachers saw her as pressuring them to change. They rated her leadership style quite positively on the context questionnaire.

In contrast, principal-teacher relationships at Sumpter were strained and distant. The principal said he had stepped into a bad situation three years before and had not been able to turn it around. His goal for the year the RIS project began was "staff changes"—"to weed out those people who really don't want to be here or who are not sensitive to the needs of the children." The Sumpter teachers may have been aware that he was contemplating a staff shake-up. They gave the most negative responses on all scales related to principal leadership on the school context questionnaire.

Teacher Collegiality and Collaboration. Teachers in both schools responded positively to questionnaire items about collaboration and co-ordination of instruction. However, the questionnaire items described what Little (1990) terms "weak" collegiality—one-on-one interactions for help or advice, rather than joint work. In fact, in both schools teachers also reported that they were isolated—the "down side" of their autonomy.

The Jones principal described the teachers as collegial, but the observers saw little evidence of genuine collaboration. Teachers did talk informally, sharing social or personal information, jokes, or classroom "war stories," and some remarked about how well they "got along." But when the observer asked directly about collaboration, one teacher looked at her in surprise and said they did not have time for that. Everyone was too "overloaded." The teachers were only somewhat aware, usually through second-hand information, of how others taught reading. They did not visit other classrooms or ask direct questions about classroom practices. One suggested that their philosophical differences reinforced this "noninterference" policy. They described very limited collaboration, for the most part sharing materials or working together on one-time special projects.

At Sumpter, the observer noticed even less communication among teachers: "It was like there was a hush over the whole place. People didn't talk together." On the questionnaire, these teachers reported the highest degree of isolation of teachers at all six schools. In fact, they seemed almost to *avoid* each other's company. They stayed in their rooms even during planning hours, shunning the small, unattractive teachers' lounge. The only ones who regularly congregated were the smokers, who met in an unpleasant room off the cafeteria. Lack of teacher collegiality was chronic at Sumpter, according to the principal, especially among the intermediate-level teachers. They were veterans who made their own decisions and did not ask for help. The curriculum specialist said that rather than working as a team, they were a "collection of individuals." Their different personalities, she said, made teaming difficult to consider.

In their interviews, Sumpter teachers also remarked on their lack of collegiality. One blamed it on the physical layout of the school; another said that having a difficult class gave her less time to socialize. All reported that the infrequent faculty meetings were the only times the whole group met. In the absence of teacher contact, one said, the curriculum specialist, who often visited classrooms to demonstrate new teaching techniques, acted as a go-between. The one topic on which they all agreed, however, was their animosity toward the principal; initially, this was the single bond among them.

Images of Students. The Jones principal described students' families as "upwardly mobile working class to middle class"; many were first-time homeowners in the modest suburban neighborhood surrounding school. Thirty-three percent of students qualified for free or reduced-price lunches, a rough estimate of low socioeconomic status. They scored close to the mean for the district on annual achievement tests. On the school context questionnaire, Jones teachers reported the most positive perceptions of students of all six RIS schools. A few said that students' home lives limited teachers' success, but such remarks were less frequent than at Sumpter, and tended to be about *individual* students rather than students in general. They expressed satisfaction with their own abilities to manage the classroom and to adapt their instruction to meet student needs. It was not clear that Jones teachers had very high academic expectations of their students, but they liked them very much.

As already mentioned, the Sumpter principal saw the diverse school population as a problem. On the questionnaire, Sumpter teachers as a whole (all grades) were more negative than any other group about their students. Because busing of low-income Hispanic children ended after third grade, the intermediate classrooms in the RIS study were not particularly diverse—90 percent Anglo, only 20 percent qualifying for free or reduced-price lunch. They scored far above the district average on achievement tests. Nevertheless, some intermediate-level teachers complained that many students came from bad homes and could not succeed. They must have been able to share information about students, because certain students and entire classes had "reputations." Teacher complaints focused more on misbehavior than low ability; that is, these students could achieve, but they were hard to manage.

Teacher Cooperation

Condition #4: If all of the above conditions are met, do teachers at this school take charge of maintaining and expanding them by working together to create a community of practice?

A school with good working conditions, in which teachers have freedom to change and are supported by a culture with norms of positive principal-teacher relationships, teacher collegiality and collaboration, and high expectations for students, might be considered the ideal context for a staff development project. But something more may be required. The teachers themselves, as a community, must play a major role in creating and maintaining this context and taking advantage of the opportunities it affords (Little, 1987). In schools that present the optimum (if rare) context for staff development, teachers have established a "collective conception of autonomy" that resolves the apparent contradiction between autonomy and collaboration (Little, 1990, p. 519). That is, they feel autonomous as a group of teachers, and share a "norm of analysis, evaluation and experimentation" (Little, 1982, p. 339). The *content* of their collaboration is crucially important. One can hear it in their shared language of practice. Their goals are to improve student learning, their own teaching capacity, and the efficacy of the school (Little, 1990, p. 524).

Pendlebury (1990) suggests that autonomy as "license" to do what one chooses is not the goal of teachers in this ideal school. Rather, the goal is "liberty as independence" within a "community of practice" (p. 272). In such a community "the independence of practitioners is not neutral but presupposes some conception of the good" (p. 273). Teachers share beliefs about what constitutes good teaching practice, what is best for students, and the proper ends of the school. These shared beliefs constrain autonomy, by holding each teacher accountable to the community (p. 275). With interdependence, "individual action is both constrained and enabled" (Little, 1990, p. 521).

Finding #4: Neither of these schools could be considered an ideal context for staff development.
Neither school could have been characterized as a community of practice. Before beginning staff development, however, Jones School appeared to have an edge over Sumpter. Initially, the RIS team had constructed contrasting images of the two schools. Even before all the context data were collected and analyzed, we had been influenced by the physical environments of the schools and our initial contacts with the teachers and principals. The danger, of course, was that these first impressions could become self-fulfilling prophecies.

A community of practice is not something that staff developers can create from scratch; it is the outcome of time, deliberate effort and support, and interpersonal compatibility. However, according to Lieberman and Miller (1984), if staff developers want their efforts to succeed, they must attempt to create a microcosm of this kind of community:

> Little will happen unless attention is paid to the necessity for building an ethos, a climate for collective effort . . . through strategies that involve teachers in experiences where they can work together as colleagues, where they can be involved in the plans, and where their concerns can be made primary. (p. 9)

At the outset of this project, we thought the success of such strategies seemed more probable at Jones than at Sumpter. We were wrong.

WHAT ACTUALLY HAPPENED

From the start, the staff developers stated explicitly that they did not have an agenda and that they wanted to address the teachers' own concerns about reading instruction. Teachers at each school responded differently to those intentions. The open-endedness of the design allowed for contrasting social constructions of the staff development process, and brought different issues and feelings to the surface in each group. Hamilton (1989) created a scheme of stages in the staff development process, outlined in Figure 7.1, that provides a way to compare the schools. (See Chapter 6 for a more detailed description of these stages.)

Jones School: Mistrust and Conflict Come to the Surface

At Jones School, tension stalled the movement of the staff development process. As Figure 7.1 illustrates, this group spent a long period in the introductory stage. The staff developers tried hard to foster a teacher-directed program, but the teachers did not seem to trust this intention. They side-stepped self-examination, asking the staff developers to tell them the "right way to teach reading" or to share their "favorite practices." The staff developers repeated that they were not there to provide the "one right way," and redirected such questions; but the teachers persisted. Yet when the staff developers from time to time did offer suggestions, the teachers rejected them or shut down (Richardson, 1990).

The seven Jones teachers did not gel as a group. Because Jones had initially been identified as the more collegial school, this did not meet the staff developers' expectations. Reactions to the group-level process ran the gamut from hostile or defensive to noncommittal or willingly participa-

Figure 7.1   Stages in the Staff-Development Process

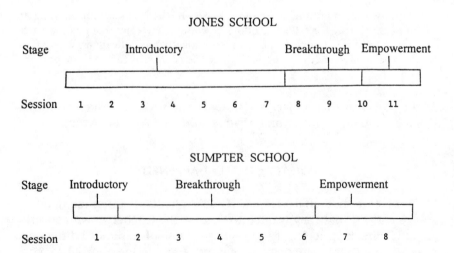

tory. Some teachers seemed willing only to attend, but not to participate actively. Some professed an interest in the project, but claimed they did not have time to become involved in collegial work. Others said, "I'm happy with what I'm doing," or "I don't need any of this." At times it also seemed that the Jones teachers treated the meetings as a social hour, a time for joking and telling stories. But this made staff development seem like a useless activity to them: another burden on their time, since they could have these kinds of conversations elsewhere during the day.

Another impediment that developed at Jones was the teachers' hesitation to share individual teaching philosophies and practices with the group. When the staff developers began asking pointed questions about the "whys" and "hows" of teaching, there was an almost visible digging-in-of-the-heels. When a staff developer pressed one teacher, Ralph, to explain his thinking, another teacher made it clear that kind of challenge was not acceptable, and defended Ralph's right to hold any view he wanted. As late as the eighth session, when a staff developer probed more deeply with Tammy, she closed down completely rather than reveal her philosophy of teaching.

There were three teachers—Emmett, James, and Ellen—who might have been able to work together under the right circumstances. They were also the most verbal in the staff development sessions. Although none of the teachers asked direct questions about their colleagues' teaching, they did listen quietly when their colleagues spoke. As a result, some teachers said, in their final interviews, that they had gotten new ideas from those who did speak up. For example, Randall and Ellen both attributed change in their practices to Emmett's contributions.

Interestingly, Emmett made it very clear in an interview that he avoided his colleagues. They "think differently," he said, and he preferred to remain aloof. He seemed to greatly enjoy expounding on his philosophy during the sessions, but when pressed about his philosophy in his final interview, he often changed the subject. Emmett was quite aware of and willing to verbalize his practices and theories, but not particularly willing to engage in open discussion of them. His self-protective individualism maintained the distance between himself and the other teachers.

A respected veteran teacher, Ellen contributed a great deal in the staff development sessions. At times, in fact, she appeared to guide, if not direct, the sessions. In contrast to Emmett, in her interviews Ellen said she felt very close to her colleagues. Yet she also alluded to "camp" lines based on reading approaches. Like Emmett, Ellen liked to think of herself as a lone nonconformist. A self-described "whole language person," she was surprised to find that Emmett also described himself that way. Furthermore, she appeared to foster division in the group by underscoring differences between her orientation and that of others. For example, she said, "I guess we'll be in different groups, right?" to Randall, when group work was discussed. It seemed that the importance she placed on being different encouraged the other teachers to emphasize their differences. The group seemed to become more individualistic, rather than more collegial, over time.

Another driving force for Ellen was her concern with finding the "one best method" of teaching reading. Starting with the first meeting, she often asked if the staff development was promoting a best method, and asked the staff developers to give the group their best suggestions on practices. Yet she also complained strongly about not feeling empowered and objected to being told what to do. The staff developers found it difficult to respond to her contradictory messages.

In contrast to our initial impressions, the team also found that the teachers felt conflicted about the principal. They described her as supportive, but several lumped her with the "bad guys" who upheld district policy. In fact, they claimed that although she supported a whole language approach to reading, she was guilty by association of wanting them to use basal readers. That is, they blamed her and the other "theys" in the system for limiting their freedom to change their practices. When questioned, the principal categorically denied this possibility.

After a number of sessions, it appeared that the Jones group was falling apart. Beneath the positive facade at Jones School there were feelings of dissatisfaction, fear, and complacency. The teachers seemed to communicate with each other only on a surface level, and did not have a shared language of practice. They talked past each other rather than engaging directly in difficult or philosophical issues. They complained about problems, but offered no solutions. They said that they liked their students, but also felt limited by their home environments—and believed that some might never learn. They professed disempowerment, claiming that the system offered them no choices. They seemed worried about revealing individual differences, but the strongest individualists also seemed resistant to discovering their commonalities. Moreover, they appeared unable to break out of the norms of the school culture, isolating themselves at every opportunity. In fact, the staff development process seemed to *add* stress to the Jones School environment.

At year's end, several of the Jones teachers denied any real results from the project; but curiously, with one possible exception, there were some observable changes in both their language and their practice. Most teachers shifted at least to some degree toward a transactive orientation, away from skills and toward an interactive, literature-based approach to reading. For example, in final observations several teachers were using nonbasal materials, or if they were using basal materials, they were emphasizing students' background knowledge. Final interviews and observations showed changes in teachers' language, for example, the incorporation of questioning into lesson plans. At the group level, there were subtle effects of a year-long group process. The teachers seemed friendlier toward each other and more protective of each others' feelings. (See Chapter 8 for details of these observed changes.)

Sumpter School: Colleagues at Last

The Sumpter teachers interpreted staff development as an opportunity to meet and discuss teaching ideas, something they ordinarily did not do. They moved past the introductory stage much more quickly (see Figure 7.1). One possible explanation for this difference was that the Sumpter teachers were adamant about moving off-campus, whereas the Jones teachers chose to hold their sessions at school. Escaping their stressful, dismal environment may have opened them up. At Jones, staying in their usual setting may have confined teachers to their usual roles. Another difference at Sumpter was the attendance of the curriculum specialist, who provided additional support for change.

As the staff development process unfolded, so did the Sumpter teachers. At first they were hesitant and timid with the staff developers and each other. They discussed constraints they felt from the principal, the students, and the school environment. Then they became curious about the new approaches to teaching they were hearing about. They asked more questions and requested classroom modeling of strategies (a pattern the curriculum specialist had established). They used the time well, bringing questions and materials to share, and viewing videotapes of their classroom practices. They also struggled against their constraints, attempting to make sense for themselves. United against their common enemy, the principal, the isolated Sumpter teachers began to look to each other for support. As the level of intimacy and trust increased, they began to come to grips with their own beliefs, with areas of disagreement and incompetence. They carefully observed the questioning techniques modeled by the staff developers and incorporated them into their own talk. One turning point came when the teachers considered themselves readers and reviewed their own learning-to-read experiences.

Their participation was similar to the proverbial snowball rolling downhill. As the sessions passed, they gathered energy, information, and self-esteem so that by the end, they basically ran the program themselves. The final session saw them fervently listening to each other asking "whys" and "hows" with the staff developers leaning back, listening.

For example, Frances at first was resistant to the staff development process, but came to enjoy the meetings. She acknowledged that no one had ever asked her about her philosophy of teaching, and in the seventh session affirmed that she found it "very important" to be aware of her philosophy. In the same session, Frances revealed her personal history, which, in turn, revealed many of the beliefs behind her practices. While describing her experiences as a reader, she came to an "aha!" moment, in which she saw what she did and why she did it. As a young reader, she had no self-esteem and was always in the low reading group. She connected this with her emphasis as a teacher on raising student self-esteem and avoiding ability grouping. Her participation in the staff development process also generated within her a willingness to experiment with literature-based reading. By the end of the school year she was working with sets of novels, and the students were responding well. Although Frances had not undergone a complete transformation, she was in the process.

Another teacher, Andrea, was in the midst of a transformation that had begun the summer before the staff development. She had decided to change despite her social context, or perhaps because of it; she believed that the practices she had adopted over 17 years of teaching did not work. She observed that certain processes did help her students read, and so she attended workshops and read books that provided teaching strategies consistent with those processes. In theoretical terms, she was moving from a skills to a whole language orientation. Until the staff development, she had shared her decision only with the curriculum specialist. Although her participation in the staff development process did not instigate Andrea's change, it did facilitate it. During the year she tried strategies, reflected on them, changed them, and decided if they worked. She used the staff development sessions to think aloud about this process and to refine her theories. She modeled change and risk-taking in action.

In contrast to the situation at Jones, the stress at Sumpter was alleviated to some degree through participation in the staff development process. When asked what they found most valuable about staff development, each teacher said resoundingly that it was the opportunity to meet with colleagues. Unfortunately, they feared that once the project finished they might revert to isolation. They also feared that the principal might discourage their creative work. "He won't let me do that" was a theme in their conversations. That is, they worried that the pressures of their school context would reassert themselves after the staff development ended.

At year's end, changes at both the individual and group levels were more evident at Sumpter. The individual teachers were clearer about their beliefs and reflected more often about their teaching practices. In a year's end self-report they indicated they were talking more often to each other about practices. At a minimum, they paid lip service to an increased interest in an interactive, literature-based approach to reading. Final classroom observations found four of the five teachers using novels, because they believed students were more "interested" in them. They anchored that interest by establishing students' background knowledge before and throughout their reading assignments. The fifth teacher was trying plays she had found in an old reading series. Although she did not emphasize prior knowledge, it was significant that she had stepped beyond her re-signed use of the basal text.

TAKING SCHOOL CONTEXT INTO ACCOUNT

Our review of the research about how context affects staff development, with examples drawn from the RIS, suggests the following generalizations and recommendations.

Assessment of School Context

Previous considerations of context effects on teacher change have barely scratched the surface of this complex relationship. As revealed in our literature review, experts in this area do not always agree. While recent staff development literature (Joyce, 1990; Joyce, Weil, & Showers, 1992; Lieberman & Miller, 1991) has begun to stress the importance of learning about "school culture," some of this advice is deceiving in its simplicity. In our example, the investigators attempted a sophisticated assessment of school context based on previous research, but the results of this assessment reinforced misleading impressions of the schools. It did not probe deeply enough to identify the micropolitical dynamics at Jones School, the norms of individualism and competitiveness that would undermine the group process.

Recommendation. The relationship between school context and staff development, and ways to more adequately assess school context, should be areas of continuing study. In the meantime, it would be helpful if staff developers were as fully aware of the context as possible at the beginning of the project and could continue to assess the context during the process.

Conflicting Teacher Beliefs

This chapter also raised the issue of teacher thinking and beliefs as aspects of the school context. The culture of a school may be character-ized as collegial, based on observations of friendly interactions. However, surface-level collegiality is one thing; actual consensus on philosophical and pedagogical issues is another. By calling forth teachers' individual philosophies, staff developers may bring fundamental, underlying conflicts to the surface. Staff developers are then challenged to create a context in which these conflicts can be openly discussed, even mediated. They must do all this while respecting each individual teacher's beliefs (Fullan & Hargreaves, 1991) and unique developmental patterns (Loucks-Horsley & Stiegelbauer, 1991).

The interactional skills required by the kind of staff development represented by PASD are daunting, in comparison with the old "workshop" model (Goldenberg & Gallimore, 1991). Staff developers in this kind of project go far beyond presenting information or arranging "activities." They go far beyond encouraging weak or contrived collegiality (Fullan & Hargreaves, 1991; Hargreaves, 1991; Little, 1990). Planning and preparation for this kind of staff development project take on an entirely different dimension.

Recommendation. In planning a project that includes serious examination of individual teacher beliefs in a group context, staff developers must consider the potential effects of revealing differences among teachers, and be prepared with strategies for mediating conflict. Again, this is an area for continuing study.

The Effects of Staff Development on School Context

It can be expected that the new generation of complex, long-term, open-ended, and teacher-driven staff development models may *alter* the school context in ways that previous staff development models did not. The context "assessed" at the beginning of the project no longer exists once this kind of project begins. Goldenberg and Gallimore (1991) suggest that authentic changes in teachers' practices are very difficult to achieve, and that contexts that facilitate and maintain such changes are equally difficult to create. In one of the RIS schools, a deliberate alteration of the context—moving off campus—seemed to have had dramatic, positive effects on teacher collegiality. Yet these effects were short-lived, as several teachers were transferred to different schools the following year. Such school district practices, and the customary isolation of teachers in most schools, make it hard to conceive of professional development as collective activity sustained by teachers after the staff developers leave.

Recommendation. The effects of staff development on school context must be further investigated. If we are to create the optimum conditions for teacher change according to Little (1982, 1990), the contradiction between the "artificial" context of staff development and the "real," everyday context of schools must be dissolved. Staff developers must challenge district and school practices that limit efforts to create collegial groups of teachers who sustain their own professional growth.

OUR FINAL RECOMMENDATION: Even if you believe that a context appears to discourage teacher change, be prepared to change your view of what can happen when teachers have the opportunity to transcend that context, reflect on their beliefs, imagine what their practice could be, and move forward with mutual support.

APPENDIX: **Design and Methodology of the School-Level Component**

A questionnaire on school climate and organization was constructed by combining scales from three questionnaires previously employed in large survey studies (Bacharach, Bauer, & Shedd, 1986; Rosenholtz, Bassler, & Hoover-Dempsey, 1986; Smylie, 1988). The intention in administering the questionnaire was not to test hypotheses about relationships among school-level variables, as in most survey research, but to develop a descriptive profile of each school on variables previously shown to be related to positive responses to staff development or to teacher innovation.

The questionnaire was distributed to all teachers in all six project schools during April and May of Year 1 of the study. The school-level researcher met with each group of teachers to explain the questionnaire's purposes and to address teacher concerns. Returns were coordinated by school staff, and as a consequence return rates varied. For the total sample, 88 of approximately 120 teachers (73%) returned their questionnaires.

A school-level file was created for each school, containing principal and classroom observer interviews, excerpts from teacher interviews, field notes from the school-level researcher and classroom observers, a school fact sheet of basic organizational and demographic information, and records of incidents or communications with the school reported to the school-level researcher. The school-level researcher provided classroom observers with directions for conducting and recording their observations. Where observers varied in the extent of their observations, the school-level researcher filled in the details through a recorded debriefing interview.

At the end of Year 1 of the study, beginning with the three experimental schools, these qualitative data sets were coded according to categories which were both grounded in the data and, in many cases, congruent with categories shown to be important in previous work on school climate and organization. Narrative case studies were written from analysis of the coded data. First drafts of the case studies were distributed to the classroom observers and principal investigators for comments and editing. Final drafts incorporated additional data from early in Year 2, from principal and teacher contacts concerning planning for Year 2 activities and from observations of classroom contexts during the administration of reading tests.

The school-level researchers calculated descriptive statistics on responses to the questionnaire for the total sample as well as for each school, on an item-by-item basis and by scales. Means for each school by scale were plotted pairing the two experimental schools (Jones and Sumpter) and the two control schools. Means for a third experimental school were not plotted; a low rate of questionnaire returns and very high staff turnover between years 1 and 2 made this data questionable in validity. However, data from this school's teachers, as well as teachers from the pilot school were included in the total sample.

REFERENCES

Anderson, G. L. (1991). Cognitive politics of principals and teachers: Ideological control in an elementary school. In J. Blase (Ed.), *The politics of life in schools* (pp. 120–138). Newbury Park, CA: Sage.

Apple, M., & Teitelbaum, K. (1985). Are teachers losing control of their jobs? *Social Education, 49,* 372–375.

Bacharach, S., Bauer, S., & Shedd, J. (1986). The work environment and school reform. *Teachers College Record, 88,* 241–256.

Ball, S. J. (1987). *The micro-politics of the school.* London: Methuen.

Barr, R. (1985). Observing first grade reading instruction: Instruction viewed with a model of school organization. In J. Niles & R. Lalik (Eds.), *Issues in literacy: A research perspective* (pp. 25–32). Rochester, NY: National Reading Conference.

Barth, R. (1986). The principal and the profession of teaching. *Elementary School Journal, 86,* 471–492.

Bifano, S. (1988, April). *Elementary principals: Espoused theory and professional practice.* Paper presented at the annual meeting of the American Educational Research Association, New Orleans.

Bird, T., & Little, J. W. (1986). How schools organize the teaching occupation. *The Elementary School Journal, 86,* 493–511.

Blase, J. (1986). A qualitative analysis of sources of teacher stress: Consequences for performance. *American Educational Research Journal, 23,* 13–40.

Blase, J., (1987a, April). *An ethnographic study of the politics of teaching: The teacher-principal relationship and dynamics of school power.* Paper presented at the annual meeting of the American Educational Research Association, Washington, DC.

Blase, J. (1987b, April). *A qualitative analysis of political interactions among teachers: Implications for the sociocultural context of the school.* Paper presented at the annual meeting of the American Educational Research Association, Washington, DC.

Blase, J. (1991a). The micropolitical perspective. In J. Blase (Ed.), *The politics of life in schools* (pp. 1–18). Newbury Park, CA: Sage.

Blase, J. (1991b). Everyday political perspectives of teachers toward students: The dynamics of diplomacy. In J. Blase (Ed.), *The politics of life in schools* (pp. 185–206). Newbury Park, CA: Sage.

Bowers, C., & Flinders, D. (1990). *Responsive teaching.* New York: Teachers College Press.

Corcoran, T., Kohli, W., & White, L. (1988, April). *District and school policies and the conditions of teaching: Collegiality and participation in decision-making in urban schools.* Paper presented at the annual meeting of the American Educational Research Association, New Orleans.

Deal, T. (1984). Educational change: Revival tent, tinkertoys, jungle, or carnival? *Teachers College Record, 86,* 124–137.

Feiman-Nemser, S., & Floden, R. (1986). The cultures of teaching. In M. Wittrock (Ed.), *Handbook of research on teaching* (3rd ed., pp. 505–526). New York: Macmillan.

Firestone, W., & Herriott, R. (1981). Images of organization and the promotion of educational change. *Research in Sociology of Education and Socialization, 2,* 221–260.

Fraatz, J. (1987). *The politics of reading.* New York: Teachers College Press.

Frymier, J. (1987, September). Bureaucracy and the neutering of teachers. *Phi Delta Kappan,* pp. 9–14.

Fullan, M., & Hargreaves, A. (1991). *What's worth fighting for?* Ontario, Canada: Ontario Public School Teachers' Federation.

Gallagher, M., Goodvis, A., & Pearson, D. (1988). Principles of organizational change. In S. Samuels and D. Pearson (Eds.), *Changing school reading programs: Principles and case studies* (pp. 11–40). Newark, DE: International Reading Association.

Goldenberg, C., & Gallimore, R. (1991). Changing teaching takes more than a one-shot workshop. *Educational Leadership, 49*(3), 69–72.

Goodlad, J. (1983). The school as workplace. In G. Griffin (Ed.), *Staff development* (the Eighty-second Yearbook of the National Society for the Study of Education, pp. 36–61). Chicago: University of Chicago Press.

Greenfield, W. D. (1991). The micropolitics of leadership in an urban elementary school. In J. Blase (Ed.), *The politics of life in schools* (pp. 161–184). Newbury Park, CA: Sage.

Griffin, G., & Barnes, S. (1986). Changing teacher practice: A research-based improvement study. In J. Hoffman (Ed.), *Effective teaching of reading: Research and practice* (pp. 145–160). Newark, DE: International Reading Association.

Guskey, T. (1986). Staff development and the process of teacher change. *Educational Researcher, 15*(5), 5–12.

Hallinger, P., & Murphy, J. (1985). Assessing the instructional management behaviors of principals. *Elementary School Journal, 86,* 217–247.

Hamilton, M. L. (1989). The practical argument staff development process, school culture and their effects on teacher's beliefs and classroom practice. Unpublished doctoral dissertation, University of Arizona, Tucson.

Hargreaves, A. (1991). Contrived collegiality: The micropolitics of teacher collaboration. In J. Blase (Ed.), *The politics of life in schools* (pp. 46–72). Newbury Park, CA: Sage.

Howey, K., & Vaughan, J. (1983). Current patterns of staff development. In G. Griffin (Ed.), *Staff development* (the Eighty-second Yearbook of the National Society for the Study of Education, Part II, pp. 92–117). Chicago: University of Chicago Press.

Huberman, M., & Miles, M. (1984). *Innovation up close.* New York: Plenum.

Johnson, S. M. (1990). *Teachers at work: Achieving success in our schools.* New York: Basic Books.

Joyce, B. (1990). *Changing school culture through staff development.* Alexandria, VA: Association of Supervision and Curriculum Development.

Joyce, B., Weil, M., & Showers, B. (1992). *Models of teaching* (4th ed.). Boston: Allyn & Bacon.

King, R. (1983). *The sociology of school organization.* New York: Methuen.

Leithwood, K., & Montgomery, D. (1982). The role of the elementary school principal in program improvement. *Review of Educational Research, 52,* 309–339.

Lieberman, A., & Miller, L. (1984). *Teachers: Their world and their work.* Alexandria, VA: Association for Supervision and Curriculum Development.

Lieberman, A., & Miller, L. (1991). *Staff development for education in the 90's* (2nd ed.). New York: Teachers College Press.

Little, J. W. (1981, April). *The power of organizational setting: School norms and staff development.* Paper presented at the annual meeting of the American Educational Research Association, Los Angeles.

Little, J. W. (1982). Norms of collegiality and experimentation: Workplace conditions of school success. *American Educational Research Journal, 19,* 325–340.

Little, J. W. (1987, April). *Assessing the prospects for teacher leadership.* Paper presented at the annual meeting of the American Educational Research Association, Washington, DC.

Little, J. W. (1990). The persistence of privacy: Autonomy and initiative in teachers' professional relations. *Teachers College Record, 91,* 509–536.

Lortie, D. (1975). *School teacher.* Chicago: University of Chicago Press.

Loucks-Horsley, S., & Stiegelbauer, S. (1991). Using knowledge of change to guide staff development. In A. Lieberman & L. Miller (Eds.), *Staff development for education in the 90's* (2nd ed., pp. 15–36). New York: Teachers College Press.

Meyer, J., & Rowan, B. (1978). The structure of educational organizations. In M. Meyer et al. (Eds.), *Environments and organizations* (pp. 78–109). San Francisco: Jossey-Bass.

Murphy, J. (1988, April). *Instructional improvement and the control of schools.* Paper presented at the annual meeting of the American Educational Research Association, New Orleans.

Owens, R. G. (1987). *Organizational behavior in education.* Englewood Cliffs, NJ: Prentice-Hall.

Page, R. (1988). Teachers' perceptions of students: A link between classrooms, school cultures, and the social order. *Anthropology and Education Quarterly, 87,* 77–99.

Pendlebury, S. (1990). Practical arguments and situational appreciation in teaching. *Educational Theory, 40,* 171–179.

Popkewitz, T.S., Tabachnick, B. R., & Wehlage, G. (1982). *The myth of educational reform.* Madison: University of Wisconsin Press.

Richardson, V. (1990). Significant and worthwhile change in teaching practice. *Educational Researcher, 19,* 10–18.

Richardson, V., & Anders, P. (1986). A study of teachers' research-based instruction of reading comprehension. Proposal in response to U.S. Department of Education, OERI, Educational Research Grant Program.

Richardson, V., & Anders, P. (1990). *Final report of the Reading Instruction Study.* Tucson: College of Education, University of Arizona. (ERIC Document Reproduction Service No. ED 324-655)

Romberg, T., & Price, G. (1983). Curriculum implementation and staff development as cultural change. In G. Griffin (Ed.), *Staff development* (the Eighty-second Yearbook of the National Society for the Study of Education, pp. 154–184). Chicago: University of Chicago Press.

Rosenholtz, S., Bassler, O., & Hoover-Dempsey, K. (1986). Organizational conditions of teacher learning. *Teaching and teacher education, 2*(2), 91–104.

Sarason, S. (1982). *The culture of the school and the problem of change.* Boston: Allyn and Bacon.

Schein, E. H. (1986). *Organizational culture and leadership.* San Francisco: Jossey-Bass.

Schwille, S., & Melnick, S. (1987, April). *Teachers' professional growth and school life: An uneasy alliance.* Paper presented at the annual meeting of the American Educational Research Association, Washington, DC.

Shannon, P. (1989). *Broken promises: Reading instruction in twentieth-century America.* Granby, MA: Bergin and Garvey.

Smylie, M. (1988). The enhancement function of staff development: Organizational and psychological antecedents to individual teacher change. *American Educational Research Journal, 25*(1), 1–30.

Whiteside, T. (1978). *The sociology of educational innovation.* London: Methuen.

8

The Study of Teacher Change

VIRGINIA RICHARDSON AND PATRICIA L. ANDERS

In the preceding chapters, a new approach to staff development has been framed in terms of rationale, goals, content, and processes. The *rationale* is based on current research and thinking about the processes of teacher change, which suggest that teachers are not recalcitrant, but change all the time. New practices and procedures are adopted by teachers if they appear to work: that is, if they are consistent with teachers' beliefs concerning learning and teaching, engage the students, and allow the teachers the degree of control felt necessary. Impressions about whether a new activity works are often tacit and personal, and may be based on beliefs that are inappropriate for the given circumstances. This new form of staff development takes into account the participating teachers' existing beliefs about teaching, learning, and the curriculum.

The *goals* of this approach to staff development are to help teachers examine their beliefs in relation to their classroom practices, and to consider alternative premises and experiment with different practices. It is hoped that by so doing, teachers will assume responsibility for and ownership of their practices. In addition, this process is designed to help teachers develop an orientation toward inquiry and change that allows them to continue the reflective process. The *content* of this type of staff development consists of the teachers' own beliefs, understandings, and practices, as well as new premises and practices based on current research and theory and introduced by the staff developers. (In the case of the staff development process described in this book, of course, the content emphasis was current research and theory in reading comprehension instruction.) The *processes* consist of individual and group components in which teachers examine, over a substantial period of time, their own and others' premises and practices, and are aided in reconstructing their practical arguments and experimenting with new practices. It is expected that teacher participants and staff developers will collaborate in the determination and implementation of the agenda.

An important question remains, and is the focus of this chapter: What methodology can be used to identify and examine those changes in the participating teachers that can be attributed, at least in part, to the staff development process? We thought that a research approach quite different from those used for more traditional staff development programs might be required: one that would not violate the basic conceptions of the collaborative process.

TRADITIONAL ASSESSMENT METHODS

In order to explore this methodological issue, we will first summarize the ways in which teacher change has been examined in more traditional staff development programs. We will then contemplate the conceptual and process differences between the more traditional, or training, models of staff development and this newer collaborative approach, and the implications of these differences for the study of teacher change.

Early Studies

The primary means of assessing the outcomes of staff development programs is to ask the participating teachers after the process if they made any changes on the basis of what they had learned in the program, and/or whether they liked it. In reviewing these studies, Howey and Vaughan (1983) concluded that teachers do not like staff development programs and do not feel that they are worthwhile. Williams (1979) wrote about the status of staff development and in-service teacher education:

> It resembles the world's search for eternal peace. The citizens of the world seek the end of war and violence, yet it always eludes their grasp. Similarly with staff development—everyone extols its merits and sees the need for it. Many even agree on what characterizes an effective staff development program. Yet the lament from the vast majority of those who are subjected to staff development activities is that they are ineffective and generally a failure. (p. 95)

Smyth (1981) concluded, solely on the basis of summaries of the views of participants, that staff development had, by-and-large, been unsuccessful.

Convinced that staff development was indeed unsuccessful, a number of scholars began to identify organizational and structural problems with most staff development programs that could lead to this perceived lack of success. For example, Fullan (1991) presented seven structural reasons for the lack of success of staff development programs. Two of these were: "one-shot workshops are widespread but are ineffective," and "follow-up evaluation occurs infrequently" (p. 316). A number of more recent studies examined school district and school organizational features that might contribute to the perceived lack of program success (Little, 1989; Pink, 1989). Organizational issues that might affect staff development were extrapolated, in part, from the effective schools literature (Cohen, 1987). Thus, these early analyses and the later organizational studies were based on conclusions that relied on self-report survey data and the results of the effective schools studies, rather than on observations in the classrooms of the participating teachers or interviews with them.

The Training Model

In the late 1970s and early 1980s, several quite different programs of research began to examine the effects of staff development programs on teachers' classroom behaviors. These were the experimental phases of the process/product research, and to a somewhat lesser degree, program implementation studies. These two types of studies both employ a training conception of change, and a research paradigm compatible with this conception. This paradigm examines the effects of the process or program on changes in participating teachers' behaviors in their classrooms.

The training model has at its core a clearly stated set of objectives and learner outcomes. For Cruickshank and Metcalf (1990), these outcomes are teaching skills; and Showers, Joyce, and Bennett (1987) added thinking processes to the list of outcomes. Sparks and Loucks-Horsley (1990) describe two assumptions inherent in the training model:

> One assumption ... is that there are behaviors and techniques worthy of replication by teachers in the classroom. ...
> The other assumption ... is that teachers can change their behaviors and learn to replicate behaviors in their classroom that were not previously in their repertoire. (p. 241)

Teacher changes in programs based on training models have been examined within a standard input/output or process/product evaluation design. Since the desired outcome is clearly understood and articulated in behavioral terms at the outset of the process, the research examines the degree to which participating teachers behave as desired by the trainers or change agents, or make changes in the desired direction. This research design has been described by Cruickshank, Lorish, and Thompson (1979), who modeled their framework on the Dunkin and Biddle (1974) design for studying the relationship between teacher behaviors (processes) and student learning (product). In the case of staff development programs, the processes are teacher training activities, and the products are changes in teacher behavior, knowledge, and attitudes. Affecting both the processes and products are presage variables (trainer characteristics) and context variables. This model was used in both implementation studies and experimental phases of the process/product studies.

The implementation literature, for example, defines successful implementation (and, therefore, product) in terms of the percentage of teachers using the new practice (Huberman & Miles, 1984), the degree of institutionalization of the practice (Berman & McLaughlin, 1978; Huberman & Miles, 1984), and the extent to which the method or practice being implemented by the teachers is similar to the method or practice that was disseminated (for example, Hall & Loucks's 1977 notion of "Level of Use"). In this literature, the processes examined are often school district and school decisions and procedures as well as the processes used to promote the change.

Teacher change in staff development programs based on the training model has been examined within process/product studies. Effects of staff development are studied in the second phase of programs designed to identify effective teacher behaviors. In the first phase, correlational studies are conducted to determine relationships between teacher behaviors and student achievement. In the second, experimental phase, groups of teachers receive staff development that focuses on these behaviors, and changes in these behaviors by the teachers are then evaluated. These studies are described in depth elsewhere (e.g., Brophy & Good, 1986; Gage, 1985). In general, these are carefully conducted experiments, with control groups, pre- and postobservation of control and treatment teachers, and pre- and postcollection of student achievement data.

Stallings, Needels, and Stayrook (1979), for example, used the initial pre-observation of teachers to identify for each teacher an initial profile of behaviors, and to set goals for behavior change using the previously conducted correlational studies to identify the ideal behavioral profile. The staff developers helped the teachers work on the problem behaviors, so that the postobservation would produce a profile that looked more like the ideal. By and large, these studies indicated that teachers participating in such staff development programs began to use the practices that were being promoted (at least when they were being observed); and the students in their classes appeared to do better on standardized achievement tests.

It is not the purpose of this chapter to critique process/product studies and their associated training components. This has been done quite adequately by others (e.g., Doyle, 1977; Fenstermacher, 1979; and Koehler, 1978). However, one criticism of the experimental process/product studies is relevant, and this relates to the paucity of research designs that examine the long-term effects of the programs. An exception was Stallings and Krasavage's (1986) study of a Madeline Hunter staff development process in Napa County, California. In the third year of the study, they found that the teachers implemented the desired behaviors much less than they had in the previous two years. The study found only limited evidence of the relationship between implementation of the behaviors and increases in student achievement in reading. The question of what happened in the third year was addressed by the authors with several hypotheses. A compelling hypothesis suggests that the Madeline Hunter model could not sustain teachers' interests:

> We believe that the innovative practices teachers learn will not be maintained unless teachers and students remain interested and excited about their own learning. . . . A good staff development program will create an excitement about learning to learn. The question is how to keep the momentum, not merely maintain previously learned behaviors. (p. 137)

This critique of the goals of a staff development program based on a training model leads directly into a discussion of the differences between the training model of staff development and the collaborative process. It is these differences that affect the nature of the research design required to examine change in the Practical Argument Staff Development (PASD) process.

ASSESSMENT OF CHANGE

Moving Away from the Training Model

We think that the research design for the evaluation of training model forms of staff development is inappropriate for the collaborative staff development described in this book for the following reasons:

1. The collaborative process is not based on a deficit model of change. Rather than beginning with the premise that teachers are not doing something correctly, the collaborative process assumes that reflection and change are ongoing processes of assessing beliefs, goals, and results. Experimental changes in practice may, in fact, lead to less than desirable effects. The important element, therefore, is the development of a change and reflection orientation to allow the teacher to continue to question both new and old practices.

2. The desired outcomes are not particular behaviors or skills, but an awareness on the part of teachers of their ways of thinking and instructional practices, and of the moral, empirical, and situational grounds for them. The purpose is procedural—to create an ecology of thinking and deliberation. Therefore, it is not possible to state, at the beginning of the process, the behavioral objectives of the process. The objectives can be stated only in general terms related to reflection and change.

3. Change is not considered to be static. That is, there is no reason to suggest that a change in practice that follows staff development will still be in place several years later. In fact, it is hoped that teachers will continue to change after completing staff development.

4. It is not expected that any group of teachers will decide on a direction for change on which all of the teachers will agree. Each teacher is free to follow his or her own lines of inquiry and change. Thus, a research design that relies on aggregated data will probably not be appropriate except for very large and encompassing questions such as "Did the teachers change practices?"

5. We are not interested, solely, in changes in behaviors and actions, but also in the rationale and justifications that accompany new practices. We want to be able to examine whether teachers are taking control of the justifications for their practices, rather than suggesting a rationale based on external influences such as school board policy. We are also interested in the degree to which teachers take responsibility for their actions and assume ownership of their practices.

Building a Collaborative Research Model

Inquiry on change in any staff development program should be an important element of the process. This is particularly critical in a collaborative staff development process since teachers are being asked to conduct inquiry into their own premises and practices. The staff developers should also practice what they preach and conduct inquiry on their own actions and beliefs. But, as suggested above, this examination of change cannot rely on the straightforward and linear process developed for the training model of change. A classic experimental design is not appropriate for this process since it would affect the conception of change inherent in staff development, leading to both static and deficit assumptions of change in which the goal of change is a common one across all participants. Such a design may also affect the nature of the staff development process by requiring prespecified goals. Above all, it does not allow for a conception of change that places the process within a larger ecology of educational thought, practice, and reform.

A change study of a collaborative process such as the Practical Argument Staff Development should, therefore, have the following characteristics:

1. An open-ended design. Since the initial objectives cannot be stated in behavioral terms, it is essential that the design allow for questions to emerge from the experiences of the particular staff development process itself. This suggests that the study be open-ended and qualitative in nature.

2. Rich data. Since it is not possible to prespecify the areas of change that teachers will select, it is important to collect a considerable amount of data so that it will be possible to examine change in a number of different areas. This data could, for example, include videotapes of the group sessions, audiotapes of the individual sessions, ethnographic notes on the school context, and so forth.

3. Multimethod approaches to assessing teacher cognition. Teachers' cognitions, beliefs, theories, orientations, and so forth, may only be extrapolated from teachers' talk, writings, or actions. Thus, it is important to examine these facets using multiple means. As Kagan (1990) suggests, in assessing teacher cognition, multimethod approaches are superior because they "capture the complex, multifaceted aspects of teaching and learning" (p. 459).

4. Presentation to participants of data collected during the staff development process. This process of development and research is nonlinear; it is *not* assumed that research elements remain independent of the development process and therefore do not affect them. In fact, the opposite is assumed: Both the collection of data and the data itself may become critical elements of the development process. For example, in the Reading Instruction Study, the initial belief interviews were transcribed and presented to the teachers on the first day of the staff development process. Many teachers remarked that the belief interviews themselves caused them to begin to think in different ways about their classroom practices.

5. Constructs of change that emerge from the process and data. Since it is not possible to state the behavioral objectives at the beginning of the process, the directions for change in practices, beliefs, and discourse about practices will emerge from the process and the data.

6. Case studies of individuals and groups of teachers. It is important to follow individual cases of change, since it is assumed both that initial beliefs and practices will vary from one teacher to the next, and that

each change program will be different. At the same time, in examining the school context and its effects on the process, separate cases of the group process are beneficial. This suggests the appropriateness of "nested cases" in which the data may be used for individual cases as well as cases at a larger unit of analysis such as a group or school (Richardson, Casanova, Placier, & Guilfoyle, 1989).

7. A collaborative process. It is important that the teacher participants be involved in the research process itself. Since this research design is based on the assumption that the research process will affect the nature of the change process, it is possible for the research and development processes to intermingle and to be shared by all participants.

In addition, it is questionable whether the use of a control group adds to our understanding of teacher change, given the assumptions inherent in the collaborative process. One assumption of the PASD process is that teachers change all the time, including control group teachers, and these changes emanate from a multitude of sources. Further, the PASD process is highly individualized; The "treatment" teachers may change in many different ways. Thus the only possible question related to the control group of teachers is whether they change at all. Given the myriad of sources available to a teacher for change purposes, it would be difficult to find a teacher who does not have these sources available, and therefore does not change. Further, it is expected that the very process of data collection would help the teachers—both control and treatment—begin to rethink their practices. Thus, pre- and postdata collection with the control teachers would be considered a treatment. (It should be pointed out that a control group of teachers *was* used in RIS for the question concerning changes in student achievement; see Chapter 9.)

These characteristics may suggest a complex research design. However, they have been unearthed as both the staff development process and its associated study of teacher change are breaking new ground. As these staff development processes continue to be developed and assessed, the designs will undoubtedly become less complex.

Questions of Validity and Worth

Two questions have not yet been addressed. The first is methodological: Can a research design employing these characteristics lead to valid conclusions about whether the staff development process affected teachers' thoughts and practices? Without a control group, it may be difficult to attribute the changes seen in individual teachers to the particular process in which they participated. It is therefore essential that the observed changes be tied to the substance of the conversations that took place during the process.

The second is conceptual and concerns the teacher change that occurs during and as an outcome of the staff development process: Is the effected change in fact desirable? The question may send us in two directions. The first is to the literature, to determine whether there is sufficient research to suggest that certain instructional practices are desirable. The literature search for the PASD process that was conducted is described in Chapter 4, and provided us with material with which to respond to this question. The second direction is to examine student learning and growth, which is explored in Chapter 9. We will next describe the conduct and results of a study of teacher change that accompanied the PASD process.

THE STUDY OF CHANGE IN THE READING INSTRUCTION STUDY

The study of teacher change within the Reading Instruction Study employed the research design characteristics described above. It began as an open-ended exploration and was data rich. Data, such as the belief interviews, were used in the teacher development and the research processes. Categories of change emerged from an interaction of the researchers and participants with the data. Case studies of individuals and groups were conducted.

The Questions

The questions of broad interest to us as we began the PASD process were:

1. Were there changes in teacher beliefs concerning reading comprehension teaching and learning that could be attributed, at least in part, to the staff development process?
2. Were there changes in actual reading comprehension instructional practices that could be attributed, at least in part, to the staff development process?
3. During the course of the staff development process, were there changes in the nature of the discourse among the participants, including the staff developers?

The follow-up study conducted two years after the completion of the project allowed us to also address these questions in terms of long-term changes.

The Data

The data used for the teacher change study included the following:

Classroom Observations. As described in Chapter 3, the Timed Narrative Record was used to record classroom events of 38 teachers. The instrument focused on what the teacher was saying, and recorded, in shorthand, teacher and student actions. The observers conducted two of these observations for each teacher, at a point when the teachers said that they were teaching reading comprehension.

In addition, at the beginning of the staff development, a subset of the teachers and a new teacher to one of the three schools—17 teachers in all—were videotaped teaching reading comprehension. Twelve of these teachers were also videotaped at the end of the staff development process. (Closure of one of the schools prevented videotaping and conducting practical arguments with one group of teachers following staff development, but those teachers were reinterviewed in the fall.)

Belief Interviews. As described in Chapter 5, belief interviews were conducted with 39 teachers at the beginning of the study, and with 17 of the teachers following the staff development process. These were one- to two-hour conversations that elicited teachers' views on learning, instruction, and reading comprehension. The final interview, which was not conducted by the staff developers, also asked the participants about their views on the staff-development process.

Practical-argument Sessions. The individual sessions in which the staff developers and teachers viewed the videotapes together were audiotaped. In these sessions, the teachers' practical arguments were elicited and developed, and alternative premises were introduced. These were conducted at the beginning and near the completion of the staff development. The full group sessions were videotaped, materials that were used in the sessions were collected, and researchers made notes on the process.

Follow-up Study. Thirteen of the teachers who participated in the original staff development process were contacted two to three years following the process and asked if they would participate once again in interviews and videotaped lessons (Richardson, 1991). All agreed. The data for this element of the change study consist of transcribed belief interviews, classroom observations and videotapes of reading comprehension instruction, and audiotapes of practical-argument sessions, in which the teacher and one of the staff developers discussed premises and alternative premises. Case studies of two of these teachers, Alec and Kristi, have been developed (Valdez, 1992) and were used in these summaries.

TEACHER CHANGE IN THE RIS STUDY

As described in Chapter 5 and more completely in Richardson, Anders, Tidwell, and Lloyd (1991), each teacher was placed on two continua that emerged from an analysis of the ethnographic belief interviews. These two continua were "Reading/Purpose of Reading" and "Teaching Reading/ Learning to Read." These two continua created four quadrants that represent theories of reading, and all teachers were placed in one of four quadrants.

Changes in Theories of Reading

The teachers in the three schools that were involved in the first year of the PASD (17 teachers) were again interviewed at the completion of the process, and the same procedures were used to determine each teacher's placement on the four quadrants. Figure 8.1 represents the changes in theoretical orientations for each teacher by school. The "x" represents the initial placement, and the "o" the placement following the staff development. The "y" for two of the teachers, Alec (Ab) and Kristi (Ca), represents their position as analyzed in the follow-up belief interview—two years later.

One can see from this figure that there were considerable shifts in theories of reading, learning to read, and teaching reading. With several exceptions, the theories shifted toward the literature and construction of meaning ends of the two continua. In other words, beliefs moved toward Quadrant III, the "Whole Language" quadrant. There were several exceptions, which are described and explained in Richardson and Anders (1990) and Richardson and Valdez (1991). For example, Alec's initial interview contradicted his practices as observed in the classroom; and it was felt, at the time of the first interview, that he was attempting to impress the staff developers with whole language research. He later concurred that this was the case, and provided a better representation of his beliefs (Quadrant I) in the second interview. However, two years later, he was solidly in the Whole Language quadrant.

While the staff developers' goals did not include moving all teachers toward theories that represented the whole language movement, the conversations in group sessions often touched on this topic. Further, the belief interviews of the staff developers themselves revealed that one was solidly in Quadrant III (Whole Language), and one was in Quadrant II (Structural), but very close to Quadrant III. Thus, the changes in teachers' beliefs represented in Figure 8.1 were in the direction that would be expected from the content of the conversations.

A content analysis of the belief interviews indicated that significant changes in beliefs were represented in the teachers' stipulative (definitional) premises concerning reading comprehension. Many moved from a short, concise definition in the first interview that implied that reading comprehension is being able to answer comprehension check questions accurately, to a much broader, deeper, longer, and more cognitively oriented definition. An example is provided from Lori's (Cf) interviews. In the first interview, when asked to define reading comprehension, she stated:

> You have to be able to start with the basics and have the background to be exposed to different words so that when you see a word in print, not necessarily the first time you have heard that word. So its understanding the words, understanding the words that are put together in a sentence.

In her second interview, she explained:

> Well, understanding what you have read is, I guess, the very top layer, you know. Besides that, I think is understanding . . . not understanding, but how you feel about the book. You know, what is between the lines, kind of. When people read different things that the author has written down they each feel differently about it and how do you feel about it and what does it make you think about and what does it mean to you. You know how the characters are feeling and how does that relate to anything that you have, that happened to you. Can you, do you understand that, or is it something that is so foreign to you. (Richardson & Anders, 1990, pp. 81–82)

Several teachers expanded on the definition of reading comprehension to comprehension in general. The teachers also acknowledged multiple purposes for reading, and suggested that the definition of reading comprehension changes depending on the purpose. An important theme in the follow-up interviews was that reading comprehension became the reading of literature, rather than performing skills and reading comprehension check exercises in a basal series.

Their statements in these final interviews indicated a change in thinking and language. The teachers talked extensively and in depth about the topic, often expressing some remaining confusion about reading comprehension. Such confusion, however, did not trouble them.

Changes in Practices

Changes in practices were determined using self-report data from the interviews, and analyses of the videotapes.

Self-reports. In the final interviews, teachers were asked if they were doing anything differently. They were also asked a number of questions that would reveal practices that could then be compared with their initial observations and interviews. The following themes emerged:

1. Less reliance on the basal reader. An example of a statement concerning basals is the following:

   > Well, I don't think I've ever said this before today, but in looking back at the basals, there really are some dumb stories in there. No wonder kids are turned off to reading some of the things that they have to read. And I'm going to be very careful next year to make sure that if I do use anything from a basal that it's going to be something that's interesting to the kids based on past experiences. (Richardson & Anders, 1990, p. 85)

2. The use of more prereading practices. A strong emphasis in the staff development program was related to practices designed to activate and build background knowledge. Several sessions in all three schools revolved around discussions of the theory and practices related to background knowledge. In two of the schools, practices were modeled in individual teachers' classrooms, and tapes of this modeling were examined by the group. This emphasis was reflected in the teachers' descriptions of changes in their teaching practices.
3. Integration of literature into other subjects. Many teachers came to the realization that reading could be taught in other subjects besides reading. One type of integration that a number of them stressed was between reading and social studies.
4. Different practices in grading/assessment. A strong theme in the discussions in all three schools concerned grading and assessing reading comprehension (Anders & Richardson, 1992). Teachers were anxious about grading, and many could not consider changing their reading programs without first considering what such changes would mean for assessment. Initially, a number of teachers graded absolutely everything, including drafts. They felt that they would be more objective if they had numerous data points for each grade, and could average them for the report card grade.

Figure 8.1 Changes in Teachers' Theories

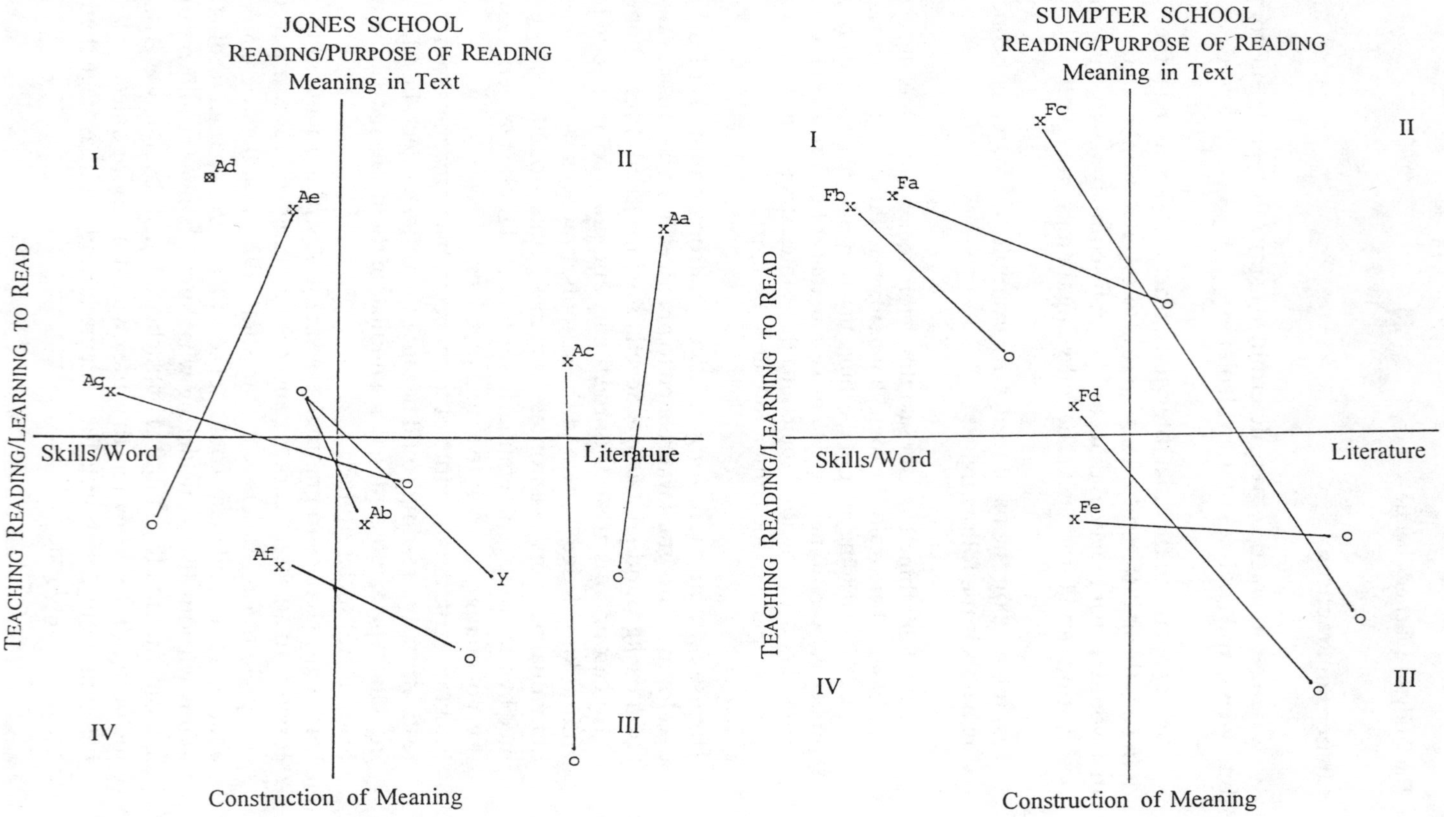

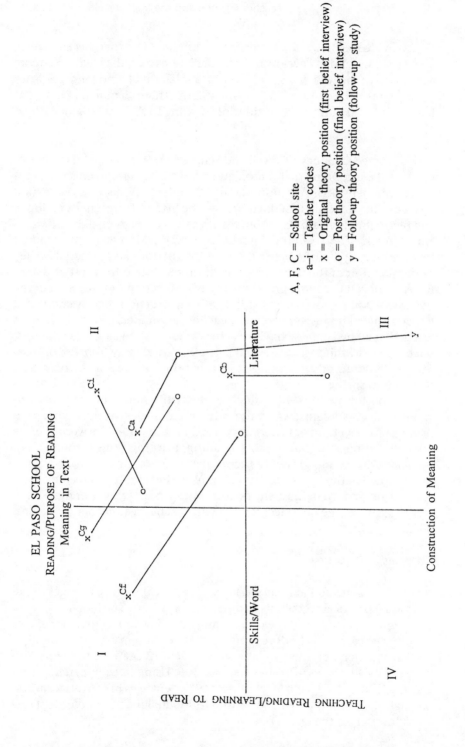

EL PASO SCHOOL
READING/PURPOSE OF READING
Meaning in Text

TEACHING READING/LEARNING TO READ

Skills/Word

Literature

Construction of Meaning

I   II   III   IV

Cg
Ci
Ca
Cf
Cb

y

A, F, C = School site
a–i = Teacher codes
x = Original theory position (first belief interview)
o = Post theory position (final belief interview)
y = Follow-up theory position (follow-up study)

As evidenced in the final interview, a number of teachers began to relax about grading, and to develop assessment systems that, they felt, were more authentic. In the follow-up study, Alec revealed that he no longer worries about standardized tests: "I don't worry about them so much. I know that I do my job and I don't like the idea of teaching to the test" (Valdez, 1992, p. 144).

Observed Changes. Tidwell and Schlegel (1991) examined the video-tapes of classroom instruction to determine changes in practices in reading comprehension instruction (see also Chapter 3). Videotapes were transcribed using a format that documented the gist of the teacher's dialogue and highlighted certain classroom features such as texts, chalkboard work, and so forth. They examined practices, overall lesson elements, student involvement, types of teacher-directed instruction, and materials. They found that four of the five teachers in Sumpter shifted from a skills-based focus in the fall to a more process-oriented focus in the spring. Four of the five teachers also moved from authoritative instruction (tightly controlled lessons, question-answer formats, teacher-dominated interactions) to a teacher-facilitated approach. The teachers at Jones showed similar changes, but on a more limited scale. Several teachers moved away from use or basal texts to literature, and the amount of teacher-directed instruction decreased from fall to spring.

In the follow-up study, Alec's and Kristi's practices continued to change. Alec's students, who were using basal readers at the completion of the staff development, were now reading literature, answering more open-ended questions about their reading, learning skills through reading and writing, and grouping themselves by choice rather than ability. Kristi turned to the use of literature groups in the teaching of reading comprehension. In fact, because she no longer used basal readers or traditional reading groups, she no longer felt that she teaches reading per se (Valdez, 1992).

Changes in Discourse

Richardson and Valdez (1991) examined the discourse changes in the individual practical arguments of nine of the teachers. The individual practical arguments involved the teacher and staff developers together examining a tape of the teacher's reading comprehension instruction, identifying the teacher's premises related to the actions seen on the tape, and considering alternative premises and practices. Using category systems from Fenstermacher (1986) and MacKinnon (1987), changes in conversation and language between the first and second individual practical argument sessions for each of the teachers were examined.

The conversation in the practical-argument sessions seemed to fall into cycles that could contain two or three of the following functions:

- *Initial Framing:* The staff developer and/or teacher brings certain aspects of teaching to the attention of the group.
- *Reframing:* The staff developer and/or teacher examine(s) the particular aspect of teaching from different theoretical viewpoints (from research and/or experience).
- *Alternative Frame:* The teacher accepts a new frame and states that he or she will consider making a change in classroom practices. This stage is not always reached in a practical argument.

In all cases, the initiation of the first function, the initial frame, led to the second, reframing function. However, these two frames did not always lead to the third. There were fewer cycles (the first two or all three functions) in the second practical argument than in the first; thus the discussions around each aspect of teaching were lengthier and deeper. In fact, it was the second stage, the reframing function, that was, in general, longer in the second practical argument than in the first. In addition, the teachers discussed changing practices more often in the second practical argument than in the first. In the first, teachers discussed change in 62 percent of the cycles; in the second, in 93 percent of the cycles.

There were also changes in the topics of conversation as well as differences in who introduced topics. Figure 8.2 lists the primary topics of conversation and who introduced them. During the first practical argument, almost every topic was consistently introduced by either the teacher *or* the staff developers; writing was the only topic brought up by both the teachers and staff developers. In the second practical argument, most topics were introduced an approximately equal number of times by both teachers and staff developers. Also, in the second argument, teachers appropriated the discussion of comprehension strategies from the staff developers.

In the follow-up study of the practical arguments of two of the teachers, Valdez (1992) found that even though there had been no formal communication between the teachers and the staff developers during the intervening two-year period, the nature and content of the conversations had continued to change. Further, the teachers exhibited an orientation to change that had been hinted at in the second practical argument but was fully revealed in the follow-up. She concluded the following:

> Discussions of change were emerging earlier and throughout the conversations; information talk about their students decreased; dialogue which encouraged teachers to examine their beliefs, understandings, and practices from several theoretical viewpoints increased; teachers began to initiate topics

Figure 8.2 Primary Topics and Who Introduced Them

Staff Developers	Equally	Teachers
First Practical Argument		
Prior Knowledge	Writing	Skills
Questioning		Vocabulary
Comprehension Strategies		Assessment
Purposes of Reading		Management
Second Practical Argument		
	Prior Knowledge	Skills
	Assessment	Comprehension Strategies
	Management	
	Literature	
	Writing	

only the staff developers had been introducing [in previous practical arguments]; discussions concerning change increased; and staff developers and teachers were mutually constructing the agenda of the conversations. (p. 170)

Valdez's (1992) discourse analysis confirmed that the conversations not only continued where they had left off several years ago, but they had moved far ahead of that point. This suggested to Valdez that the conversations had been continuing in both the teachers' and the staff developers' minds during the intervening years. In reflecting on their classroom practices, the teachers had taken over the role of the "Other" in the practical argument process and were asking themselves the "why" questions.

CONCLUSIONS: THE STUDY OF TEACHER CHANGE

This chapter examined two approaches to staff development: the training model and the collaborative process. We have suggested that the research designs required to assess teacher change that may be attributed to these two different approaches differ dramatically, to prevent violating the basic conceptions of change inherent in the approaches. The purpose of the training model is to impart specific behaviors to teachers with the assumption that these will be replicated by them in their classrooms. The training model has been examined within a process/product research framework in which the process consists of the content and procedures of the staff development itself, and the product represents changes in the teachers' behaviors in their classrooms.

The collaborative process as represented by PASD has much more open-ended goals than the training model. Teachers may differ widely in the changes they wish to make. Further, a major goal is to encourage changes in beliefs and cognitions, in addition to changes in classroom practices. This approach to practice requires a more qualitative research design, in which the constructs of change may emerge from the data, and the research process itself becomes one element of staff development.

This discussion is not meant to be critical of the training model, nor of the process/product research design. We are suggesting, however, that the staff development approach should drive the development of the research design rather than vice versa. Issues of validity will be examined differently in these two approaches: from a quantitative approach in process/product research (e.g., Borg & Gall, 1983) and a qualitative one in the research design used in the PASD process (e.g., Erickson, 1986).

The design for the assessment of change in the PASD process allowed us to examine many facets of change—to discover and develop cognitive and discourse constructs that perhaps had not been in the minds of the staff developers at the beginning of the process, and others that had been only faint and unarticulated glimmers. It also produced findings of changes in teaching practices and beliefs that are quite convincing. These findings present a picture of a change process that releases teachers from surface-level and externally derived beliefs about reading and the teaching of reading, and leads them toward a cycle of developing and questioning internalized conceptions of the curricula and their enactments.

Most important, our findings suggested to us that the PASD process has the potential to free teachers from a reliance on external conditions, such as parents, school board policies, and administrators to explain their teaching, and to allow them to develop sophisticated, theoretical premises that justify their practices. Ideally, it leads to a change orientation that compels them to reflect on their practices and continue to ask themselves why they are doing what they are doing, and if there are other practices that can be used to achieve their goals. A quote from one of the teachers in the follow-up belief interview reveals the continued presence of "why" questions in reflective moments. When asked what carried over for her from the staff development, Louise (Ac) said: "The ability to question myself when I didn't want to. When I felt like, why should I, but I did anyway. I think they really helped me to see that that's important and to not be so limited in my way of thinking."

REFERENCES

Anders, P., & Richardson, V. (1992). Teacher as game-show host, bookkeeper, or judge? Challenges, contradictions, and consequences of accountability. *Teachers College Record, 94*(2), 382–396.

Berman, P., & McLaughlin, M. (1978). Implementation of educational innovations. *Educational Forum, 2,* 347–370.

Borg, W., & Gall, M. (1983). *Education research: An introduction* (4th ed.). New York: Longman.

Brophy, J., & Good, T. (1986). Teacher behavior and student achievement. In M. Wittrock (Eds.), *Handbook of research on teaching* (3rd ed., pp. 328–375). New York: Macmillan.

Cohen, M. (1987). Improving school effectiveness: Lessons from research. In V. Richardson-Koehler (Ed.), *Educators' handbook: A research perspective* (pp. 474–490). New York: Longman.

Cruickshank, D., Lorish, C., & Thompson, L. (1979). What we think we know about inservice education. *Journal of Teacher Education, 30,* 342–346.

Cruickshank, D., & Metcalf, K. (1990). Training within teacher preparation. In W. Houston (Ed.), *Handbook of research on teacher education* (pp. 469–497). New York: Macmillan.

Doyle, W. (1977). Paradigms for research on teacher effectiveness. In L. Shulman (Ed.), *Review of Research in Education, 5,* 3–16.

Dunkin, M., & Biddle, B. (1974). *The study of teaching.* New York: Holt, Rinehart & Winston.

Erickson, F. (1986). Qualitative methods in research on teaching. In M. Wittrock (Ed.), *Handbook of research on teaching* (3rd ed., pp. 119–161). New York: Macmillan.

Fenstermacher, G. D. (1979). A philosophical consideration of recent research on teacher effectiveness. *Review of Research in Education, 6,* 157–185.

Fenstermacher, G. D. (1986). Philosophy of research on teaching: Three aspects. In M. Wittrock (Ed.), *Handbook of research on teaching* (3rd ed., pp. 37–49). New York: Macmillan.

Fullan, M. (1991). *The new meaning of educational change.* New York: Teachers College Press.

Gage, N. L. (1985). *Hard gains in the soft sciences: The case of pedagogy.* Bloomington, IN: Phi Delta Kappa.

Hall, G., & Loucks, S. (1977). A developmental model for determining whether the treatment is actually implemented. *American Educational Research Journal, 14*(3), 263–276.

Howey, K., & Vaughan, J. (1983). Current patterns of staff development. In

G. Griffin (Ed.), *Staff development* (Eighty-second Yearbook of the Society for the Study of Education, pp. 92–117). Chicago: University of Chicago Press.

Huberman, A., & Miles, M. (1984). *Innovation up close: How school improvement works.* New York: Plenum Press.

Kagan, D. (1990). Ways of evaluating teacher cognition: Inferences concerning the Goldilocks Principle. *Review of Educational Research, 60,* 419–470.

Koehler, V. (1978). Classroom process research: Present and future. *Journal of Classroom Interaction, 13*(2), 3–11.

Little, J. (1989). District policy choices and teachers' professional development opportunities. *Educational Evaluation and Policy Analysis, 11*(2), 165–180.

MacKinnon, A. (1987). Detecting reflection-in-action among preservice elementary science teachers. *Teaching and Teacher Education, 3,* 135–145.

Pink, W. (1989, April). *Effective staff development for urban school improvement.* Paper presented at the annual meeting of the American Educational Research Association, San Francisco.

Richardson, V. (1991). *A study of long-term changes in teachers' beliefs and practices* (Proposal submitted to U.S. Department of Education, Office of Educational Research and Improvement). Tucson: College of Education, University of Arizona.

Richardson, V., & Anders, P. (1990). *Final report of the reading instruction study.* Tucson: College of Education, University of Arizona. (ERIC Document Reproduction Service No. ED 324-655)

Richardson, V., Anders, P., Tidwell, D., & Lloyd, C. (1991). The relationship between teachers' beliefs and practices in reading comprehension instruction. *American Educational Research Journal, 28*(3), 559–586.

Richardson, V., Casanova, U., Placier, P., & Guilfoyle, K. (1989). *School children at-risk.* London: Falmer.

Richardson, V., & Valdez, A. (1991, April). *Changes in teachers' beliefs about and theories of reading comprehension.* Paper presented at the annual meeting of the American Educational Research Association, Chicago.

Showers, B., Joyce, B., & Bennett, B. (1987). Synthesis of research on staff development: A framework for future study and state-of-art analysis. *Educational Leadership, 45*(3), 77–87.

Smyth, J. (1981, April). *Two for the price of one: Staff development through the utilization of findings from research on teaching.* Paper presented at the annual meeting of the American Educational Research Association, Los Angeles.

Sparks, D., & Loucks-Horsley, S. (1990). Models of staff development. In R. Houston (Ed.), *Handbook of research on teacher education* (3rd ed., pp. 234–250). New York: Macmillan.

Stallings, J., & Krasavage, E. (1986). Program implementation and student achievement in a four-year Madeline Hunter follow-through project. *Elementary School Journal, 87*(2), 117–138.

Stallings, J., Needels, M., & Stayrook, N. (1979). *How to change the process of teaching basic reading skills in secondary schools* (Final report to the National Institute of Education). Menlo Park, CA: SRI International.

Tidwell, D., & Schlegel, M. (1991, April). *Teachers' reading comprehension practices: Impact of a staff development program on classroom instruction.* Paper presented at the annual meeting of the American Educational Research Association, San Francisco.

Valdez, A. (1992). *Changes in teachers' beliefs, understandings, and practices concerning reading comprehension through the use of practical arguments: A follow-up study.* Unpublished doctoral dissertation, College of Education, University of Arizona, Tucson.

Williams, R. (1979). A political perspective on staff development. In A. Lieberman & L. Miller (Eds.), *Staff development: New demands, new realities, new perspectives* (pp. 95–105). New York: Teachers College Press.

9

The Study of Student Change

CANDACE S. BOS AND PATRICIA L. ANDERS

Implicit in most programs of staff development is the assumption that staff development will result in improved student learning. Other chapters in this volume define staff development and summarize various types of staff development: those intended to solve immediate and critical problems in a classroom, school, or district; those designed to impart or deliver knowledge and practices for teachers to implement; and, of late, programs that create a context for teachers to explore their beliefs and practices by providing opportunities for reflection. This chapter focuses on one question: What happens to the quality of students' learning when their teachers participate in staff development designed to focus on teacher change through reflection and integration of research-based practices?

This seems like a straightforward question, but it is in fact complex. The complexities emerge from the nature of schooling, the culture of schools, and the range of research designs and measures available for the study of staff development programs. These issues framed our search for how to address the question of student reading achievement. The thesis of this chapter is that these complexities represent considerations that affect the development of staff development and the measurement of a program's success.

THE CULTURE OF SCHOOLS AND THE NATURE OF SCHOOLING

Staff development programs occur within the culture of the participating schools. Goodlad (1983), in a discussion of his *Study of Schooling* descriptive research project, argues persuasively that the best descriptor of "satisfying schools" is one that characterizes the relationships between and among people in a school. (For similar findings, see Little, 1987; Rosenholtz, 1989; and Sarason, 1971.) Goodlad (1984) implies that students in more satisfying schools—those schools with collegial faculties who trusted each other and worked together—were more successful than those in less satisfying schools.

Another finding in the Goodlad (1983) study was that teachers' pedagogies, for the most part, did not differ from school to school. In most classrooms the observed teaching practices were lecture and student recitation. Student performance was judged to be positive, however, in those few classes where instructional practices were those that theory and research would support—that is, interactive and cooperative.

A generalization that might be drawn from this finding is that a reflective staff development program designed to provide teachers with opportunities to learn about alternative practices should result in improved student learning. Goodlad (1983), however, contravenes this possible generalization.

> Even if a teacher were fortunate enough to engage in countervailing practices, the setting for using them is not likely to be receptive and reinforcing. . . . Countervailing practices are demanding and difficult virtually by definition; for implementation they require institutional support and legitimization. This will not occur unless school staffs are willing to take their teaching out of the closet of the classroom, admit to the need to improve, and make it, along with the rest of the daily program, the focus of school-wide, on-site staff development. (pp. 57–58)

Goodlad's recommendation is easier said than done. Lloyd (1973) found what Lortie (1975) described well in his classic study: The individual teacher is the center of the culture of schools. "Coming out of the closet" to share and constructively criticize and reflect on one's practices is not part of the established norms of school culture. Therefore, attempting to achieve teacher change using a reflective model of staff development is an uphill climb. Nonetheless, as presented in the other chapters in this volume, the hill can be climbed with the help of critical and supportive friends in a climate of inquiry, collaboration, and cooperation (Courter & Ward, 1983; Englert, 1993; Fenstermacher & Richardson, 1993; Little, 1987).

Measuring the efficacy of the staff development program and the progress of the participating teachers' students is also challenging. Anders and Richardson (1992) report that a "culture of testing" permeates schools and society. Shepard (1989) states the case strongly:

> In the U.S. today standardized testing is running amok. Newspapers rank schools and districts by their test scores. Real estate agents use test scores to identify the "best" schools as selling points for expensive housing. Superintendents can be fired for low scores, and teachers can receive merit pay for high test scores. Superintendents exhort principals and principals admonish teachers to raise test scores. (p. 4)

Planners and researchers involved in staff development need not be to-tally dependent on standardized measures for evaluating their programs. A range of possibilities exists and the next section describes the typical designs adopted.

STAFF DEVELOPMENT PROGRAMS AND THE RESEARCH DESIGN

Staff development programs are as diverse as the people who create, con-duct, and participate in them. Hence, we are suggesting that the research design and the student assessment measures be sensitive to the type of staff development being conducted. The issue is not *if* staff development pro-grams should be evaluated in relation to student learning; rather, the issue is selecting the design and measures that best fit the staff development program.

During the 1970s and 1980s, many of the staff development programs were externally driven. That is, new curricula, methods, or instructional programs were imported to the classroom vis-à-vis teacher training. (See Chapter 6 for a discussion of types of staff development programs.) These programs were a "good fit" for the process/product designs. The desired teacher and student outcomes were articulated in terms of behavioral objectives that were typically measured by norm-referenced tests. Examples of such staff development programs include those conducted and evalu-ated by Emmer, Sanford, Evertson, Clements, and Martin (1981); Good and Grows (1979); and Stallings, Needels, and Stayrook (1983).

During the late 1980s and through the present, collaborative types of staff development are the focus of a growing number of teacher change projects (e.g., Englert, 1993; Goldenberg & Gallimore, 1991; Matlin & Short, 1991; see also Chapter 8 of this volume). As discussed in Chapter 6, goals and content for collaborative types of staff development are dynamic and develop through conversations among teachers, administrators, and facili-tators/researchers.

The research designs and related measures of student achievement for these programs should account for the dynamic aspects of collabora-tive staff development. For example, the measures of student achieve-ment need to be valued by the participants and should be compatible with the theory and evolving goals of staff development. Furthermore, recent studies recommend that collaborative types of staff development utilize multiple-year research designs to measure effects (e.g., Englert, 1993; Gaskins, in press; Chapter 8 of this volume; Saunders, Goldenberg, & Hamann, 1992).

TWO EXAMPLES OF COLLABORATIVE STAFF DEVELOPMENT

Two multiple-year, collaborative staff development programs with theoretically balanced research designs are the Early Literacy Project (ELP) and the Benchmark School Project. The ELP, a four-year research project funded by the U.S. Department of Education, was conducted by Englert, Raphael, and their colleagues (Englert, 1993; Englert, Raphael, & Mariage, in press). The researchers worked within a collaborative teacher-researcher community to construct a model of teaching and learning that "pushed past the barriers of strategy instruction to address the overarching concern of how do we get children to have the 'skill and will' to learn and succeed in literacy" (Englert, 1993, p. 2). The teachers and researchers worked within a culture of special education classrooms serving primary-grade students who are described as "preconventional readers and writers." The ELP curriculum grew out of weekly meetings in which the teachers and researchers discussed the literacy needs of their primary grade students. The content for the early literacy instruction was developed within the guiding principles of a constructivist theory of literacy and strategy instruction (Englert & Palincsar, 1991).

The ELP also addressed the developmental and long-term nature of teacher learning (Duffy, 1993; Fullan, 1991) by employing a multiple-year research design. Three teachers were involved in the first and second years of the project. Three additional teachers joined the project during the third year, and three more during the fourth year. Each year, teacher and student measures were collected for contrast teachers (i.e., effective teachers who utilized many components of interactive early literacy instruction but not in a holistic, integrated manner), and also for each group of three teachers to allow for the comparison of teachers at different stages of implementation.

The student learning measures were local measures developed and valued by the researchers and teachers: written retellings of expository text similar to the texts used in the classroom, student compositions, and student metacognitive strategy interviews, for example. The study also utilized standardized measures of literacy valued by district-level administrators, including the *Slosson Oral Reading Test* (Slosson, 1963) and the *Durrell Analysis of Reading Difficulty* (Durrell, 1955).

Analysis of the student measures during the third year of the project reveals an appropriate match between the collaborative staff development and the research design. First, the effects of the staff development on student learning were stronger for the second-year teachers than the first-year teachers, supporting the developmental nature of teacher learning (Englert,

1993). Second, the importance of local measures was highlighted by the results of the first-year teachers; while significant differences between the first-year and contrast teachers were evident for the local measures, significant differences were not as consistent for standardized measures. As Griffin (1991) argues, assessment measures should be suited to the change that is to be observed. Districts have accountability responsibilities and tend to use standardized achievement tests as a tool for meeting those responsibilities. Indeed, that is a reasonable use of those tests. It is an error, however, to assume that standardized achievement tests are sensitive to the sorts of change experienced by these teachers and their students.

A second example of a collaborative, long-term staff development program has been undertaken at Benchmark School (Gaskins, in press; Pressley et al., 1991). A private school for underachieving students in grades 1 through 8, Benchmark School provides systematic instruction based on the teachers' interpretations of research findings related to strategic reading and learning. Over the past 12 years, teachers have been selected and prepared to use and develop instruction consistent with the strategy research. In this project, staff development is closely attuned to classroom instruction and assessment.

The staff development program at Benchmark can be characterized as collaborative staff development that provides teachers with empirical information through supervision, journal articles, attendance at research conferences, and the opportunity to interact with visitors who present their research in strategy instruction. These external resources are reported to be important to the teachers (Pressley et al., 1991), but perhaps equally important is the information the teachers provide each other. The staff of Benchmark School communicate adeptly with each other about strategy instruction and have created a community of collegial professionalism.

Benchmark School provides the opportunity to study long-term collaborative staff development because student achievement is measured using both standardized and local measures of reading and writing, including paragraphs, summaries, interpretation of text information, and outlining. Results from both local and standardized measures indicate that students made significant gains after one year of strategy instruction, but that student gains were more dramatic during the second year.

Collaborative types of staff development require research designs and measures that are valued by participating teachers and are sensitive to change. The Early Literacy Project and the Benchmark School Project are examples of a "good match" for collaborative types of staff development.

RIS PROJECT: ASSESSMENT MEASURES

The Reading Instruction Study (RIS) project, as described in Chapters 6 and 8, was a collaborative and dynamic staff development process. This section describes the reading assessment measures used and the procedures and outcomes of the assessments. We conducted this study to learn how the students' reading performance changed when their teachers participated in the staff development process.

We originally planned three types of student measures: a standardized district-administered measure of reading, the *Iowa Test of Basic Skills* (ITBS) (Hieronymus & Hoover, 1986a, b); a standardized test designed to be consistent with an interactive theory of reading, the *Illinois Goal Assessment Program* (IGAP) (Valencia, Pearson, Reeve, & Shanahan, 1988); and local teacher-developed measures. We successfully implemented the first two measures, but were unsuccessful in developing the local measures. As described elsewhere (see Chapters 4 and 6), the teachers with whom we worked were steadfastly committed to the value of "objective" standardized measures. Also, they were not convinced of the efficacy of "research-based practices." The combination of these strongly held beliefs restricted the possibilities available to us for developing local measures.

Iowa Test of Basic Skills

We used the ITBS because it was the state-mandated, district-administered achievement test. On the reading portion of the test, the reading process is represented as complex and assumes that a good reader is one who apprehends the author's meaning, grasps the significance of the ideas presented, evaluates them, and draws correct conclusions (Hieronymus & Hoover, 1986b). The test also assumes that the reading process is made up of subskills grouped into three general categories: facts (recognizing and understanding stated factual details and relationships), inferences (inferring underlying relationships), and generalizations (developing generalizations from a selection). The reading comprehension portion uses a wide selection of texts found in schools including newspapers, magazines, encyclopedias, government publications, textbooks, and original literary works. The passages vary in length from a few sentences to a full page of text. All items contain a single correct response in a multiple-choice format. Using a statistical model of test development, degree of item difficulty and item discrimination are the criteria used for item selection. Consideration is also given to the match between the items and the skills objectives listed within the reading domain.

Illinois Goal Assessment Program

A growing concern exists regarding the mismatch between typical standardized measures of reading (e.g., ITBS) and current theories of the reading process (Calfee & Hiebert, 1991; Johnston, 1983; Valencia & Pearson, 1986). Recent research describes reading as a constructive and interactive process (Anderson & Pearson, 1984). The reader is strategic and thoughtful, and uses clues from the text, background knowledge of both content and strategies for reading, the reading context, and other resources to construct meaning from the text. Such a model suggests that skilled reading is reflected in the reader's awareness of how, when, and why to use resources for the goal of constructing meaning, and that expert readers use this knowledge flexibly across different reading situations (e.g., Baker & Brown, 1984; Pearson & Valencia, 1987).

These concerns compelled us to look for an additional standardized measure that better reflected current theory and practice. The reading portion of the *Illinois Goal Assessment Program* has been developed from this current interactive perspective of reading. Not only does the theory supporting the IGAP differ from that of traditional standardized tests, but the format is also considerably different from the conventional. For example, the IGAP consists of full-length stories or expositions. Passages present coherent stories or information that represent the levels of complexity, topic relevance, length, and difficulty found in grade-appropriate materials. A semantic map (Pearson & Johnson, 1978) of each passage was constructed as a check on structural integrity and readability and to provide a guide for the development of test items. For our study, six passages were selected, including three narrative passages and three expository passages.

Another difference is the way that comprehension is "checked." On the IGAP 15 multiple-choice items were developed for each passage. The *Constructing Meaning* items are of three different question types: textually explicit, inferential, or transfer/application. Readers are encouraged to select as many responses as appropriate, from one to three, to answer the question. "The rationale behind such a format is that most questions, particularly inference and application, do have more than one correct answer" (*IGAP: Reading*, 1988, p. 13).

Another section not found on a traditional standardized test is the *Topic Familiarity* section. This section was developed to reflect research findings that emphasize the importance of activating and integrating background knowledge (Anderson & Pearson, 1984). This section of the IGAP is designed to assess how much students know about a topic before they read the passage and also serves as a means for activating students' background knowledge about the topic of the passage. The item format for this section consists of telling students the topic about which they will read and providing a list of 15 statements. After hearing the topic, students are asked to predict the likelihood that the content of each statement will be included in the passage by responding yes, maybe, or no.

Finally, the IGAP includes a *Reading Strategies* section designed to measure students' metacognitive reading strategies. Using a scenario in which the students are presented with a hypothetical problem related to understanding the information or identifying key information from the passage, students make judgments that require them to be aware of and to judge the usefulness of cognitive strategies related to reading. Two scenarios with five items apiece are used for each passage.

Local Norming Study. The IGAP was developed and normed for third-, sixth-, eighth-, and eleventh-graders in Illinois. Since we intended to use the sixth-grade test with fourth-, fifth-, and sixth-graders in Arizona, we conducted our own norming study. We also wanted to determine if the IGAP was developmentally appropriate across all three grades, and if the concurrent validity of the IGAP and the ITBS for each grade level was comparable to that found with the sixth-grade Illinois norming sample between the IGAP and the *Stanford Achievement Test*. If these criteria were met, then we would have support for using the IGAP in our effectiveness study.

To develop our own norms, 787 students in grades 4, 5, and 6 from the five schools participating in the project were assessed. Of the total number of students, 374 were male and 413 were female. Students were from grade 4 (n = 296), grade 5 (n = 251), and grade 6 (n = 240). The test was administered in the students' classrooms by RIS-trained graduate students and by professors at the school sites.

First we compared student performance by grade level. The means and standard deviations for the scaled scores on the three reading activities assessed are presented in Table 9.1. Both visual and statistical analyses of the data support the developmental trend across the three grade levels. Analyses of variance (ANOVA) across grades revealed a significant effect for grade on Topic Familiarity, Constructing Meaning, and Reading Strategies. We also computed the correlations for each grade level between the IGAP Constructing Meaning and ITBS reading portion (Grade 4, r = .53; Grade 5, r = .60; Grade 6, r = .58). These correlations are similar to the correlation for the Illinois sixth-grade norming sample between the IGAP reading portion and the *Stanford Achievement Test* reading portion (r = .63).

Results of the norming study provided support for the use of the reading portion of the IGAP as a measure of reading achievement. Both the developmental criterion and the similar concurrent validity criterion were

Table 9.1 IGAP Means and Standard Deviations: Norming Study

Reading Activity	Grade 4	Grade 5	Grade 6
Constructing Meaning	212.09	260.71	293.30
	(79.30)	(92.61)	(87.36)
	($n = 284$)	($n = 249$)	($n = 234$)
Topic Familiarity	230.57	253.22	278.50
	(80.32)	(77.74)	(82.54)
	($n = 296$)	($n = 251$)	($n = 238$)
Reading Strategies	233.03	251.00	275.68
	(77.72)	(85.06)	(90.47)
	($n = 272$)	($n = 200$)	($n = 232$)

met. Based on the theoretical framework of the IGAP, we hypothesized that the IGAP would be more sensitive to the effects of staff development than the ITBS.

EFFECTIVENESS STUDY

To ascertain the qualitative differences between students of teachers who participated in the RIS staff development and those who did not, we used the IGAP and the reading portion of the ITBS. Students who participated in the effectiveness study were the students of the participating teachers in the two staff development schools (Jones and Sumpter) and the contrast school (Wilson). A sample of 276 students participated in the first year of the effectiveness study. These students completed the ITBS and the IGAP during the pretest (spring or fall 1988) and posttest (spring 1989) administrations.

A sample of 159 students participated in the second year of the effectiveness study. They were the students of the participating teachers in Jones and Wilson and they completed the ITBS and IGAP at the pretest (spring or fall 1989) and posttest (spring 1990) administrations. Characteristics of the students in the effectiveness study are presented in Table 9.2.

For the first year, teachers in the staff development schools participated in the staff development described in Chapter 6. Teachers in the

Table 9.2 Student Characteristics for the Effectiveness

Characteristics	Grade 4	Grade 5	Grade 6	Total
Year 1 ($n = 276$)				
Number of Students	91	80	105	276
Jones (Staff Dev.)	29	31	32	92
Sumpter (Staff Dev.)	17	17	23	57
Wilson (Contrast)	45	32	50	127
Sex				
Male	42	32	54	128
Female	49	48	51	148
Year 2 ($n = 159$)				
Number of Students				
Jones (Staff Dev.)	33	23	15	71
Wilson (Contrast)	36	24	28	88
Sex				
Male	33	29	18	80
Female	35	19	25	79

contrast school did not participate in any staff development except that regularly scheduled by the district. For this first year of the study, we compared student performance for the participating teachers in each staff development school with student performance for the participating teachers in the contrast school. The staff development schools were separated for these analyses because the school cultures and implementation of the staff development process varied for each school (Hamilton & Richardson, in press; see also Chapter 7).

During the second year of the study, the RIS staff development was no longer formally implemented at Jones and Sumpter and teachers in the contrast school, Wilson, participated in a more traditional staff development program. We provided the teachers at Wilson with a menu of topics on reading about which we could facilitate discussion. The topics included the list of foci and practices from our literature review (see Chapter 4 of this volume) plus other topics, including "mainstreaming," "retelling for comprehension assessment," and "text sets." The teachers selected "vocabulary" and "text elements" from our foci and practices list and also selected "mainstreaming," "retelling for comprehension assessment," and "text sets." We presented their topics of choice throughout the year at times convenient to the staff.

For this second year of the study, we compared the performance of the students in the classrooms of the five continuing teachers at Jones with that of the students in the classrooms of the seven teachers at Wilson. (Student achievement at Sumpter was not evaluated because all but one teacher retired or changed schools during the second year of the study.) For the reading portion of the ITBS we used the norm equivalent scores, and for the three portions of the IGAP we used scaled scores.

Statistical information for student performance may be found in Tables 9.3 (first year) and 9.4 (second year). During the first year of the study,

Table 9.3 ITBS and IGAP Adjusted Means and Standard Deviations: Year 1

Test	Staff Development School		Contrast School Wilson
	Jones	Sumpter	
ITBS			
Reading	42.05	50.6	47.05
	(20.1)	(24.8)	(25.5)

$F\,(2,257) = 1.098$, when previous year's performance used as covariate: $F\,(1,257) = 295.46$, $p < .0001$

IGAP			
Topic Familiarity	276.64	280.11	277.77
	(97.0)	(93.0)	(92.3)

$F\,(2,271) = .02$ when performances in Fall used as covariate: $F\,(1,271) = 27.693, p < .0001$

Constructing Meaning	256.16	282.40	251.15
	(102.4)	(102.7)	(101.7)

$F\,(2,261) = 3.423, p < .03$, with significant covariate: $F\,(1,261) = 223.497, p < .0001$

Reading Strategies	286.28	293.28	249.28
	(98.0)	(105.9)	(107.9)

$F\,(2,243) = 5.006, p = .007$, with significant covariate: $F\,(1,243) = 32.687, p < .0001$

Table 9.4 ITBS and IGAP Adjusted Means and Standard Deviations: Year 2

Test	Staff Development School Jones	Contrast School Wilson
ITBS		
Reading	42.85	43.67
$F(1,156) = .21$	(18.43)	(15.97)
IGAP		
Topic Familiarity	228.74	211.89
$F(1,149) = 1.20$	(95.72)	(98.49)
Constructing Meaning	201.32	180.55
$F(1,154) = 2.38$	(97.95)	(80.92)
Reading Strategies	231.79	216
$F(1,143) = 1.01$	(87.95)	(105.96)

there were no significant differences among the three schools for the students' performance on the ITBS when their previous year's performance on the test was used as a control. This suggests that the ITBS, as a measure of student achievement and gain in achievement, was not sensitive to the staff development.

On the other hand, the Reading Strategies portion of the IGAP indicated some differences during the first year on two of the three portions. For Topic Familiarity no significant differences among the three schools were evident. However, differences among the three schools were evident in their students' performance on the Constructing Meaning section. Further analyses indicated that differences in performance were evident between Wilson and Jones, with the staff development school scoring significantly higher. This was also the case with the Reading Strategies section. Analyses indicated that there were differences for the two staff development schools in comparison with the contrast school, with the staff development schools scoring higher.

However, the differences among the schools on the IGAP did not continue into the second year, as is evident in Table 9.4. No significant differences between Jones (staff development school) and Wilson (contrast school) were evident on either the ITBS or the three portions of the IGAP.

DISCUSSION AND CONCLUSIONS

This chapter focuses on the question: What happens to the quality of students' learning when their teachers participate in staff development designed to focus on teacher change through reflection and integration of research-based practices? The fifth question as posed in the original proposal to OERI (Does the use of research-based teaching of reading practices affect student reading achievement in a positive direction?) was modified to reflect the more collaborative nature of the staff development that actually ensued during the project.

An attribute of a well-developed and comprehensive staff development program, regardless of its collaborative nature, is that it takes into account student outcomes (Howey & Vaughan, 1983). As demonstrated in the RIS and in two other examples cited here (the Early Literacy Project and the Benchmark School Project), measuring student outcomes in constructivist staff development programs is challenging and complex. Nonetheless, since improving the quality of student learning is one goal of staff development, we have no choice but to describe the nature of student change. In planning staff development programs, selecting a research design and measures that provide a "good match" between the type of staff development and the anticipated change is necessary. This is important to justify the staff development program and to accommodate teachers' purposes for participating in the program (Berman & McLaughlin, 1978; Harootunian & Yagar, 1980; McLaughlin & Marsh, 1978).

In the RIS, a collaborative type of staff development was enacted with the teachers. It provided the opportunity for teachers to focus on their valuative, empirical, situational, and stipulative premises, and to discuss them in relation to recent research on the teaching of reading comprehension. Traditionally, student achievement has served as a measure for the effectiveness of externally driven staff development with the use of process/ product design (Brophy & Good, 1986; Gage, 1985). While existing evidence from experimental studies tends to support a causal relationship between a number of teaching behaviors and academic achievement (Gage, 1985; Good & Grows, 1979; Stallings, 1975), shortcomings and limitations in the model have been reported (see Chapter 6). The RIS contributes to a small but growing body of research that attempts to describe the relationship of constructivist staff development and student performance (Englert, 1993; Gaskins, in press).

Broadly, the results of the effectiveness study for the RIS support the premise that students' reading changed when their teachers participated in staff development. During the first year of the study, when the staff development program was ongoing, student performance for Constructing Meaning and Reading Strategies was significantly higher at Sumpter (the school where staff developers had the phenomenological sense of being successful) than at Wilson (the contrast school). At Jones, where the staff development was perceived by the researchers as less successful, student performance was still significantly higher for Reading Strategies than at Wilson. During the second year of the study, when staff development was no longer ongoing at Jones and Sumpter, but Wilson teachers received staff development focused on topics teachers chose from a menu provided by the RIS team, significant differences for reading achievement between the two schools were no longer evident.

When this broad interpretation of change is viewed more closely, however, the fact that there were no significant differences among the schools on the ITBS stands out. The results of the effectiveness study support our hypothesis that the IGAP was more sensitive to our staff development than was the ITBS, and are consistent with the findings of Englert and her colleagues (Englert et al., in press), who found that local measures were more sensitive to change than were skill-oriented standardized measures. Hence, it makes sense to develop and use local measures. Several possibilities come to mind: teachers' evaluations of their own classrooms and practices as case studies; action research conducted collaboratively by teachers and staff developers; teachers' systematic observation of students' behaviors and cognitions such as is evident in student portfolios and other behaviors—for example, number of books checked out from the library.

Another consideration within this broad interpretation of the results is that students at both Jones and Sumpter demonstrated their use of reading strategies more effectively than did students in the contrast school. Richardson and Anders (see Chapter 8) note that teachers' beliefs and practices toward interactive instruction changed at Jones and Sumpter. Hence, a connection may be drawn between teachers' beliefs and practices about reading and their students' performance.

It is also interesting to note that during the first year of the study, only students at Sumpter, where the staff development was perceived by the researchers as "working," showed higher scores on the Constructing Meaning section of the IGAP. This section of the IGAP probably created the most tension for students because they were to select up to three responses for each item. This type of item encourages flexibility and divergent thinking. As described in Chapter 6, the Sumpter teachers "took over" the staff development much sooner than did the Jones teachers. We speculate that perhaps the Sumpter teachers' sense of independence and flexibility was transmitted to their students.

No differences were evident among the three schools for student performance on the Topic Familiarity section of the IGAP. In Illinois, this section has not been used as an outcome measure, but as a method to activate background knowledge before reading, and to determine how much students know about the topic before they read. A comparison of the correlations between Topic Familiarity and Constructing Meaning for the first-year fall and spring administrations of the IGAP indicate that the correlations were higher for the spring administration in the two staff development schools. This provides some evidence of either increased background knowledge or increased ability to activate that knowledge.

No significant differences were found between the students of Wheeler and Jones schools during the second year of the study. This finding supports the recommendation that staff development continue for more than one year. Similar to the findings of the multiple-year Early Literacy Project, analysis of the Valdez (1992) follow-up study reveals that teachers' beliefs and practices continued to change. If the RIS had continued, we might have seen dramatic changes in student reading performance.

The RIS staff development process encourages empowerment, diversity, and flexibility—aspects difficult to measure using standardized, group-administered student assessments. Like others in the field of reading (Johnston, 1983, 1984; Pearson & Valencia, 1987), we encourage the further development of assessments that capture the complex, holistic nature of the reading process. This recommendation is consistent with Sparks and Loucks-Horsley's (1990) call for evaluation of programs that are not focused on training. It is not enough to ask teachers to make conscious decisions concerning *what* and *how* to teach (Nitsaisook & Anderson, 1989, p. 301); it is also necessary to help teachers develop empirical rationales for their decisions, and to develop student measures that are consistent with those rationales.

REFERENCES

Anders, P., & Richardson, V. (1992). Teacher as game-show host, bookkeeper, or judge? Challenges, contradictions, and consequences of accountability. *Teachers College Record, 94,* 382–396.

Anderson, R. C., & Pearson, P. D. (1984). A schema-theoretic view of basic processes in reading. In P. D. Pearson (Ed.), *Handbook of reading research* (pp. 255–292). New York: Longman.

Baker, L., & Brown, A. L. (1984). Metacognitive skills and reading. In P. D. Pearson (Ed.), *Handbook of reading research* (pp. 353–394). New York: Longman.

Berman P., & McLaughlin, M. W. (1978). *Federal programs supporting educational change. Vol. VIII: Implementing and sustaining innovations.* Santa Monica, CA: Rand Corporation.

Brophy, J. E., & Good, T. L. (1986). Teacher behavior and student achievement. In M. C. Wittrock (Ed.), *Handbook of research on teaching* (3rd ed., pp. 328–375). New York: Macmillan.

Calfee, R., & Hiebert, E. (1991). Classroom assessment of reading. In R. Barr, M. L. Kamil, P. Mosenthal, & P. D. Pearson (Eds.), *Handbook of reading research* (Vol. 2, pp. 281–309). New York: Longman.

Courter, R. L., & Ward, B. A. (1983). Staff development for school improvement. In G. G. Griffin (Ed.), *Staff development* (Eighty-second Yearbook of the National Society for the Study of Education, pp. 185–209). Chicago: University of Chicago Press.

Duffy, G. G. (1993). Rethinking strategy instruction: Four teachers' development and their low achievers' understanding. *Elementary School Journal, 93,* 231–248.

Durrell, D. D. (1955). *Durrell Analysis of Reading Difficulty.* New York: Harcourt Brace Jovanovich.

Emmer, E., Sanford, J., Evertson, C., Clements, B., & Martin, J. (1981). *The classroom management improvement study: An experiment in elementary school classrooms.* Austin: Research and Development Center for Teacher Education, University of Texas. (ERIC Document Reproduction Service No. ED 178-460)

Englert, C. S. (1993, April). *A principled search for understanding: Strategic instruction for special needs students.* Paper presented at the annual meeting of the American Educational Research Association, Atlanta.

Englert, C. S., & Palincsar, A. S. (1991). Reconsidering instructional research in literacy from a sociocultural perspective. *Learning Disabilities Research and Practice, 6,* 225–229.

Englert, C. S., Raphael, T. E., & Mariage, T. (in press). Developing a school-based discourse for literacy learning: A principled search for understanding. *Learning Disabilities Quarterly.*

Fenstermacher, G. D, & Richardson, V. (1993). The elicitation and reconstruction of practical arguments in teaching. *Journal of Curriculum Studies, 25,* 101–114.

Fullan, M. G. (1991). *The meaning of education change.* New York: Teachers College Press.

Gage, N. L. (1985). *Hard gains in the soft sciences: The case of pedagogy.* Bloomington, IN: Phi Delta Kappa.

Gaskins, I. W. (in press). Classroom applications of cognitive science: Teaching poor readers how to learn, think, and problem solve. In K. McGilly (Ed.), *Classroom lessons: Integrating cognitive theory and classroom practice.* Boston: Bradford Books/MIT Press.

Goldenberg, C., & Gallimore, R. (1991). Changing teaching takes more than a one-shot workshop. *Educational Leadership, 49*(3), 69–72.

Good, T., & Grows, D. A. (1979). The Missouri mathematics effectiveness project: An experimental study of fourth-grade classrooms. *Journal of Educational Psychology, 71,* 355–362.

Goodlad, J. I. (1983). The school as workplace. In G. G. Griffin (Ed.), *Staff development* (Eighty-second Yearbook of the National Society for the Study of Education, pp. 36–61). Chicago: University of Chicago Press.

Goodlad, J. I. (1984). *A place called school: Prospects for the future.* New York: McGraw-Hill.

Griffin, G. A. (1991). Interactive staff development: Using what we know. In A. Lieberman & L. Miller (Eds.), *Staff development for education in the 90's* (2nd ed., pp. 243–260). New York: Teachers College Press.

Hamilton, M. L., & Richardson, V. (in press). Effects of the school culture on the process of staff development. *Elementary School Journal.*

Harootunian, B., & Yagar, G. P. (1980, April). *Teachers' conceptions of their own success.* Paper presented at the annual meeting of the American Educational Research Association, Boston.

Hieronymus, A. N., & Hoover, H. D. (1986a). *Iowa Test of Basic Skills.* Chicago: Riverside.

Hieronymus, A. N., & Hoover, H. D. (1986b). *Iowa Test of Basic Skills Manual for School Administrators.* Chicago: Riverside.

Howey, K. R., & Vaughan, J. C. (1983). Current patterns of staff development. In G. G. Griffin (Ed.), *Staff development* (Eighty-second Yearbook of the National Society for the Study of Education, pp. 92–117). Chicago: University of Chicago Press.

Illinois Goal Assessment Program: Reading—Technical manual. (1988). Springfield: Illinois State Board of Education.

Johnston, P. H. (1983). *Reading comprehension assessment: A cognitive basis.* Newark, DE: International Reading Association.

Johnston, P. H. (1984). Assessment in reading. In P. D. Pearson (Ed.), *Handbook of reading research* (pp. 147–184). New York: Longman.

Little, J. W. (1987). Teachers as colleagues. In V. Richardson-Koehler (Ed.), *Educators' handbook: A research perspective* (pp. 491-519). New York: Longman.

Lloyd, D. M. (1973). The effects of staff development inservice programs on teacher performance and student achievement. Unpublished doctoral dissertation, University of California at Los Angeles.

Lortie, D. C. (1975). *Schoolteacher: A sociological study.* Chicago: University of Chicago Press.

Matlin, M. L., & Short, K. G. (1991). How our teacher study group sparks change. *Educational Leadership, 49*(3), 68.

McLaughlin, M. W., & Marsh, D. D. (1978). Staff development and school change. *Teachers College Record, 80,* 69–93.

Nitsaisook, M., & Anderson, L. W. (1989). An experimental investigation of the effectiveness of inservice teacher education in Thailand. *Teaching and Teacher Education, 5,* 287–302.

Pearson, P. D., & Johnson, D. D. (1978). *Teaching reading comprehension.* New York: Holt, Rinehart & Winston.

Pearson, P. D., & Valencia, S. (1987). Assessment, accountability, and professional prerogative. In J. E. Readence & R. S. Baldwin (Eds.), *Research in literacy: Merging perspectives* (Thirty-sixth yearbook of the National Reading Conference, pp. 3–16). Rochester, NY: National Reading Conference.

Pressley, M., Gaskins, I. W., Cunicelli, E. A., Burdick, N. J., Schaub-Matt, M., Lee,

D. S., & Powell, N. (1991). Strategy instruction at Benchmark School: A faculty interview study. *Learning Disability Quarterly, 14*, 19–48.

Rosenholtz, S. (1989). *Teachers' workplace: The social organization of schools.* New York: Longman.

Sarason, S. (1971). *The culture of the school and the problem of change.* New York: Allyn and Bacon.

Saunders, W., Goldenberg, C., & Hamann, J. (1992). Instructional conversations beget instructional conversations. *Teaching and Teacher Education, 8,* 199–218.

Shepard, L. A. (1989). Why we need better assessments. *Educational Leadership, 46*(6), 4–7.

Slosson, R. L. (1963). *Slosson Oral Reading Test.* East Aurora, NY: Slosson Educational Publications.

Sparks, D., & Loucks-Horsley, S. (1990). Models of staff development. In W. R. Houston (Ed.), *Handbook of research on teacher education* (pp. 234–250). New York: Macmillan.

Stallings, J. A. (1975). Implementation and child effects of teaching practices in Follow Through classrooms. *Monographs of the Society for Research in Child Development, 40,* (Serial No. 163). Vienna, VA: Society for Research in Child Development.

Stallings, J., Needels, M., & Stayrook, N. (1983). *How to change the process of teaching basic reading skills in secondary schools: Phase II and Phase III.* Menlo Park, CA: SRI International.

Valdez, A. (1992). *Changes in teachers' beliefs, understandings, and practices concerning reading comprehension through the use of practical arguments: A follow-up study.* Unpublished doctoral dissertation, College of Education, University of Arizona, Tuscon.

Valencia, S. W., & Pearson, P. D. (1986). *New models for reading assessment* (Reading Education Rep. No. 71). Champaign: Center for the Study of Reading, University of Illinois.

Valencia, S. W., Pearson, P. D., Reeve, R., & Shanahan, T. (1988). *Illinois Goal Assessment Program: Reading.* Springfield: Illinois State Board of Education.

10
A Theory of Change

VIRGINIA RICHARDSON AND **PATRICIA L. ANDERS**

In Chapter 1, we talked about how and why we began this inquiry on teacher change and staff development, and how the nature of the inquiry changed as we moved forward. It began as a consideration of teachers' use of current research on reading comprehension, and moved in a number of additional directions. For example, the project investigated theories of teacher change, examined the relationship between teachers' beliefs and practices, advanced and explored a new form of staff development, reconsidered the nature of reading research and its helpfulness to educational practice, and studied the effects of different school contexts on the change process. We fully expect that we will continue to reconceptualize and reinterpret our experiences with this project as we pursue our explorations of teaching and learning. But for now, this chapter affords us the opportunity to summarize what we have learned about teacher change and about the staff development process in which we and a group of teachers participated.

At the beginning of the project, our goals and the processes we would use to achieve them were only partially formulated. As we entered the process, we knew that it would have to diverge from traditional, externally mandated staff development, about which much has been written. We also hoped that teachers would begin to feel more empowered, and we wished to bring current research on reading comprehension into the conversations. What emerged was a process that eventually led to changes in beliefs and practices for both teachers and staff developers. We, as staff developers, developed and articulated a descriptive theory of teacher change, a normative theory of teaching, and ideas for the improvement of our own practices as staff developers. Further, we acquired many ideas—both substantive and methodological—for further inquiry in this area. Finally, because of our emerging theories, we have developed a sense of educational reform that contradicts many of the inherent assumptions in current reform movements.

TEACHER CHANGE

Teachers have been receiving considerable critical attention in the media for a number of years. The attention has created a public conception of the teacher who is a stodgy, lazy individual, who sticks to the old ways of doing things. This conception derives from a theory of change that suggests that teachers are recalcitrant, and resist change—an unfortunate way of thinking, for several reasons. It continues a tradition of teacher-bashing that destroys morale and a sense of empowerment within the teaching profession. Further, the assumption that teachers resist change is not entirely valid; the sense of recalcitrance and resistance relates only to change that is externally mandated. That is, teachers may resist changing to a practice that someone *outside* the classroom decides is of importance for teachers to do *inside* the classroom. As Morimoto (1973) suggested:

> When change is advocated or demanded by another person, we feel threatened, defensive, and perhaps rushed. We are then without the freedom and the time to understand and to affirm the new learning as something desirable, and as something of our own choosing. Pressure to change, without an opportunity for exploration and choice, seldom results in experiences of joy and excitement in learning. (p. 255)

In fact, as we and others who have observed in classrooms have discovered, teachers change all the time. They reorganize their classrooms, try different activities and texts, change the order of topics in the curriculum, attempt different interpersonal skills, and so on. Teachers often see this change as being reactive. They adjust their behavior to the different groups of students in their classrooms and to individual student's needs. They respond to parents who make demands on behalf of their children, and adjust their classrooms on the basis of policies set by the school board or administrators. They also try new activities in the classroom in the hope that their students will become more involved in learning than they have previously, with other activities.

When teachers experiment with new activities in the classroom, the new practices are assessed on the basis of whether they "work." Activities that are tried by teachers are those that do not violate their beliefs about teaching and learning. When these activities work, it means that they engage the students, do not violate the teacher's particular need for control, and help the teachers respond to system-determined demands such as high test scores. Activities are quickly dropped if the teacher senses that they do not work. If they do work, they are absorbed into the teacher's repertoire of activities, and are subsequently not often thought of in terms of a change in practice.

A teacher's judgment about whether an activity is working is highly personal, and is often made quickly, during a time of complex classroom action. This judgment is often based on tacit beliefs and personal needs and may lead to classroom actions that violate other educative beliefs held by the teacher. For example, the need to control student behavior drove the assessment system for many of the teachers in this study; grading was used as a method of controlling student behavior rather than providing feedback to students and their parents about the students' progress. This was demonstrated in a discussion about assessment in one group session. When asked what would happen if we did away with report cards, one teacher suggested that "we might as well just send the students home" (Anders & Richardson, 1992).

The beliefs driving action are often deep and complex, and sometimes contradictory. Fenstermacher and Richardson (1993) describe a case that took place over the course of the Practical Argument Staff Development (PASD) process. One teacher justified her practice of asking students to read aloud on the basis of her belief that reading comprehension is being able to recognize a word and say it correctly (pp. 107–111). After comparing her own oral and silent reading processes and discovering that they were very different, she changed her premise concerning the definition of reading comprehension to the ability to read silently, with understanding. As a result, she decided that her students should spend more of their time reading silently. However, she still asked the students to read aloud a substantial amount of the time. In a further exploration of this practice, she articulated beliefs related to student motivation: that students will read a passage silently only if they are motivated to do so. She felt that the teacher could not affect that motivation process; therefore, in order to get the students to read, and assure herself that they were reading, she asked them to read aloud. Thus, her need for control and beliefs about motivation outweighed her new belief about learning to read.

The process of experimenting with new activities and judging whether they work does not happen only within the confines of the classroom. Teachers work within the social context of a school and a school district. As suggested in Chapter 7, teachers' norms are socially constructed; thus, it is possible to observe ways of thinking held by many teachers in one school that differ from those in another school. This suggests that the development of teachers' beliefs is affected by many factors, and broader understandings of change should include an examination of school culture as well as individual change processes.

One of the norms that we encountered as we began conversations with teachers was their view of teacher change as externally determined. We could see this initially with many of the teachers whose explanations for their practices focused on mandates and pressures from outside the class-room. For example, we were told by the teachers that they were using basal readers because the school board dictated that basal readers be used in teaching reading a certain percentage of the time. Assessment systems with large numbers of data points were required, they explained, because many parents come to the school to complain about their children's grades. A large number of data points would convince the parents that the teachers were correct and objective in their assessments. One possible effect of this externally justified view of change is a feeling of disempowerment. Expla-nations based on external forces did not allow teachers to explore their own premises and take control of the justifications for their practices.

The descriptive theory of change developed in this chapter is useful in understanding teachers' classroom actions; it also provides a framework for considering how teachers can be helped to move toward change that fulfills their educative goals. But first, it is important to consider what it is we want of teachers. The next section describes an image of teaching that builds on this concept of teacher change, and provides a direction for pro-fessional development.

A NORMATIVE CONCEPTION OF TEACHING

Until recently, the dominant perceptions of teachers among educators has been that they are the recipients and consumers of research and practice. Lagemann (1987) attributes the roots of this perception to Charles Judd (1918), by tracing, historically, the plural worlds of educational research and practice. She reports that Judd believed that research should be the domain primarily of men because they were better suited to its careful and scientific nature. The nurturing nature of women, on the other hand, was better suited to teaching. It follows that teachers should be the recipients and consumers of the results of well-designed studies to improve their teaching. This view was not without its detractors, however. Dewey (1933), a contemporary of Judd, challenged this view, as do many educators today—including ourselves.

The current conception of a teacher describes a person who mediates ideas and constructs meaning and knowledge, and acts on them. The ideas may be derived from many sources: staff development; other teachers; read-ings in research, theory, and literature; or reflection on experience. New understandings are constructed on the basis of these ideas as they interact with existing understandings. It is these understandings that drive practice.

However, the knowledge constructed by a teacher on the basis of experience is personal and may remain tacit. Teachers make decisions on the basis of a personal sense of what works, but without examining the beliefs underlying a sense of "working," teachers may perpetuate practices based on questionable assumptions and beliefs. Thus, the concept of teacher as inquirer provides a vision of a teacher who questions assumptions and is consciously thoughtful about goals, practices, students, and the larger contexts of school and community.

This vision is incomplete without consideration of teachers' goals, which largely determine the substance of their reflection. As has been pointed out previously (Richardson, 1990; Zeichner & Tabachnick, 1991), one critique of the early reflection literature that was based on Schön (1983) is that there was no discussion about what one reflects *on*. Reflection was described by Schön as something that is undertaken by professionals, and is probably good for them as professionals. However, his theory does not provide a basis for an assessment of the substance of reflective thought. In Chapter 2 of this book, Fenstermacher suggests that standing apart from one's experience as a teacher and reflecting on it must be undertaken within the framework of a clear sense of purpose. For Fenstermacher, this purpose should be grounded in the aim to foster "acquisition of enlightenment, the realization of high ideals of human culture, the ability to exercise the responsibilities of informed citizenship, and the capacity to conduct oneself according to common standards of decency, respect, and regard." He proposes that this type of reflection on the part of the teacher is educative for both teacher and student, and that it provides students with an important model: an empowered and enlightened learner who takes responsibility for his or her own learning, actions, and justifications.

The question for staff development, then, is *how* we can help teachers become inquiring, reflective individuals whose educative goals are in the forefront of their reflection, and who are able to model a process of learning that will help to liberate and enlighten their students. Such a staff development process must operate from the same vision. That is, it too must provide a model of reflection, inquiry, and learning that will be useful to teachers as they pursue their goals with their students. We move, now, to a discussion of an attempt at such a staff development process, the Practical Argument Staff Development process.

THE STAFF DEVELOPMENT PROCESS

At the beginning of the process, we were aware that the traditional externally set staff development process is not a good vehicle to help teachers meet the ideal of the teacher inquirer. The traditional model does not allow teachers to participate in building the agenda as an integral element throughout the process, nor does it provide support for the pursuit of individually determined inquiries on beliefs and practices.

We needed a more constructivist approach, one that would bring teachers in a school together to examine school norms, share beliefs, examine new knowledge in reading comprehension, and allow us to work individually with teachers as they examined their premises and practices. The practical argument described by Fenstermacher (1986; see also Chapter 2) became the foundation for the development of the process. The individual component was designed to help teachers examine their own beliefs and practices, change and develop new beliefs, and experiment with new practices. The group component allowed teachers to develop a sense of their colleagues' expertise and knowledge, to air their own, and to examine and critique new practices as a group.

This was not, however, an easy process to implement. We were working against norms that had been established over decades in schools across the country. These norms made it difficult for the teachers to talk with each other about their beliefs and expertise. In fact, after years of external mandates and negative images in the media, many of these teachers were not aware of their deep-seated, situational knowledge; nor did they have a sense that this knowledge was worth sharing with their colleagues.

In addition, there is a somewhat schizophrenic attitude toward university people who bring staff development to teachers in elementary and secondary schools. On the one hand, they are considered the "experts," because they hold formal knowledge about the processes of schooling and learning. On the other, there is a resentment toward these experts who come in with neat new ideas, many of which are not appropriate to the specific settings of the teachers' classrooms, and then go back to their quiet, scholarly lives and think up more new practices. University people are not considered "teachers" even though they help to prepare teachers. Hence, our challenge as staff developers was to move beyond these norms and attitudes, to help the teachers understand and value their own expertise, and to critically examine some of the new knowledge related to reading comprehension that we introduced into the conversations.

What We Learned

As we conducted our inquiry into the staff development process, we acquired important information in regard to agenda setting, the role of the Other, and the role of research on reading comprehension.

Setting the Agenda. We came to the staff development process with an idea of content in mind—current research on reading comprehension. While the teachers volunteered for the staff development process, the general content had been selected in advance. Our challenge, then, was to turn the control of the content and agenda over to the participants. This was difficult to do, particularly in one school where the teachers expected the staff developers to select the practices they thought the teachers should try (see Chapter 7). The RIS staff development process broke with traditional in-service training programs, in which trainers both set the agenda and control the content and process.

As described in Chapters 5 and 8, the participants eventually took over the agenda, content, and processes. This happened faster in one school than in another, a finding that could be attributed, in part, to the different cultures of the two schools. The question remains, however, whether the process could be moved along faster with less frustration on the part of both participants and staff developers.

Were these same teachers and staff developers to work together in the same way at this time, without any modification at all, the development might well proceed much more smoothly simply because of greater familiarity with the process. The collaborative process is now better understood and appreciated in the schools in this area because of other programs that have recently been introduced. One example is a study-group process on the use of literature introduced by Kathy Short (Short, 1992). Another is the teacher researcher work being conducted by teachers belonging to the Teachers Applying Whole Language (TAWL). Teachers in this organization have a conference each year in which they present their work to their colleagues. These programs and others like it have prepared teachers to think differently about the processes of staff development and change. Further, the inquiry process we conducted, in combination with a growing literature on collaborative staff development, has provided us with a better sense of what we are doing and why, and how we, as staff developers, should proceed.

The Role of the Other or Staff Developer. The collaborative process described in this book requires staff developers with a nontraditional conception of their role. No longer does the staff developer prepare lectures and activities around a classroom practice with the hope that the teachers will implement it in their classrooms. The staff developer does not play the role of "expert," imparting wisdom to the teachers.

Instead, the staff developer works as one of many experts in a collaborative process. All of the participants have expertise related to the content of the conversation. The teachers have practical knowledge based on experience and reflection on experience, and knowledge of the context in which the teaching takes place. Often, they also have well-developed theories of practice, as well as formal knowledge acquired in graduate courses and workshops. The staff developer's expertise includes knowledge of formal theory and research in a particular content or pedagogical area, and process skills. As described in Chapter 6, the content knowledge must be deep and flexibly held, so that it can be brought to the attention of the group at appropriate points during the conversation. The staff developer should also be knowledgeable about inquiry processes that help teachers move beyond the often tacit assessment of a practice—"it works"—toward an inquiry approach to teaching. This inquiry orientation allows for an examination of personally held values, goals, and empirical beliefs, as well as student learning and development.

The process skills include facilitating group conversations in nonthreatening ways, and modeling how beliefs can be revealed and related to practice. This staff development process also requires the developer to model the process of relating experientially acquired practical knowledge with formal theory and research. Of importance in this process—and perhaps the most difficult aspect—is the introduction, in nonthreatening and nonjudgmental ways, of alternative premises and practices based on current research and theory.

It is this latter function that distinguishes the role of the Other or staff developer from the role of the psychological counselor. It is true that a staff developer would benefit from an understanding of the Rogerian principles of realness, caring, and nonjudgmental understanding (Meador & Rogers, 1984). However, there is also a content understanding that enters into this role, and that understanding is related both to the goals of educational practice and to the formal educational research and theory that help us reach those goals. These two elements of content help teachers to develop the critical adjuncts of reflective practice described by Fenstermacher in Chapter 2: "a normative view of education and how one's own knowledge and the knowledge available to educators in general bear on practice."

Again, this role will become easier as all participants gain experience with the collaborative process. We found it extremely difficult at first because we were experimenting with a new role, and the teacher participants were asked to accept a new conception of staff developer. During the follow-up study in which Richardson participated, the teacher participants were much more comfortable with and actually seemed to relish the process. Further, they were beginning to model the process in their own classrooms, with questions that asked their students to examine their beliefs, and consider alternatives (Valdez, 1992).

The Role of Research on Reading Comprehension. During the 1970s and 1980s, a major shift took place in reading research and practice. Those of us responsible for the Reading Instruction Study (RIS) had been participants in the creation of new theories and practices related to the teaching of reading comprehension. At the beginning of this project, we were inclined to agree that if teachers would use the new practices, their students' reading comprehension would improve. We still agree that there are more and less effective ways of teaching comprehension; however, we have learned some things about research and practice that have shifted the ways we think about and value the research enterprise.

The research we reviewed during the first year of the project was primarily experimental or quasi-experimental in design. The long tradition of reading research has valued quantitative, hypothesis-driven research over other modes of inquiry. Hence, it is this type of research that is published in research journals and was available for our review. Hypothesis-driven research requires that the researcher make certain assumptions about what is being studied, that variables (such as time, teacher behaviors, students, and settings) be controlled, and that predictions be confirmed or rejected on the basis of "objective" measures. This mode of inquiry constrains what might be learned about children as they are learning to read, and often lacks ecological validity. The teacher can read research and respond: "but, what if . . ."; "that would never work with my kids"; and so forth. Thus, we found that the research did not "ring true" for the teachers with whom we worked; and faced with the realities that the teachers described to us, we could not confidently recommend the practices (see Chapter 4).

In addition, researchers have their own culture and language about teaching and learning. To members of the research community, a mere citation can represent a body of knowledge and a theoretical framework that helps members of that community construct meaning similar to that of other members. Teachers also have their own culture and language about teaching and learning, which is often not the same as that of researchers. Certainly, there are areas of overlap; however, there are enough differences that the researcher and the teacher often mean different things when using similar language.

We learned from the study that reading instruction research is important as a starting place for new practices. But it is only that. We found that practices need to be contextualized, and to be reconstructed by individual teachers in the context of the teacher's goals and perceptions of students. This process of contextualization and reconstruction is aided if the teachers work in collaboration with their colleagues. In many cases, the theoretical foundation for a particular practice was not a part of the teachers' belief systems. In such cases, the practices made little or no sense to the teachers. We found it necessary, therefore, to ground our discussions of practices in their theoretical rationale. Time was spent comparing the theoretical assumptions of the researchers with those of the teachers. More often than not, some aspects of a practice needed to be changed to make it "work" in a particular teacher's classroom. The decision to change a practice cannot be made with fidelity if the theoretical rationale of both the researcher and the teacher are not well understood by those participating in the implementation of the practice.

How We Would Do It Differently

We are impressed with the direction that some staff development programs have been taking since we initiated our program. The advent of teacher study groups (Joyce, Weil, & Showers, 1992; McDonald, 1986; Short, 1992) is one such development. Anders has conducted a similar staff development process with teachers during the summer; teachers formulate their own questions, choose professional and scholarly literature to use as a resource to address those questions, and participate in discussion and journal activities that contribute to the personal construction of instructional theory and practice.

Given the collaborative nature of these programs and what we learned from our own, we would be inclined, if we were to undertake such a study again, to increase the degree of collaboration on all fronts. That is, we would spend more time sharing and constructing goals for the staff development process and for the inquiry to be undertaken. We would not impose objectives, although we would openly and forthrightly share our goals for the staff development. We would acknowledge and discuss the presumed power differential between university and school-level professionals and would spend time establishing our relationship. We recognize that for the teachers to participate equally and collaboratively, a new community needs to be established.

The follow-up study conducted by Richardson (1991) and Valdez (1992) suggested that, over time, we had developed such a community. The teachers were ready to forge ahead and displayed none of the lack of trust or concern about the university experts that they had initially. Likewise, the researcher was more revealing and conversational about her own dilemmas as a teacher educator. The teachers with whom we had worked had taken control and seemed to have developed and articulated a change orientation. This disposition toward critical analysis of both practice and theory had created an environment conducive to the systematic experimentation with practices and to the connecting of beliefs and practice.

THE RESEARCH PROCESS

The Reading Instruction Study combined three very different approaches to inquiry: analytic, in the study, categorization, and assessment of the literature; descriptive, in the study of classroom processes, teacher beliefs, school context, and student learning; and action-oriented in the development, implementation, and testing of the school staff development process. The study also operated at several levels within the schooling system. At one level, it examined the nature of reading comprehension in the literature, and in the minds and practices of individual grade 4, 5, and 6 teachers. At a more global level, the study investigated the larger context in which the teaching of reading takes place: the norms of teachers in particular schools and the testing culture that governs society's understanding of the success of schools and teachers. Third, the study examined teacher change both in general terms and as a result of a particular approach to staff development.

The methodology could be described as eclectic. It involved school context studies and belief interviews, open-ended narrative observations, and the development of analysis systems that were derived from the data rather than predetermined. It included the examination of student scores on several standardized tests, and relationship studies. It was dominated by a qualitative approach to educational inquiry. The sample size was small, and the study initially focused on the meanings that the teacher participants brought to their teaching of reading comprehension. Later on, the focus shifted to the way in which the staff development proceeded and the changes in participants' beliefs and practices—both teachers and staff developers—that could be attributed to the process. Several questions required a quantitative approach to research; thus, our methodology shifted when we looked at the relationship between the staff development process and student achievement. Much of the action research and data analysis moved toward critical theory as we worked with teachers in understanding the underlying assumptions that affected power relationships in the classroom and in the staff development process. Our analysis of the effects of society's concern with assessment and testing on teachers is an example of such a critical analysis (Anders & Richardson, 1992).

While we began with a sense of the data to be collected and very broad questions to be explored, the specific questions and ways of analyzing the data emerged during the course of and following the staff development. If we were to repeat the study, would we collect different data? Yes. It became clear during the staff development process that our original narrative observations, focused entirely on the teacher, did not provide us with student-response data. We had tied the observations too closely to the specific question we were addressing: Do teachers use research-based practices in the teaching of reading comprehension? While the data allowed us to answer this question, other, equally interesting, questions that emerged during the course of the study could not be answered. For example, we could not examine changes in the nature of student involvement before and following the process with the data we had collected. Fortunately, the videotapes of a subset of teachers' reading instruction, collected as one element of the staff development process, provided us with more complete data on classroom activities, including student actions. But these were collected a semester following the initial observations. We now believe that videotapes of each of the 39 teachers as they were involved in reading comprehension instruction would have been more valuable than the narrative observations.

Another type of data that would have been extremely valuable both for us and for the teachers is students' responses to interview questions about *their* views of learning, reading comprehension, and teaching. For example, in a staff development process in one of the schools, the teachers became intrigued with how their students viewed reading comprehension, given the differing views of the process on the part of the teachers themselves. They asked their students to write a short piece about reading, and were surprised that so many of their students viewed reading as something you do in groups, with a basal reader. They had developed a schooling-specific view of reading. Did the students view reading differently at the completion of the process? We could not answer this and other questions involving the students with the data we had collected.

Of most interest to us, however, as we think back on the research design and methodology, is the degree to which the research and staff development processes intermingled and merged as we went along. The data became part of the staff development process as we provided teachers with the transcribed belief interviews, and as the videotapes of the staff development sessions, as well as the transcriptions of belief interviews and practical arguments, became part of our thinking and planning as staff developers. The staff development process itself became data for our studies, through the videotapes. The research process and the staff development practice, then, were not independent of each other. We suspect that any inquiry-oriented staff development process will commingle research and practice in a similar manner.

POLICIES FOR ENCOURAGING REFLECTIVE TEACHING

The staff development process described in this book is time consuming, and requires dialogue in a trusting atmosphere among individual teachers and staff developers, as well as among groups of teachers. How can this be encouraged and supported at the local, state, and federal levels? This question requires that we briefly examine the current policy arena in relationship to the theory of teacher change and the conception of the teacher as reflective inquirer that have been developed in this book.

There are two barriers to the establishment of support systems that would lead us toward the vision of the inquiring teacher. One relates to the difficulty in establishing the sense of autonomy as felt by teachers at the conclusion of the PASD process described here. While one often hears and reads rhetoric that pays lip service to reflection, teacher autonomy, and participatory decision making, official policies and the actions of policymakers still reveal a strong need to control educational goals and sometimes the instructional means for reaching them. Smyth (1992) has discussed this phenomenon with lessons from Australia that seem relevant to the United States. He suggests that the devolution of decision making implied in such policies as school-based management allows policymakers to centralize control of educational priorities while handing over decisions about the ways in which schools will achieve them. This is a money-saving device as well, he suggests:

> Giving the appearance of endorsing decentralized forms of school governance is a way of strategically responding to the need to reduce government spending (with decisions seemingly made closer to the workplace) while achieving tighter control and accountability through choice and free market mechanisms. (p. 273)

Thus, one has to question whether policymakers really want teachers to be autonomous. In Chapter 2, Fenstermacher quotes Dearden's (1975) description of autonomy:

> . . . what he thinks and does in important areas of life cannot be explained without reference to his own activity of mind. That is to say, the explanation of why he thinks and acts as he does in these areas must include a reference to his own choices, deliberations, decisions, reflections, judgments, plannings or reasonings. (p. 63)

Pendlebury (1990) describes a communitarian approach to autonomy that is more relevant to groups of teachers working within a school. This type of autonomy requires an ongoing involvement of community members in "critical discussion[s] of the goods, standards and procedures which is necessary for a thriving practice" (p. 274). Such autonomy might lead to quite different goals and standards from school to school depending on the setting in which the schools are located. An examination of current policies, such as national standards and national teacher exams, however, indicates an increased emphasis on centralizing the decisions about educative goals. Such policies make it more difficult than in the past for teachers to be autonomous in participating in the educative agenda setting.

The second barrier to reflective teaching is related to the popularity of structural and systemic change policies that seem easy to propose, although (to the policymakers) inexplicably difficult to implement. Many national and state educational change policies focus on altering structural relationships between and among organizations (for example, establishing professional development schools,[1] or requiring college of education faculty to spend time in real schools); changing the roles of educators (for example, that of the principal in site-based management); and the development of standards and assessment systems designed to alter teachers' behaviors through a stick—sometimes carrot-and-stick—approach. By focusing on structures, organizations, standards, and examinations, these policies hold the individual practitioner and student at arm's length. They fail to acknowledge the expertise and authority of the practitioner, and that education in our schools is primarily an interactive process among teachers and students. They ignore the fact that positive change may require time and extended conversation among those closest to students, in a risk-free atmosphere. In other words, these policies still suggest that someone other than the teacher in the local setting knows best how to work with the students in his or her class, and they attempt to exert control, from afar, over teachers' intentions, educative goals, and practices.

And yet, as McLaughlin (1990) points out, "change continues to be a problem of the smallest unit" (p. 12). We have described a staff development program that emphasizes person-to-person conversations between and among professionals who work within classroom and school contexts that contain common and unique characteristics. This process requires the involvement of individuals who work toward nonjudgmental understandings of their own and others' beliefs and practices, and are willing to experiment with new practices in an inquiring manner. These professionals must also be allowed to examine and alter their conceptions of the purposes of schooling and their own instruction.

What types of policies can be developed to promote change that focuses on such a vision? We certainly cannot mandate that teachers be reflective. Nor would we advise the enactment of policies that require structural changes that are thought to be necessary in order for reflection to take place, such as a policy that requires schools to give one-half day per week to teachers for planning purposes. Structural change, we believe, is often thought of as an easy and inexpensive way to change teaching practice. Deep change, however, requires the involvement of the participants in the deliberation concerning both the goals and the processes of change. In fact, the very process of group conversation about teaching and schooling will have more effect on classroom practices than structural change or mandated behavior.

Two articles in Shulman and Sykes' *Handbook of Teaching and Policy* (1983) may provide some guidance for us on policies to encourage teachers to become inquirers. Elmore's (1983) chapter on complexity and control of the educational system suggests that policies should enhance capacity rather than regulate compliance to mandates. The important actors, he suggests, are individual teachers and students, and "very few, if any, of them are subject to direct administrative control" (p. 356). Because of this, Elmore suggests, policies should focus resources as close as possible to the point of delivery. In the same volume, Fenstermacher and Amarel (1983) examine the responsibility of the teacher in resolving the conflict between means and ends in education. This conflict arises from competing claims among the interests of the students, the state, and humanity. A distal authority cannot develop policy that assumes that responsibility, because it is the teacher who knows the students and the local context. They conclude:

> Policy and the rules and regulations that flow from it are misused if their purpose is to instruct teachers on what and how to teach. Policy is neither the instrument nor the content of education. It is the temporary resolution of competing potentials and demands to optimize the attainment of ends we seek. (p. 407)

There is no alternative, therefore, to the development of policies that support the capacity of local groups of teachers and administrators, students and parents, to deliberate about the goals of education and the appropriate means to achieve them. Support is also required for teachers to understand and assess their own practices and beliefs in relation to the goals that they have participated in establishing.

CONCLUSION

This book represents a story of learning: learning about teacher change, learning about how to enhance change that is significant and worthwhile. In the process, the many individuals involved in the project altered their own ways of thinking and their educational practice. We are convinced that such change comes about only through dialogue and conversation among those engaged in the many facets of the educational process. These conversations take place in a trusting atmosphere and are framed within constantly examined normative conceptions of the aims of education.

We cannot ignore the basic nature of education and change in our federal, state, and local policies. Emphasis on structural, organizational, or systemic change, if it ignores the fundamental notion that education and development of students and teachers are interactive and time-consuming in nature, will always produce disappointing and unanticipated results. Policies must be developed within an atmosphere of trust and mutual respect.

The teachers with whom we worked were not selected on the basis of "effectiveness." They were teachers who volunteered to work with us. Nonetheless, these were effective teachers, committed to the education of their students. They wanted to do well, and were willing to study and change their practices in order to do so. Even those with many years of experience were not "recalcitrant." Change in these teachers was individually determined; the timetables and ways of changing varied from teacher to teacher. Working with these teachers was a joy for us, and allowed us to consider and change our own practices as teacher educators. We hope that the notions of teacher change developed in this book will begin to frame national, state, and local policies designed to enhance the capacity of educators to meet the needs of our students and communities.

NOTE

1. We are not suggesting that there is necessarily a problem with professional development schools. However, a policy that simply focuses on the bureaucratic interrelationships of two organizations (a college/university and an elementary/secondary school) may miss—in fact, may possibly inhibit—the type of interpersonal process that is required for significant and worthwhile change to occur.

REFERENCES

Anders, P., & Richardson, V. (1992). Teacher as game-show host, bookkeeper, or judge? Challenges, contradictions, and consequences of accountability. *Teachers College Record, 94*, 382–396.
Dearden, R. F. (1975). Autonomy and education. In R. F. Dearden, P. H. Hirst, & R. S. Peters (Eds.), *Education and reason* (pp. 58–75). London: Routledge and Kegan Paul.

Dewey, J. (1933). *How we think.* Boston: D. C. Heath.

Elmore, R. F. (1983). Complexity and control: What legislators and administrators can do about implementing public policy. In L. S. Shulman & G. Sykes (Eds.), *Handbook of teaching and policy* (pp. 342–369). New York: Longman.

Fenstermacher, G. D. (1986). A philosophy of research on teaching: Three aspects. In M. C. Whittrock (Eds.), *Handbook of research on teaching* (3rd ed., pp. 392–407). New York: Macmillan.

Fenstermacher, G. D, & Amarel, M. (1983). The interests of the student, the state, and humanity in education. In L. S. Shulman & G. Sykes (Eds.), *Handbook of teaching and policy* (pp. 392–407). New York: Longman.

Fenstermacher, G., & Richardson, V. (1993). The elicitation and reconstruction of practical arguments in teaching. *Journal of Curriculum Studies, 25*(2), 101–114.

Joyce, B., Weil, M., & Showers, B. (1992). *Models of teaching* (4th ed.). Boston: Allyn & Bacon.

Judd, C. H. (1918). *Introduction to the scientific study of education.* Boston: Ginn & Company.

Lagemann, E. C. (1987). The politics of knowledge: The Carnegie Corporation and the formulation of public policy. *History of Education Quarterly, 27*(2), 205–220.

McDonald, J. P. (1986). Raising the teacher's voice and the ironic role of theory. *Harvard Educational Review, 56*(4), 355–378.

McLaughlin, M. (1990). The Rand change agent study revisited: Macro perspectives and micro realities. *Educational Researcher, 19*(9), 11–16.

Meador, B. D., & Rogers, C. R. (1984). Person-centered therapy. In R. J. Corsini (Ed.), *Current psychotherapies* (3rd ed.). Itasca, IL: Peacock.

Morimoto, K., with Gregory, J., & Butler, P. (1973). Notes on the context for learning. *Harvard Educational Review, 43*(2), 245–257.

Pendlebury, S. (1990). Community, liberty and the practice of teaching. *Studies in Philosophy and Education, 10*(4), 263–280.

Richardson, V. (1990). The evolution of reflective teaching and teacher education. In R. Clift, W. R. Houston, & M. Pugach (Eds.), *Encouraging reflective practice in education* (pp. 3–19). New York: Teachers College Press.

Richardson, V. (1991). *A study of long-term changes in teachers' beliefs and practices.* Proposal submitted to U.S. Department of Education, Office of Educational Research and Improvement. Tucson, AZ: College of Education, University of Arizona.

Schön, D. (1983). *The reflective practitioner.* New York: Basic Books.

Short, K. (1992). "Living the process": Creating a learning community among educators. *Teaching Education, 4*(2), 35–42.

Shulman, L. S., & Sykes, G. (Eds.). (1983). *Handbook of teaching and policy.* New York: Longman.

Smyth, J. (1992). Teachers' work and the politics of reflection. *American Educational Research Journal, 29*(2), 267–302.

Valdez, A. (1992). *Changes in teachers' beliefs, understandings and practices concerning*

reading comprehension through the use of practical arguments: A follow-up study.
Unpublished dissertation, College of Education, University of Arizona, Tuc-
son.
Zeichner, K., & Tabachnick, B. R. (1991). Reflections on reflective teaching. In
B. R. Tabachnick & K. Zeichner (Eds.), *Issues and practices in inquiry-oriented
teacher education* (pp. 1–21). London: Falmer.

About the Contributors

Patricia L. Anders is a professor of Language, Reading, and Culture at the University of Arizona. She was co-principal investigator of "The Reading Instruction Study," the project on which this book is based. She brought to this project a long-time interest in the relationship of theory and practice in the teaching of reading. Her scholarship and practice have focused on reading and writing in the content areas, teacher beliefs and practices, and theoretically grounded reading comprehension practices. Professor Anders received her doctorate from the University of Wisconsin in 1976 after teaching in both Madison and Racine, Wisconsin.

Candace S. Bos, Ph.D., is a professor of Special Education at the University of Arizona, where she coordinates the graduate program in Learning Disabilities. She is well known for her research in reading comprehension, content area learning, and interactive models of teaching as they relate to students at risk or students who have learning disabilities. She is co-author of a major textbook in learning disabilities, *Strategies for Teaching Students with Learning and Behavior Problems* (3rd. ed.; Allyn & Bacon, 1994), and co-editor of a recent book on conducting research in the field of learning disabilities, *Research in Learning Disabilities: Theory, Methodology, Assessment, and Ethics* (Springer-Verlag, 1994). She is currently President-Elect of the Division for Learning Disabilities of the Council for Exceptional Children.

Gary D Fenstermacher is Professor of Education at the University of Arizona, Tucson. His areas of specialization are philosophy of education, teacher education, and educational policy analysis. He recently completed a six-year term as dean of the college of education at the university and has now returned to full-time teaching and research. His interest in practical reasoning began more than a decade ago, in an effort to understand the connections between theory, research, and practice.

Mary Lynn Hamilton, currently an assistant professor in the Department of Curriculum and Instruction at the University of Kansas, Lawrence, coordinates the Instructional Leadership Program, an alternative doctoral program, and facilitates coursework for preservice students. Her current research focuses on examining teachers' knowledge and beliefs through both self-study and the study of other teachers' practices. Of particular interest to her are the implications that culture has for knowledge and belief. Her most recent publication, "Think You Can: The Influence of Culture on Beliefs" (in Day, Calderhead, & Denicolo, Eds., *Research on Teacher Thinking*; Falmer, 1993), received the 1993 Distinguished Research in Teacher Education Award from the Association of Teacher Educators of Kansas.

Carol V. Lloyd teaches and does research in the Department of Teacher Education at the University of Nebraska at Omaha. Her undergraduate and graduate classes focus on issues related to teaching reading, student learning, and teachers as decision makers. Her research focuses on the interrelationships between teaching and learning within classroom contexts.

Judy N. Mitchell is Department Chair and Professor of Language, Reading and Culture in the College of Education, University of Arizona. She is interested in the characteristics and structure of written language as text and its relationship to comprehension and composition. Her work involves reading and language theory, research, and practice from an interdisciplinary perspective.

Peggy Placier received her Ph.D. from the University of Arizona and is currently Assistant Professor of Foundations of Education in the College of Education, University of Missouri-Columbia. Her research and teaching interests include language and culture, educational policy rhetoric, school culture, and multicultural education. She is also involved, with Mary Lynn Hamilton and others, in a collaborative study of the socialization of beginning professors in colleges of education.

Virginia Richardson is a professor of Teaching and Teacher Education in the College of Education, University of Arizona. Her interests are teacher beliefs and change, research on teaching education, and qualitative research methodology.

Deborah L. Tidwell is an assistant professor of reading in the Department of Curriculum and Instruction at the University of Northern Iowa and Director of the University's Reading Clinic. Her current research focuses on beliefs and practices of educators in the areas of literacy development and multicultural education.

Index